A Policy for Skilled Manpower

NATIONAL MANPOWER COUNCIL

A Policy for
Skilled Manpower

A STATEMENT BY THE COUNCIL
with
FACTS AND ISSUES PREPARED
BY THE RESEARCH STAFF

New York 1954

COLUMBIA UNIVERSITY PRESS

LIBRARY OF CONGRESS CATALOG CARD NUMBER: 54-12810

COPYRIGHT 1954 COLUMBIA UNIVERSITY PRESS

PUBLISHED IN GREAT BRITAIN, CANADA, INDIA, AND PAKISTAN
BY GEOFFREY CUMBERLEGE: OXFORD UNIVERSITY PRESS,
LONDON, TORONTO, BOMBAY, AND KARACHI

MANUFACTURED IN THE UNITED STATES OF AMERICA

65

The National Manpower Council

Preface

THIS VOLUME is the fourth publication of the National Manpower Council. The Council was established at Columbia University in the spring of 1951, under a grant from the Ford Foundation, to study significant manpower problems and to contribute to the improved development and utilization of the country's human resources.

Its first study, *Student Deferment and National Manpower Policy*, appeared in April, 1952, and was followed in May, 1953, by *A Policy for Scientific and Professional Manpower*. In March, 1954, the Council published the *Proceedings of a Conference on the Utilization of Scientific and Professional Manpower*. This conference, held by the Council in October, 1953, brought together sixty-six experts for a five-day meeting at Arden House, the Harriman Campus of Columbia University. The deliberations aided the Council's present study by illuminating the role of technicians in our economy.

As in its earlier investigations, the Council has received generous cooperation from many experts. Without the benefit of their knowledge, experience, and judgment, the Council would not have been able to frame a comprehensive approach for dealing with the skilled manpower component of the nation's labor force, nor could it have formulated policy recommendations designed to contribute to the further development of our resources of skilled workers and technicians.

The Council realizes that its study of skilled manpower is not definitive and that it may raise more questions than it answers. But the Council will be gratified if it has stimulated interest in a segment of the nation's manpower which is relatively neglected, even though it is critically important to our security and economic progress. The Council hopes that its concern with these eight or nine million skilled workers and technicians will stimulate much needed research and also contribute to strengthening these manpower resources by encouraging action in local communities, among employers and trade unions, and within the governmental sphere. The Council will seek to help implement its policy recommendations by holding a national conference in the spring of 1955.

At every stage of the study the Council held conferences to secure information not otherwise available. The participants in these conferences are listed in the Acknowledgments, and the Council is deeply grateful for their assistance. Various Council members played a key role in planning and conducting specific conferences: Dr. Leo Bartemeier, Mr. A. J. Hayes, Mr. Wilbur C. Munnecke, Dr. Roland R. Renne, Miss Sara Southall. The Chairman participated in the San Francisco conference in March, 1954.

The Fund for the Advancement of Education cooperated with the Council in calling the conference on secondary education in New York in February, 1954, which was presided over by Dr. Alvin C. Eurich, Vice-President of the Fund. Dr. John E. Ivey, Jr., Director of the Southern Regional Education Board, and Dr. Philip Weltner of Oglethorpe University arranged the conference with Southern industrialists held in Atlanta in April, 1954. The second Atlanta conference was arranged by Dr. Brailsford R. Brazeal, Dean of Morehouse College. The conference on the problems of skill in the armed services, held in the Pentagon in March, 1954, was made possible by the cooperation of the then Assistant Secretary of Defense for Manpower, Dr. John A. Hannah; Mr. James M. Mitchell, Deputy Assistant Secretary of Defense; and Dr. Gus C. Lee, Director, Manpower Utilization, in the Office of the Assistant Secretary of Defense. Mr. Dean Brossman of the Stamford-Greenwich Manufacturer's Council arranged the conference held in Stamford, Connecticut, in August, 1954.

The administrative work connected with the preparation and staging of these conferences, which contributed so much to advancing the Council's study, was carried out with high competence by Miss Bryna Ball, Administrative Assistant of the Council's staff.

The chapters which comprise Part Two of this volume, "Facts and Issues about Skilled Manpower," grew out of materials prepared for the Council by its staff. The Council is indebted to the many organizations and individuals named in the Acknowledgments for their valuable assistance in preparing these materials.

Special note should be made of the fact that Dr. Seymour L. Wolfbein, Dr. Harold Goldstein, and Mr. Richard Lewis, of the Bureau of Labor Statistics, U. S. Department of Labor, were most helpful throughout the study. The staff had the benefit of their detailed comments on the chapters in Part Two. The staff likewise called frequently for assistance upon Mr. Matthew Radom of the Standard Oil Company of New Jersey, who also read the chapters. Essential information on several aspects of skilled manpower was made available by the Bureau of Apprenticeship of the Department of Labor. Mr. John S. McCauley, Chief of the Research and Statistics Branch of the Bureau, and Dr. O. L. Harvey, formerly Chief of the Branch and now Special Assistant, Office of the Secretary of Labor, were particularly helpful.

The following conference participants also assisted the Council by their careful reading of selected chapters: Dr. Alvin C. Eurich, Mr. Algie A. Hendrix, Mr. Alexander R. Heron, Mr. Carl Huhndorff, Dr. John E. Ivey, Jr., Dr. Francis Keppel, Dr. Morris Krugman, Mr. Karl R. Kunze, Mr. Louis W. Lerda, Mr. Archie A. Pearson, Mr. Paul Rehmus, and Dr. Ralph Tyler. The Council was also aided by Major General Howard McC. Snyder, the Advisor of the Conservation of Human Resources Project, Graduate School of Business, Columbia University; and by the Project's Consultant in Psychiatry, Dr. Sol W. Ginsburg.

From the beginning of this study both the Council and the staff have profited from the advice of its consultant, Professor Harold F. Clark of Teachers College, Columbia University. Professor Moses Abramovitz of Stanford University also served in a consultative capacity to the staff on special problems. Professor

Acknowledgments

ORGANIZATIONS

Educational

American Association of Junior Colleges
American Vocational Association, Inc.
Board of Education of the City of New York
Los Angeles City Board of Education
National Association and Council of Business Schools
National Citizens Commission for the Public Schools
National Council of Technical Schools
National Education Association, National Association of Secondary School
   Principals, United Business Education Association
National Home Study Council
New York State Education Department

Government

Department of Defense
Department of Health, Education, and Welfare, Office of Education
Department of Labor, Bureau of Apprenticeship, Bureau of Employment
   Security, Bureau of Labor Statistics
Department of the Air Force
Department of the Army
Department of the Navy, including U. S. Marine Corps
Selective Service System
Veterans Administration

Labor

American Federation of Labor
Congress of Industrial Organizations
International Association of Machinists

Other

American Registry of Physical Therapists
American Registry of X-Ray Technicians
American Society of X-Ray Technicians
New York State Council of Retail Merchants, Inc.
Registry of Medical Technologists of the American Society of Clinical
   Pathologists

CONFERENCE PARTICIPANTS

AUGUST, 1953

Washington, D. C.

Hiram E. Barg, Milwaukee Vocational and Adult Schools, Milwaukee, Wisc.

Harold F. Clark, Teachers College, Columbia University, New York, N. Y.

Nelson Cruikshank, American Federation of Labor, Washington, D. C.

Michael Fox, Railway Employes' Department, American Federation of Labor, Chicago, Ill.

Edward E. Goshen, Bureau of Apprenticeship, Department of Labor, Washington, D. C.

Harry I. Hadley, Department of the Army, Washington, D. C.

A. J. Hayes, International Association of Machinists (AFL), Washington, D. C.

Carl Huhndorff, International Association of Machinists (AFL), Washington, D. C.

Lawrence L. Jarvie, State University of New York, Albany, N. Y.

Vernon Jirikowic, International Association of Machinists (AFL), Washington, D. C.

Chester E. Johansen, Federal Telecommunication Laboratories, a Division of the I. T. & T. Corp., Nutley, N. J.

Otto Klitgord, New York City Community College of Applied Arts and Sciences, Brooklyn, N. Y.

Louis W. Lerda, Esso Standard Oil Company, New York, N. Y.

Richard Lewis, Bureau of Labor Statistics, Department of Labor, Washington, D. C.

Charles C. Limburg, Department of the Air Force, Washington, D. C.

N. M. Mitchell, Barnes Textile Associates, Inc., Boston, Mass.

Guichard Parris, National Urban League, New York, N. Y.

Joseph H. Piconke, United Automobile, Aircraft & Agricultural Implement Workers of America (CIO), Detroit, Mich.

Matthew Radom, Standard Oil Company of New Jersey, New York, N .Y.

E. H. Reed, International Harvester Company, Chicago, Ill.

Homer C. Rose, Department of the Navy, Washington, D. C.

William Leavitt Stoddard, The Lincoln and Therese Filene Foundation, Boston, Mass.

Walter Studdiford, Bureau of Employment Security, Department of Labor, Washington, D. C.

Conrad Taeuber, Bureau of the Census, Department of Commerce, Washington, D. C.

JANUARY, 1954

Chicago, Illinois

Thomas G. Ayers, Commonwealth Edison Company, Chicago, Ill.

Garret L. Bergen, Marshall Field & Company, Chicago, Ill.
John T. Bobbitt, Argonne National Laboratory, Lemont, Ill.
Ray Brown, University of Chicago Clinics, Chicago, Ill.
W. G. Caples, Inland Steel Company, Chicago, Ill.
LeRoy W. Clemence, Abbott Laboratories, North Chicago, Ill.
Ralph Hoitsma, Standard Oil Company of Ohio, Cleveland, Ohio
Wilbur C. Munnecke, Chicago *Sun-Times,* Chicago, Ill.
W. J. Reilly, International Harvester Company, Chicago, Ill.
John W. Root, Holabird, Root and Burgee, Chicago, Ill.
Kenneth A. Rouse, A. B. Dick Company, Niles, Ill.
J. C. Sherrick, Holabird, Root and Burgee, Chicago, Ill.
J. N. Stanbery, Illinois Bell Telephone Company, Chicago, Ill.

JANUARY, 1954

Detroit, Michigan

Preston Amerman, Detroit Edison Company, Detroit, Mich.
H. E. Armitage, S. S. Kresge Company, Detroit, Mich.
Harlan R. Arthur, Ford Motor Company, Dearborn, Mich.
Dr. Leo Bartemeier, Detroit, Mich.
Conrad Batchelder, American Brass Company, Detroit, Mich.
Thomas Beaver, Ford Motor Company, Dearborn, Mich.
Algie A. Hendrix, General Motors Corporation, Detroit, Mich.
Walter F. Holcomb, Parke, Davis & Company, Detroit, Mich.
William L. Hurley, Baker, Simmonds & Company, Detroit, Mich.
George Jacoby, General Motors Corporation, Detroit, Mich.
Read Jenkins, J. L. Hudson Company, Detroit, Mich.
Robert Marsden, Burroughs Corporation, Detroit, Mich.
Richard V. O'Brien, J. A. Utley Company, Royal Oak, Mich.
Archie A. Pearson, Ford Motor Company, Dearborn, Mich.
John R. Robertson, Chrysler Corporation, Detroit, Mich.
Arthur D. Sutherland, Home Life Insurance Company of New York, Detroit, Mich.
K. W. Thompson, Michigan Bell Telephone Company, Detroit, Mich.

FEBRUARY, 1954

New York, New York

Philip Coombs, Fund for the Advancement of Education, New York, N. Y.
Alvin C. Eurich, Fund for the Advancement of Education, New York, N. Y.
Burton Fowler, Germantown Friends School, Germantown, Pa.
Matthew P. Gaffney, New Trier Township High School, Winnetka, Ill.
Nathaniel L. Gage, College of Education, University of Illinois, Urbana, Ill.
George F. Gant, Southern Regional Education Board, Atlanta, Ga.
Dr. Sol W. Ginsburg, New York, N. Y.

Paul Hanna, School of Education, Stanford University, Stanford, Calif.

Francis Keppel, Graduate School of Education, Harvard University, Cambridge, Mass.

Morris Krugman, New York City Board of Education, Brooklyn, N. Y.

Morris Meister, Bronx High School of Science, Bronx, N. Y.

Eugene P. Northrop, National Science Foundation, Washington, D. C.

Reverend Brother Alphonsus L. Pakenham, Power Memorial Academy, New York, N. Y.

Paul Rehmus, Portland, Oregon

William F. Russell, Teachers College, Columbia University, New York, N. Y.

William G. Saltonstall, The Phillips Exeter Academy, Exeter, N. H.

Leo F. Smith, Rochester Institute of Technology, Rochester, N. Y.

Procter Thomson, University of Chicago, Chicago, Ill.

Ralph Tyler, Center for Advanced Study in the Behavioral Sciences, Chicago, Ill.

MARCH, 1954

San Francisco, California

William A. Andrews, Jr., Bullock's, Los Angeles, Calif.

Fred A. Cutter, Cutter Laboratories, Berkeley, Calif.

W. W. Davison, Standard Oil Company of California, San Francisco, Calif.

James B. DuPrau, Columbia Geneva Steel Corporation, San Francisco, Calif.

Julian M. Edwards, The Pacific Telephone and Telegraph Company, San Francisco, Calif.

Gerald Henry, California Packing Corporation, San Francisco, Calif.

Alexander R. Heron, Crown Zellerbach Corporation, San Francisco, Calif.

Karl R. Kunze, Lockheed Aircraft Corporation, Burbank, Calif.

P. T. Sinclair, Crown Zellerbach Corporation, San Francisco, Calif.

H. K. Swenerton, Gladding, McBean & Company, Los Angeles, Calif.

A. B. Tichenor, Matson Navigation Company, San Francisco, Calif.

J. M. Trickett, Food Machinery and Chemical Corporation, San Jose, Calif.

James D. Zellerbach, Crown Zellerbach Corporation, San Francisco, Calif.

MARCH, 1954

Chicago, Illinois

Glen T. Barton, Agricultural Research Service, Department of Agriculture, Washington, D. C.

Harold F. Clark, Teachers College, Columbia University, New York, N. Y.

Charles M. Hardin, University of Chicago, Chicago, Ill.

Lowell S. Hardin, School of Agriculture, Purdue University, Lafayette, Ind.

Carl P. Heisig, Agricultural Research Service, Department of Agriculture, Washington, D. C.

W. E. Hendrix, University of Chicago, Chicago, Ill.

Homer L. Hitt, Louisiana State University, Baton Rouge, La.
D. Gale Johnson, University of Chicago, Chicago, Ill.
Sherman Kessler, New Ross, Ind.
Charles P. Loomis, Michigan State College, East Lansing, Mich.
William R. Rothenberger, Frankfort, Ind.
Theodore W. Schultz, University of Chicago, Chicago, Ill.
Sara E. Southall, Santa Fe, N. Mex.
Joseph W. Willett, University of Chicago, Chicago, Ill.

MARCH, 1954

Washington, D. C.

Bun Benton Bray, Manpower Utilization and Labor Relations, Department of the Navy, Washington, D. C.

E. D. Carstater, Bureau of Naval Personnel, Department of the Navy, Washington, D. C.

Colonel W. E. Clark, Directorate of Personnel Procurement and Training, Department of the Air Force, Washington, D. C.

John T. Dailey, Bureau of Naval Personnel, Department of the Navy, Washington, D. C.

Roy K. Davenport, Office of the Adjutant General, Department of the Army, Washington, D. C.

Donald B. DuBois, Department of the Air Force, Washington, D. C.

Lt. Colonel H. H. Dunwoody, Manpower Control Branch, Department of the Army, Washington, D. C.

Colonel B. D. Godbold, Office of Manpower Requirements, Department of Defense, Washington, D. C.

Captain G. A. Griffin, Aviation Training Division, Department of the Navy, Washington, D. C.

Harry I. Hadley, Personnel Research and Procedures Division, Department of the Army, Washington, D. C.

A. Prentice Kenyon, Bureau of Naval Personnel, Department of the Navy, Washington, D. C.

Gus C. Lee, Office of Manpower Utilization, Department of Defense, Washington, D. C.

James M. Mitchell, Department of Defense, Washington, D. C.

Colonel C. L. Moir, Directorate of Personnel Procurement and Training, Department of the Air Force, Washington, D. C.

Aaron B. Nadel, Committee and Panel on Personnel and Training, Department of Defense, Washington, D. C.

Captain K. L. Nutting, Bureau of Naval Personnel, Department of the Navy, Washington, D. C.

Lt. Colonel D. M. Ramsey, Department of the Army, Washington, D. C.

Lt. Colonel H. J. Rice, Training Section, Marine Corps, Washington, D. C.

Colonel W. M. Rodgers, Military Personnel Management Division, Department of the Army, Washington, D. C.

Lt. Colonel J. C. Scott, Division of Aviation, Marine Corps, Washington, D. C.

Colonel H. F. Smith, Directorate of Personnel Procurement and Training, Department of the Air Force, Washington, D. C.

Colonel H. E. Townsend, Department of Defense, Washington, D. C.

Harold Wool, Manpower Utilization Controls Division, Office of Manpower Utilization, Department of Defense, Washington, D. C.

APRIL, 1954

Washington, D. C.

Solomon Barkin, Textile Workers Union of America (CIO), New York, N. Y.

Hyman H. Bookbinder, Congress of Industrial Organizations, Washington, D. C.

Edwin C. Brown, Rhode Island State Federation of Labor (AFL), Providence, R. I.

Oscar A. Ehrhardt, St. Louis Industrial Union Council (CIO), St. Louis, Mo.

Sam Ezelle, Kentucky State Federation of Labor (AFL), Louisville, Ky.

Milton Fried, Amalgamated Clothing Workers of America (CIO), New York, N. Y.

Thomas Gibson, United Automobile, Aircraft & Agricultural Implement Workers of America (CIO), Detroit, Mich.

William Gomberg, International Ladies' Garment Workers' Union (AFL), New York, N. Y.

William J. Hart, United Steelworkers of America (CIO), Philadelphia, Pa.

Peter Henle, American Federation of Labor, Washington, D. C.

Carl Huhndorff, International Association of Machinists (AFL), Washington, D. C.

Everett M. Kassalow, Congress of Industrial Organizations, Washington, D. C.

Kenneth J. Kelley, Massachusetts State Federation of Labor (AFL), Boston, Mass.

R. N. Marginot, International Brotherhood of Electrical Workers (AFL), Washington, D. C.

Joseph H. Piconke, United Automobile, Aircraft & Agricultural Implement Workers of America (CIO), Detroit, Mich.

Stanley H. Ruttenberg, Congress of Industrial Organizations, Washington, D. C.

Boris Shishkin, American Federation of Labor, Washington, D. C.

APRIL, 1954

Atlanta, Georgia

Harry Alston, National Urban League, Atlanta, Ga.

William M. Boyd, Atlanta University, Atlanta, Ga.

Brailsford R. Brazeal, Morehouse College, Atlanta, Ga.
Robert H. Brisbane, Morehouse College, Atlanta, Ga.
Walter R. Chivers, Morehouse College, Atlanta, Ga.
Grace Towns Hamilton, Atlanta Urban League, Atlanta, Ga.
Mozell C. Hill, Atlanta University, Atlanta, Ga.
John Hope II, Fisk University, Nashville, Tenn.
J. P. Lydon, Lockheed Aircraft Corporation, Marietta, Ga.
George Mitchell, Southern Regional Council, Atlanta, Ga.
Phenizee Ranson, Georgia State Employment Service, Atlanta, Ga.
Robert A. Thompson, Atlanta Urban League, Atlanta, Ga.
Samuel Z. Westerfield, Atlanta University, Atlanta, Ga.
Edward B. Williams, Morehouse College, Atlanta, Ga.

APRIL, 1954

   Atlanta, Georgia

Robert C. Anderson, Southern Regional Education Board, Atlanta, Ga.
C. L. Barrineau, Redstone Arsenal, Huntsville, Ala.
Raymond E. Bisha, Louisville & Nashville Railroad Company, Louisville, Ky.
Charles Bullock, Bureau of Labor Statistics, Department of Labor, Atlanta, Ga.
Robert C. Chinn, Ford Motor Company, Hapeville, Ga.
C. W. Cole, E. I. du Pont de Nemours & Company, Augusta, Ga.
G. L. Crawford, Southern Technical Institute, Chamblee, Ga.
William E. Crooks, Celanese Corporation of America, Rome, Ga.
I. Y. East, International Paper Company, Mobile, Ala.
John K. Folger, Southern Regional Education Board, Atlanta, Ga.
John E. Ivey, Jr., Southern Regional Education Board, Atlanta, Ga.
J. P. Lydon, Lockheed Aircraft Corporation, Marietta, Ga.
N. R. Maleady, General Electric Company, Rome, Ga.
Captain Robert E. Perkins, U. S. Navy, Charleston Naval Shipyard, Charleston, S. C.
E. A. Shelley, Tennessee Valley Authority, Knoxville, Tenn.
D. H. Standard, Harris Foundry & Machine Company, Cordele, Ga.
Philip Weltner, Oglethorpe University, Oglethorpe University, Ga.
Colonel A. N. Willis, U. S. Army (Ret.), Combustion Engineering-Superheater, Inc., Chattanooga, Tenn.
Daniel E. Woodman, The Woodman Company, Inc., Decatur, Ga.

AUGUST, 1954

   Stamford, Connecticut

Gilbert Brooks, Stamford Branch of the Bridgeport Engineering Institute, Stamford, Conn.

Dean Brossman, The Stamford-Greenwich Manufacturers' Council, Stamford, Conn.

William Brown, Homelite Corporation, East Portchester, Conn.

Reed Clark, Yale & Towne Manufacturing Company, Stamford, Conn.

John Miller, Pitney-Bowes, Inc., Stamford, Conn.

Paul Osterby, Norma-Hoffman Bearings Corporation, Stamford, Conn.

Harry Roos, Electrolux Corporation, Old Greenwich, Conn.

Sarah F. Smith, Board of Education, Stamford, Conn.

INDIVIDUALS*

Dwight Adams, Los Angeles City Board of Education, Los Angeles, Calif.

P. E. Babcock, Vocational Education Service, Atlanta, Ga.

Melvin L. Barlow, University of California, Los Angeles, Calif.

Earl E. Bedell, Board of Education, Detroit, Mich.

Harry Beilin, University of Minnesota, Minneapolis, Minn.

W. R. G. Bender, E. I. du Pont de Nemours & Company, Wilmington, Del.

B. G. Blackwood, United Automobile, Aircraft & Agricultural Implement Workers of America (CIO), Washington, D. C.

Jesse P. Bogue, American Association of Junior Colleges, Washington, D. C.

Lawrence Borosage, formerly Office of Education, Department of Health, Education, and Welfare, Washington, D. C.

Harold J. Bowers, Department of Education, Columbus, Ohio

Francis C. Buros, White Plains Public Schools, White Plains, N. Y.

Howard A. Campion, Los Angeles City Board of Education, Los Angeles, Calif.

John Carleton, International Association of Machinists (AFL), Atlanta, Ga.

Harry J. Carman, Columbia University, New York, N. Y.

James M. Cass, National Citizens Commission for the Public Schools, New York, N. Y.

Hollis L. Caswell, Teachers College, Columbia University, New York, N. Y.

Paul Chipman, International Association of Machinists (AFL), Atlanta, Ga.

Ansel R. Cleary, Bureau of Apprenticeship, Department of Labor, Washington, D. C.

Herbert C. Clish, San Francisco Public Schools, San Francisco, Calif.

William H. Cole, Los Angeles City Board of Education, Los Angeles, Calif.

Mary M. Condon, State Department of Public Instruction, Helena, Mont.

Claude V. Courter, Cincinnati Public Schools, Cincinnati, Ohio

Philip A. Cowen, State University of New York, Albany, N. Y.

U. Cleal Cowing, Public Schools of Springfield, Springfield, Mass.

James W. Crown, Chicago Vocational School, Chicago, Ill.

Jack Crunk, International Association of Machinists (AFL), Atlanta, Ga.

A. L. Cunningham, School City of Gary, Gary, Ind.

Robert P. Curry, Cincinnati Public Schools, Cincinnati, Ohio

* Not previously listed

Lily Mary David, Bureau of Labor Statistics, Department of Labor, Washington, D. C.

Adam E. Diehl, Los Angeles City Board of Education, Los Angeles, Calif.

David H. Dingilian, Los Angeles City Board of Education, Los Angeles, Calif.

Arthur Dondineau, Board of Education, Detroit, Mich.

Harry M. Douty, Bureau of Labor Statistics, Department of Labor, Washington, D. C.

John J. Duggan, Board of Education, Chicago, Ill.

Paul E. Elicker, National Association of Secondary School Principals, National Education Association, Washington, D. C.

Charlotte D. Elmott, Santa Barbara City Schools, Santa Barbara, Calif.

F. E. Engleman, State Department of Education, Hartford, Conn.

Fred W. Erhard, Bureau of Apprenticeship, Department of Labor, Washington, D. C.

W. N. Fenninger, State Education Department, Albany, N. Y.

Warren G. Findley, Educational Testing Service, Princeton, N. J.

Hamden L. Forkner, Teachers College, Columbia University, New York, N. Y.

Stuart Garfinkle, Bureau of Labor Statistics, Department of Labor, Washington, D. C.

Robert Gilchrist, Board of Education, Pasadena, Calif.

N. B. Giles, formerly Office of Education, Department of Health, Education, and Welfare, Washington, D. C.

J. Lyman Goldsmith, Los Angeles City Board of Education, Los Angeles, Calif.

Harold B. Gores, Newton Public Schools, Newtonville, Mass.

Hollis Guy, United Business Education Association, National Education Association, Washington, D. C.

Major General N. B. Harbold, Department of the Air Force, Washington, D. C.

Major General Harlan N. Hartness, Department of Defense, Washington, D. C.

O. L. Harvey, Department of Labor, Washington, D. C.

Carl A. Heinz, Bureau of Employment Security, Department of Labor, Washington, D. C.

J. B. Hershman, National Council of Technical Schools, Valparaiso, Ind.

John F. Hilliard, Office of Defense Mobilization, Washington, D. C.

Nicholas Hobbs, George Peabody College for Teachers, Nashville, Tenn.

Lincoln Holroyd, Esso Standard Oil Corporation, Elizabeth, N. J.

H. D. Hopkins, National Association and Council of Business Schools, Washington, D. C.

R. W. Howes, State Department of Education, Hartford, Conn.

Frank W. Hubbard, National Education Association, Washington, D. C.

A. J. Jaffe, Bureau of Applied Social Research, Columbia University, New York, N. Y.

B. Lamar Johnson, University of California, Los Angeles, Calif.
Eric H. Johnson, Illinois Curriculum Program, Springfield, Ill.
Frank P. Johnston, State Education Department, Albany, N. Y.
Toivo P. Kanninen, Bureau of Labor Statistics, Department of Labor, Washington, D. C.
David L. Kaplan, Bureau of the Census, Department of Commerce, Washington, D. C.
Franklin J. Keller, Metropolitan Vocational High School, New York, N. Y.
Homer Kempfer, National Home Study Council, Washington, D. C.
Warren A. Koerner, Board of Education, Chicago, Ill.
William D. Kraengel, Board of Education, New York, N. Y.
William B. Langsdorf, Pasadena City College, Pasadena, Calif.
Warren K. Layton, Board of Education, Detroit, Mich.
Gerald B. Leighbody, State Education Department, Buffalo, N. Y.
Louis Levine, U. S. Employment Service, Department of Labor, Washington, D. C.
Harry J. Linton, Department of Education, Schenectady, N. Y.
Seymour Lipset, Columbia University, New York, N. Y.
J. Kenneth Little, Office of Education, Department of Health, Education, and Welfare, Washington, D. C.
William P. Loomis, Office of Education, Department of Health, Education, and Welfare, Washington, D. C.
H. H. London, University of Missouri, Columbia, Mo.
Edward G. Ludtke, Office of Education, Department of Health, Education, and Welfare, Washington, D. C.
Carl G. McAndrew, E. I. du Pont de Nemours & Company, Wilmington, Del.
John S. McCauley, Bureau of Apprenticeship, Department of Labor, Washington, D. C.
Arthur L. McGrath, Board of Education, Detroit, Mich.
G. F. Malick, The Canton Public Schools, Canton, Ohio
Howard E. Marvin, Pasadena City Schools, Pasadena, Calif.
Charles Matthias, Atlanta Industrial Union Council (CIO), Atlanta, Ga.
Jeanne Miller, Technical Education News, New York, N. Y.
M. D. Mobley, American Vocational Association, Inc., Washington, D. C.
Charles N. Morris, Teachers College, Columbia University, New York, N. Y.
J. Cayce Morrison, State Education Department, Albany, N. Y.
Charles O'Dell, U. S. Employment Service, Department of Labor, Washington, D. C.
William Pabst, Brooklyn Technical High School, Brooklyn, N. Y.
C. W. Patrick, San Diego City Schools, San Diego, Calif.
James H. Pearson, Office of Education, Department of Health, Education, and Welfare, Washington, D. C.
William Poole, Standard Oil Development Corporation, Elizabeth, N. J.
Brigadier General H. B. Powell, Department of the Army, Washington, D. C.

Benjamin Remland, New York City Board of Education, Brooklyn, N. Y.

Felix C. Robb, George Peabody College for Teachers, Nashville, Tenn.

W. Lyle Roeseler, State Department of Public Instruction, Helena, Mont.

Ralph M. Rogers, Los Angeles City Board of Education, Los Angeles, Calif.

Edward J. Russell, Public School Department, Pittsfield, Mass.

Andrew J. Scholar, Board of Education, Chicago, Ill.

Lowell Selby, Dade County Public Schools, Miami, Fla.

William E. Severn, City School District, Corning, N. Y.

C. E. Shaw, E. I. du Pont de Nemours & Company, Wilmington, Del.

Charles B. Shuman, Illinois Agricultural Association, Chicago, Ill.

John T. Shuman, The School District of the City of Allentown, Allentown, Pa.

Irving H. Siegel, The Twentieth Century Fund, Washington, D. C.

Brigadier General Dale O. Smith, National Security Council, Washington, D. C.

Elmer R. Smith, Department of Public Schools, Providence, R. I.

Herbert H. Sommers, Board of Education, Chicago, Ill.

Benjamin J. Stern, New York City Board of Education, Brooklyn, N. Y.

Ralph H. Stone, Veterans Administration, Washington, D. C.

Brigadier General W. S. Stone, Department of the Air Force, Washington, D. C.

Joseph Strobel, State Education Department, Albany, N. Y.

Philip Q. Stumpf, Paulsboro Public Schools, Paulsboro, N. J.

Donald E. Super, Teachers College, Columbia University, New York, N. Y.

Sol Swerdloff, Bureau of Labor Statistics, Department of Labor, Washington, D. C.

Ernest R. Thiel, Indianapolis Public Schools, Indianapolis, Ind.

Gwyn Thomas, Manufacturers Association of Syracuse, Inc., Syracuse, N. Y.

W. R. Thomas, Dade County Public Schools, Miami, Fla.

Albert S. Thompson, Teachers College, Columbia University, New York, N. Y.

Archie M. Turrell, Muir College, Pasadena, Calif.

Captain E. K. Van Swearingen, Department of the Navy, Washington, D. C.

Pearl A. Wanamaker, State Superintendent of Public Instruction, Olympia, Wash.

Gilbert G. Weaver, American Vocational Association, Inc., Washington, D. C.

Ralph C. Wenrich, University of Michigan, Ann Arbor, Mich.

Alvin E. Westgaard, Milwaukee Public Schools, Milwaukee, Wisc.

H. F. Williams, Jr., The Evansville Manufacturers and Employers Association, Evansville, Ind.

Calman Winegarden, Bureau of Labor Statistics, Department of Labor, Washington, D. C.

Helen Wood, Bureau of Labor Statistics, Department of Labor, Washington, D. C.

Contents

Tables

PART ONE

A Policy for Skilled Manpower

Summary of Recommendations by the National Manpower Council

OUR future progress and strength depend upon a conscious and deliberate concern with our manpower resources. Recognition that our most precious single resource consists of the skills, capacities, and creativeness of our people is not enough. For the sake of contributing to the greater well-being of each individual and strengthening the nation as a whole, it is also necessary for us to assure the further development of our manpower resources and their more effective utilization. To take such action we must view our human resources as a whole, and not only as they now are, but as they can be developed.

In the past we have acted as if each manpower problem exists in isolation — whether it be the waste of potential ability and talent, shortages of teachers and nurses, or the adequacy of a community's facilities for training technicians. Consequently, we are easily diverted from a search for sound solutions for complex and difficult problems and tend to rely upon simple and short-sighted answers.

Five major long-range objectives must be pursued if we are to strengthen the nation's resources of skilled workers and technicians. These are:

To strengthen the contributions made by secondary education to the acquisition of skill

To develop a more effective program for vocational guidance

To provide more equal opportunities for all individuals to acquire skill

To improve the facilities and methods used to train skilled and
technical manpower

To increase knowledge about our manpower resources.

These objectives can be achieved only through a continuing and
many-sided effort sustained by an informed public opinion and
requiring the cooperation of the schools, employers, labor organizations, voluntary groups, the armed services, and local, state, and
Federal government.

With respect to strengthening the contributions made by secondary education to the acquisition of skill, the National Manpower Council recommends that:

1. Local and state governments encourage men and women
   of ability to enter and remain in the teaching profession
   by establishing more desirable conditions of employment,
   including salaries commensurate with their training and
   responsibilities

2. Boards of education and school officials concentrate on
   achieving the key purposes of secondary education — to
   prepare the individual for citizenship, for a worthwhile life,
   and for work — by insuring that all students, excepting the
   small minority unable to profit from it, pursue a common
   program at least through the second year of high school
   which concentrates on teaching them to communicate
   effectively in writing and speech, to handle elementary
   mathematical operations, and to apply their knowledge to
   solving the problems they will encounter in life and work

3. Boards of education and school officials insure that students
   are permitted to specialize intensively in vocational subjects
   only after they have completed two years of high school,
   and that able and interested vocational students also are
   provided with the opportunity to qualify for college
   entrance

4. Local and state educational officials, in cooperation with
   special advisory committees comprising employer and la-

bor representatives, critically reappraise existing vocational education programs in order to insure their effectiveness in the light of current changes in technology, employment standards, and on-the-job training practices; the growth of junior and community colleges and technical institutes; and the training programs of the armed services

5. The Congress review existing Federal legislation providing grants-in-aid for vocational education purposes in order to ascertain whether the objectives, scale, and methods of allocation of funds are enabling the Federal government to make the most effective contribution to the development of the nation's resources of skilled manpower.

With respect to developing a more effective program for vocational guidance, the National Manpower Council recommends that:

1. State and local governments and boards of education recognize that the provision of essential educational and vocational guidance services is a major responsibility of secondary education by increasing substantially and rapidly the funds and staff available for guidance and counseling purposes

2. School officials use their guidance and counseling staff primarily for vocational guidance purposes and, when expanded resources of staff and funds permit, also for counseling students with personal adjustment problems

3. School officials make vocational guidance available no later than the ninth year and have it continue throughout the high school course, and that they assign to the classroom teacher major responsibility for helping the student to make sound educational and occupational decisions

4. School officials take the lead in their communities to assure a vigorous cooperative effort, in which industry, business, labor, government, the armed services, and civic groups participate, to provide occupational information and other

types of assistance essential for effective vocational guidance.

With respect to providing more equal opportunities for all individuals to acquire skill, the National Manpower Council recommends that:

1. All employers hire and promote employees and all unions admit individuals to membership without regard to their race, creed, color, national origin, or sex

2. Employers and unions and the Joint Apprenticeship Councils and Committees eliminate the practice, wherever it exists, of barring individuals from admission to apprenticeship programs because of their race or national origin

3. The President insure that the heads of Federal departments and agencies eliminate discrimination based on race, creed, color, national origin, or sex wherever it remains in Federal employment; and that the full authority of the Federal government be used to prevent such discrimination in all work performed for it under contract.

With respect to improving the facilities and methods used to train skilled and technical manpower, the National Manpower Council recommends that:

1. Unions and employers and the Joint Apprenticeship Councils and Committees review regularly the content and length of training time of apprenticeship programs in order to insure their efficiency and effectiveness

2. Employers seek to provide greater opportunities for their employees to acquire increased skills through a planned system of varied job assignments, broader training on and off the job, and increasing the training competence of their supervisory staffs

3. State and city governments undertake comprehensive surveys to determine whether existing training facilities are adequate to meet the requirements for skilled and technical manpower

4. The Congress, by adjusting pay and other service benefits, enable the armed forces to reduce excessive turnover and to encourage re-enlistment, so as to retain a larger core group of qualified technicians, specialists, and noncommissioned officers

5. The Secretary of Defense direct the Secretaries of the Army, Navy, and Air Force to utilize, wherever appropriate, the facilities and personnel available in the civilian community in meeting the training requirements of the services.

With respect to increasing knowledge about our manpower resources, the National Manpower Council recommends that:

1. The universities and foundations encourage and support research to increase our knowledge about manpower resources with particular reference to the complex process of occupational choice; the types of information essential for effective vocational guidance; the role of skilled and technical manpower in economic development; the impact of governmental policies upon the supply of skilled manpower resources; and the relation between how people are trained and their subsequent work performance

2. The Secretary of Defense direct the Secretaries of the Army, Navy, and Air Force to evaluate the varied experiences of the services with training and make their significant findings and their new methods available for civilian use

3. The President direct the appropriate agencies of the government to provide periodic and comprehensive appraisals of the country's available resources of skilled and technical workers and to seek improvements in the methods of estimating future manpower requirements.

A Statement by the National Manpower Council

IN THE PAST Americans could risk being just as complacent about their human resources as they had been about their resources of water, iron, or oil. Today, any attitude of complacency is short-sighted and dangerous. Our present position and our future needs require that we concern ourselves with the long-range development and effective utilization of all our trained manpower resources.

The skilled manpower segment in our civilian working population of sixty-four million consists of eight or nine million skilled workers and less than half a million technicians. These resources of skilled manpower play a critical role in producing almost half of the world's goods. We depend upon them for our food, clothing, housing, and public utilities. They assist our doctors and dentists in providing essential health services. They help operate our transportation systems and communication facilities. They help transform into reality the dreams and the diagrams of the scientist and engineer. They build, install, control, maintain, and repair the machines in our factories and offices. They are needed to operate our atomic installations and to produce, service, and repair our automobiles and telephones, our television sets and refrigerators, our vacuum cleaners and washing machines. The armed forces must depend upon highly trained personnel in uniform, and upon skilled workers and technicians as civilian producers of weapons, vehicles, ships, planes, tanks, and communication equipment.

In its previous studies, the National Manpower Council dealt with our resources of scientific and professional workers. Here it considers another vital segment of our manpower — the highly skilled men and women whose formal education usually stops with high school or junior college. Concern with manpower resources must begin with concern for the education and training of all our people. The best possible education and training for all, in order to help them prepare for life and work, must be the nation's constant goal. The National Manpower Council's primary concern is with the *quality* of the nation's human resources — that is with the training, capacities, skills, competences, and creativeness of the American people.

IDENTIFYING SKILLED AND TECHNICAL WORKERS

As new ways of producing goods and services emerge, the tasks which men and women perform change. Technological innovations result in breaking down some skilled trades into separate tasks, each of which is learned fairly quickly and easily, as in shoemaking and glassmaking. Certain skilled occupations have thus been made relatively unimportant, if not obsolete. But advances in science and technology also create new skills and new skilled occupations.

The measure of skilled work is relative and changing, and the classification of workers as unskilled, semi-skilled, and skilled must always be somewhat arbitrary. Three criteria can be used to decide who is a skilled worker or technician. First, the individual must possess the distinctive abilities required for a specific occupation. These distinctive abilities go beyond those acquired in the process of growing up, such as reading, writing, driving a car or a tractor, or using a saw. Second, the skilled worker must achieve a particular level of competence. Every skilled occupation has its own standards of what tasks the worker must be able to master in a given time and the quality of acceptable work. Third, the skilled worker or technician must have had training to acquire his distinctive abilities and competence. No one becomes a skilled worker without making some special effort.

Distinctive abilities, competence in work, and special training — these are the features which distinguish the one worker in seven or eight who today merits being called skilled. They explain why the supply of skilled manpower cannot be increased overnight. They make it clear why, when shortages of skilled workers arise, an effort is made to change the way in which goods and services are produced so as to enable less skilled employees to handle the work.

SKILLED OCCUPATIONS

Skilled workers and technicians are found in hundreds of different occupations. In addition to foremen and workers in manufacturing and construction trades traditionally considered skilled, the skilled manpower resources of the nation include workers in the clerical, sales, and service fields; in mining, lumbering, transportation, and communications; and in technical occupations. The largest skilled groups are in maintenance and repair, metal machining, and construction. In these fields there are skilled occupations comparable in size with the largest of the professions — teaching and engineering — but most skilled groups are relatively small.

Many skilled workers are in trades which have long histories. This is true of the glass blower, the carpenter, the machinist, the draftsman, the millwright, the typesetter, the baker, and the barber. Other occupations, such as those of the aircraft mechanic, the electronic technician, the meteorological aide, the orthopedic technician, and the X-ray technician, are relatively new. In many occupations the old name frequently obscures the new and different skills that workers have acquired. The work of the electrician today bears only slight resemblance to that of his predecessor half a century ago.

TECHNICIANS

The number of technical workers is increasing rapidly. Their growing importance reflects both advances in science and technology, and a steadily rising demand for services that can best be provided by professional personnel working together with persons of less than professional training. Except for draftsmen and surveyors, most technical workers represent new kinds of occupational groupings — engineering aides, testing technicians, laboratory assistants, and a variety of medical and dental technicians.

Technicians are more likely to be trained in educational institutions than are the more traditional skilled workers. Most technicians have some knowledge of theory in their field. Moreover, many of them work so closely with professional personnel that it is common practice to describe them as sub- or semi-professional workers. Yet the features which technicians and other kinds of skilled workers share in common are at least as significant as the differences between the two groups. Technical workers, consequently, represent a distinctive group within the total skilled manpower component of the labor force.

TRAINING OF SKILLED AND TECHNICAL MANPOWER

Skilled workers and technicians are trained in many different ways. Their training may be acquired in formal programs, informally, or in both ways. It may take the form of apprenticeship or enrollment in a technical institute or in a community or junior college. It may occur through observation and imitation, or planned instruction on the job. It may involve study in a night school class or through a correspondence course. It may be obtained in the armed services through a combination of classroom instruction and on-the-job experience. In the very diversity of the ways in which people can acquire skill the nation has a source of strength.

At least three out of every five skilled workers and technicians acquire their abilities and competence through informal training. Because informal training is a part of work experience, a considerable number of workers are always being prepared for jobs requiring more skill than the tasks they are currently performing. The various methods of skill training do not, however, produce uniform results. The skilled worker who is the product of apprenticeship training has been prepared for an occupation rather than a specific job and is likely to be better equipped to meet the challenges of new problems than is the worker who "picks up" his skills. A formal training program which is not narrowly centered on meeting immediate production needs will provide the employer with more resourceful and adaptable workers than unplanned, informal training. On the other hand, since skills are so extensively acquired on the job, the processes of promotion and changing jobs contribute significantly to the development of skilled manpower.

The distinctive abilities and competence which differentiate skilled workers are not quickly acquired. Few skilled occupations can be learned, through either formal or informal methods, in less than two years, and for most skilled occupations the training is longer. But, just as there is no single way of becoming a skilled worker, so there is no specified training time. The time required to prepare an individual for a skilled job is affected by many factors. His aptitudes, background, the amount and quality of his schooling, and his access to opportunities for training play decisive roles. Graduation from a good high school may give young men and women significant advantages in later acquiring the skills of a trade. The training he receives in the armed services may carry a young man a considerable distance along the road to becoming a skilled worker. An unwillingness to forego present income, however, may deter a person from continuing in school or from entering an apprenticeship program. Because of race, sex, ethnic origin, or religion, individuals may be cut off from some opportunities for training or barred from jobs which lead to the acquisition of skills.

The length of training also depends on the nature of the particular occupation. Apprenticeship training, for example, runs from a minimum of two years, as in the case of construction ironworkers and women bookbinders, to five and six for photoengravers, and as many as eight for diesinkers. Most apprenticeship training requires four years. The training period for most technician occupations is two or three years. When training is indistinguishable from the work experience itself and the climb up the skill ladder is accomplished through promotion and changing jobs, it may take a decade or more before a worker reaches a skilled job with corresponding pay.

THE ARMED SERVICES AS TRAINING INSTITUTIONS

Our military requirements have wide-ranging implications for our skilled manpower resources. To maintain the armed forces at their present strength of about three million, at least two out of every three young men in the country spend two, three, or four years on active duty. The general level of skill and of technical knowledge required in the armed forces today is much higher than it was only a decade ago. Continuing progress in research and development will raise the level rapidly in the years immediately ahead.

Almost half of the enlisted men in the services are currently classified as technical or skilled, or as noncommissioned officers. Since most begin their military service at eighteen or nineteen, relatively few are skilled when they enter the armed forces. For many, fulfilling their obligation to their country interrupts their education or their training for work. Even though Selective Service regulations provide that young men enrolled in approved apprenticeship programs are eligible for deferment, only a small number are deferred. Most men complete their apprenticeship after they come out of service.

Yet compulsory service should not be viewed primarily as an interruption in a man's education or his training for work. Nor are the armed services merely users of vast numbers of trained manpower. On the contrary, they play a vital, though still far from clearly understood, role in the development of skilled and technical manpower. For many young men they provide the initial experience in working together with others. For many others the services provide training opportunities that are frequently not available in civilian life. The training he acquires during a two-year term of service rarely makes a man skilled. However, many men who serve for four years or more have the opportunity to acquire a high order of skill or technical competence. Veterans have been able to step into skilled jobs in such fields as electronics and airplane and automobile production, maintenance, and repair on the basis of what they learned in service.

About half of the men who enter the armed forces receive some kind of technical training, much of it narrowly specialized. The range of skills taught in the services and the training methods used are almost as varied as in civilian life. In the Army, which relies more heavily than the other services upon formal instruction, 500 different courses are being taught in thirty-five schools. Courses of formal instruction lasting sixteen weeks or more — that is, about a fourth of the effective time a draftee is in uniform — are used by the Army to prepare men for specialized assignments. Almost one in every five enlisted men currently completes such a course. In the Air Force and Navy, substantial numbers of enlisted men also receive specialist training in service schools and on the job. Over a quarter of a million men, moreover, are making use of the opportunity provided by the United States Armed Forces Institute to study a wide range of nonmilitary subjects.

PREVIOUS POLICY ON SKILLED MANPOWER

Only recently have we come to realize that the development and effective utilization of our human resources cannot be left to chance. In the past, concern with the adequacy of our skilled manpower assumed national dimensions only in times of emergency, as in World War II and, to a lesser extent, during the fighting in Korea. At other times, problems involving skilled workers, which resulted from changes in technology, the opening up of new industries, or the rapid expansion of enterprises in new locations have challenged the individual employer rather than the nation as a whole.

Throughout most of our history, however, we pursued one major national policy that was designed to provide the United States with an adequate labor supply. Until the 1920's, we added annually to our labor supply large numbers of skilled workers from Europe. The expansion of public education also contributed to strengthening the nation's skilled manpower supply. The growth of publicly supported secondary education has been influenced by the establishment, through the Smith-Hughes Act of 1917, of a system of Federal aid for vocational education in the high schools. More recently, the country's skilled manpower resources have been strengthened by the Federal government's encouragement of apprenticeship training, the education and training opportunities made available to veterans, and the growth of publicly supported community and junior colleges and technical institutes.

EFFECTS OF NATIONAL ACTION ON SKILLED MANPOWER RESOURCES

Today, the actions of the Federal government affect, both directly and indirectly, the development and utilization of skilled and technical manpower. Large appropriations for defense materially increase the demand for skilled workers and technicians. The armed services provide training for various skilled and technical occupations. Because the acquisition of skill depends so greatly on training which is part of work experience, Federal policies aimed at maintaining high levels of employment also contribute to the development of skilled and technical manpower.

The Federal government also plays a large part in opening up opportunities for the acquisition of skill to members of minority groups. It seeks to do away with discriminatory employment practices in civilian industry where it has the authority. The Supreme Court recently laid the basis for an unsegregated public school system. Currently the Federal government contributes about $30 million a year for vocational education in the fields of agriculture, trade and industrial occupations, home economics, and the distributive occupations. This sum, administered through the Office of Education in the Department of Health, Education, and Welfare, however, is only a small part of what the states and local communities spend on the joint Federal-state program of vocational education. Such governmental agencies as the Atomic Energy Commission and the Tennessee Valley Authority support various training activities.

The Department of Labor is charged by law with carrying out specific responsibilities directly related to increasing our national resources of skilled manpower. It encourages apprenticeship training through the Bureau of Apprenticeship. The Bureau of Labor Statistics and the Bureau of Employment Security play key roles in developing basic data that are indispensable for estimating future skilled and technical manpower requirements and for vocational guidance.

LOOKING AHEAD

The immediate employment outlook in specific communities provides a poor vantage point for evaluating the nation's resources of skilled manpower. A longer-range view is essential, even though it will not provide us with accurate forecasts of the requirements for different types of skilled workers and technicians. Constant change characterizes our economy. New ways of making goods, new products, new skills and knowledge, and new occupations will appear in the future as they have appeared in the past. Consequently, the more our skilled workers secure broad training that enables them to adapt easily to changing conditions, the stronger we will be.

The peaceful resolution of international differences and the prevention of war constitute the mainspring of American foreign policy. Yet we must continue to be prepared against the eventuality of a major war. By lifting the general level of skill and thereby providing a larger potential supply of skilled workers and technicians, we can better meet the problems of full-scale mobilization for atomic warfare.

We are sometimes likely to forget that the rate of our economic progress depends in considerable measure on the quantity and quality of our available skilled manpower. Many small, but important, improvements in technology are made by skilled and technical workers. Moreover, the rapidity with which major innovations can be introduced into the economy depends in part upon the availability of skilled manpower. This is no less true for the armed services than it is for the civilian sector of the economy. Shortages of skilled manpower can retard economic progress, and there are limits to the extent to which additional machines can be used as substitutes for skilled workers and technicians. Many difficulties that underdeveloped countries experience in trying to improve their economic position, even when they have enough capital, arise from inadequate numbers of supervisory and skilled personnel. Even in the United States the interrelations between skilled manpower and economic progress can be seen in the problems encountered in speeding the industrialization of the South, or in attracting new industries to such areas as the anthracite coal mining counties of Pennsylvania.

We lack an adequate inventory of our resources of skilled and technical manpower. Hence, it is not surprising that there are no reliable forecasts of the nation's future requirements for skilled and technical workers. However, the general direction of important future developments can be perceived. The rapid growth of the technician group is likely to continue. The percentage of the work force in manufacturing and construction industries will probably decline, while the proportion of workers in the clerical, sales, and service fields will probably increase. If the demand for health services continues to increase substantially, the number of technicians in the medical and dental fields is likely to continue to grow rapidly.

Private and governmental expenditures for research and development are speeding up advances in scientific knowledge and technology that create new skills. This is apparent from what has already happened in such fields as atomic energy, electronics, and chemicals. Future technological changes will, as in the past, lead to the use of larger, more complex, and costlier machines and equipment. Human errors arising from the employment of poorly trained workers could destroy facilities and materials worth hundreds of thousands and even millions of dollars. The marked trend toward increasingly automatic systems of production, as well as the further mechanization of office operations, will probably eliminate the need for many semi-skilled workers who now perform narrowly specialized and routine tasks, and will require programs for retraining such workers. Highly skilled workers and technicians will be needed, however, for the production, installation, maintenance, repair and control of such self-directing, self-tending automatic machines as scientists and engineers are currently developing.

GUIDES FOR ACTION

Our future progress and strength depend upon a conscious and deliberate concern with our manpower resources. Recognition that our most precious single resource consists of the skills, capacities, and creativeness of our people is not enough. For the sake of contributing to the greater well-being of each individual and strengthening the nation as a whole, it is also necessary for us to assure the further development of our manpower resources and their more effective utilization. To take such action we must view our human resources as a whole, and not only as they now are, but as they can be developed.

In the past we have acted as if each manpower problem exists in isolation — whether it be the waste of potential ability and talent, shortages of teachers and nurses, or the adequacy of a community's facilities for training technicians. Consequently, we are easily diverted from a search for sound solutions for complex and difficult problems and tend to rely upon simple and short-sighted answers.

Five major long-range objectives must be pursued if we are to strengthen the nation's resources of skilled workers and technicians. These are:

To strengthen the contributions made by secondary education to the acquisition of skill

To develop a more effective program for vocational guidance

To provide more equal opportunities for all individuals to acquire skill

To improve the facilities and methods used to train skilled
and technical manpower

To increase knowledge about our manpower resources.

These objectives can be achieved only through a continuing and
many-sided effort sustained by an informed public opinion and
requiring the cooperation of the schools, employers, labor organizations, voluntary groups, the armed services, and local, state, and
Federal government.

STRENGTHENING THE SECONDARY SCHOOLS

One of the most important developments in American life has
been the remarkable growth in secondary education. Few boys
and girls went to high school in 1900. Today, four out of five young
people receive some secondary schooling, and three out of five
graduate from high school. About 8 million boys and girls are now
enrolled as daytime students in some 24,000 public secondary
schools. We are now entering upon another period of rapid growth,
and it is expected that by 1965 our publicly supported secondary
schools will have about 12 million daytime students — an increase
of 50 percent over the present enrollment. In the next few years,
therefore, we will be setting the pattern for secondary education
for a period of expansion.

Secondary education seeks to prepare our youth for assuming
the privileges and responsibilities of citizenship and for leading a
meaningful and worthwhile life. It fulfills another key purpose
by helping to prepare them for work — both those who continue
with their formal schooling and those who enter employment
immediately upon leaving high school. Preparation for work is an
integral part of secondary education because high school provides
all students with an opportunity to increase the skills which form
the foundation for work. These skills consist of the ability to
communicate effectively in writing and speech, to handle elementary mathematical operations, and to utilize knowledge to
cope thoughtfully with problems. From his school experience,

moreover, the student acquires basic work habits. He learns to follow a regular schedule, to meet performance standards, and to respond to incentives in the form of grades, privileges, awards, and opportunities for further study.

Preparation for citizenship, for the growth of the individual, and for work are related and complementary purposes of secondary education. They are not in conflict with one another, or even in competition, although the debates that engage educational leaders sometimes suggest that they are. The secondary schools can make their maximum contribution to the development of the nation's manpower resources by insuring that their students are equipped to communicate effectively, to do mathematical operations, and to respond thoughtfully to problem situations, for without these basic skills the abilities and competence required for skilled and technical work cannot be acquired.

The positive value that Americans assign to education and the practical benefits which the individual derives from formal schooling have combined to keep more of our young people in school longer. High school graduation is increasingly becoming a qualification for desirable employment, and the armed forces urge young people to complete high school before beginning their military service. High school graduation is not only a prerequisite for advanced schooling, but it is also extremely important in securing access to the opportunities for acquiring skill in industry and the armed services.

Throughout the country, communities are critically evaluating the education of their children. This is a healthy development. In the past we have been more preoccupied with school buildings and the number of years our children spend in school than with the quality of their education. We are just beginning to understand the difficult tasks that face the high schools of the country because their student bodies comprise boys and girls who vary greatly in family background, intellectual ability, motivation, and educational need. More by accident than conscious design we have required the schools to assume responsibilities for the development of our children which lie beyond the reach of their limited funds and teaching resources. We are beginning to recognize that as citizens we must provide more financial support if we want the schools to do a tolerable, let alone a superior, job in accomplishing their major educational tasks.

The key to good education is good teaching. When able men and women are discouraged from entering upon a teaching career or leave after a few years because of poor salaries and low prestige, it becomes extremely difficult for the nation to realize its educational goals. Exceptional teachers are always at a premium, and the schools face no greater challenge than to learn how to make the most effective use of those they have. In concentrating attention on the problem of shortages of teachers, we have neglected developing more effective ways of utilizing our available teaching personnel. The need to recruit and maintain an adequate number of competent high school teachers of mathematics and the physical sciences deserves special comment. Lack of instruction or poor instruction in these subjects can cut off many boys and girls from opportunities to prepare properly for skilled and technical occupations.

During the past three decades vocational education has secured an established place within secondary education. Vocational schools and courses are not designed to produce fully trained skilled workers and technicians. They do, however, aim to provide young people with the fundamentals of specific occupations and to prepare them to acquire further skills more readily either on the job or through additional schooling. As the proportion of young people attending high school increased and as the school-leaving age rose, vocational education sought to meet the occupational needs of many who did not plan to go on to college. Since 1917, Federal funds, matched and exceeded by state and local appropriations, have spurred the growth of vocational education, while Federal law and administrative practice have influenced its forms and objectives.

Although general and vocational education are intermingled in the same school systems, sharp differences still exist between educational leaders in the two fields. In some states and communities these differences are intensified by separate administrative structures for vocational education. Partly because of the size and diversity of the high school population, the separation of vocational education from general secondary education is becoming less distinct. The number of separate vocational high schools is relatively small, and vocational instruction has been diffused throughout the secondary school system. Four fifths of the 2,000 high schools offering trade and industrial vocational courses under the Federal-state program are not vocational schools. Federally supported vocational agriculture courses are offered in 10,000 high schools. In addition, many high school students are enrolled in industrial arts and business courses which lie outside the Federal-state program.

To make certain that vocational education is fully responsive to changes in technology and to the ways in which skilled and technical manpower resources are developed in the United States, it is necessary to guard against certain errors which have been made in the past. One of these errors is to conceive of vocational courses as a means of preparing students for specific jobs rather than as providing them with a broad base for later training. A second is to relate the vocational instruction provided in school solely to the needs of one or two major employers in the community, or to traditional occupations, thus neglecting new fields of work. A third error is to direct less able and poorly motivated students into vocational courses on the ground that their educational needs cannot be met in any other way. A fourth lies in failing to provide vocational, as well as general, high school students with as much mastery over the basic mental skills as they are capable of acquiring. And a fifth error is to compel vocational students to pursue programs of study which severely reduce their opportunity of going on to college, if they later decide to do so.

In order to strengthen the contributions of secondary education to the development of our resources of skilled workers and
technicians, the National Manpower Council recommends that:

1. Local and state governments encourage men and women of
   ability to enter and remain in the teaching profession by
   establishing more desirable conditions of employment, including salaries commensurate with their training and
   responsibilities

2. Boards of education and school officials concentrate on
   achieving the key purposes of secondary education — to
   prepare the individual for citizenship, for a worthwhile
   life, and for work — by insuring that all students, excepting
   the small minority unable to profit from it, pursue a common program at least through the second year of high
   school which concentrates on teaching them to communicate effectively in writing and speech, to handle elementary
   mathematical operations, and to apply their knowledge to
   solving the problems they will encounter in life and work

3. Boards of education and school officials insure that students
   are permitted to specialize intensively in vocational subjects only after they have completed two years of high
   school, and that able and interested vocational students
   also are provided with the opportunity to qualify for college
   entrance

4. Local and state educational officials, in cooperation with
   special advisory committees comprising employer and labor
   representatives, critically reappraise existing vocational
   education programs in order to insure their effectiveness in
   the light of current changes in technology, employment
   standards, and on-the-job training practices; the growth of
   junior and community colleges and technical institutes;
   and the training programs of the armed services

5. The Congress review existing Federal legislation providing
   grants-in-aid for vocational education purposes in order to

ascertain whether the objectives, scale, and methods of allocation of funds are enabling the Federal government to make the most effective contribution to the development of the nation's resources of skilled manpower.

DEVELOPING A MORE EFFECTIVE VOCATIONAL GUIDANCE PROGRAM

The freedom of the individual to choose his occupation and work is an article of American faith. In a complex, highly specialized, and changing society, the individual needs help to make effective use of this freedom. Particularly during their high school years young people need assistance to clarify their understanding of their aptitudes, interests, and vocational goals; to learn about the range of occupations, not only in their own but in other communities; to relate their present schooling to their future work and career; and to become informed about the opportunities for further education and training. When a person makes an educational or occupational decision without due consideration of his strengths and his opportunities, he wastes his potential abilities, and the community's manpower resources are correspondingly weakened.

Shortly after the turn of the century, a few secondary schools undertook to provide their students with vocational guidance. Today, vocational guidance and counseling are recognized as important functions of the secondary school. Yet, except for a small number of communities, these functions are not being satisfactorily performed. Most students do not receive the assistance they require to make the best educational and occupational decisions. Some counselors base their advice solely on the results of intelligence or aptitude tests. In some schools counselors seek to persuade their students to reach a particular decision rather than to help them make their own. The occupational information essential for sound vocational guidance is limited, and, moreover, it is frequently in a form that makes it difficult for the counselor as well as the student to use.

In recent years many schools have vastly extended the scope of their guidance responsibilities by broadening their objectives to include the counseling of students on problems of personal adjustment. Neither funds nor personnel are available to enable most schools to achieve these objectives. At present there are about 18,000 persons in the junior and senior high schools who perform counseling duties for a school population of eight million. Only a small minority are full-time counselors specially trained for their tasks. Until more and better trained personnel become available, it is important for the schools to reconsider the nature of their counseling commitments.

The test of an effective program of vocational guidance lies in the success it has in helping the individual to take full advantage of the opportunities available to him — in short, to increase his true freedom of choice. Information presented in usable form that extends the occupational horizons of boys and girls, gives them a sense of the characteristics and future prospects of different occupational fields, and indicates the preparation required to enter them is basic for an effective guidance program.

Many agencies play important roles in vocational guidance, but the secondary school is in a strategic position to affect the largest number of young people during crucial years of their lives. The school can help the student understand the importance of his educational and occupational choices by having the teacher provide relevant knowledge as a part of regular classroom instruction. In achieving this end, the schools will have to utilize their professionally trained guidance experts to advise, assist, and support the classroom teacher, who will have to carry most guidance responsibilities. School officials, moreover, can encourage employers, unions, governmental officials, and others in the community to cooperate in the preparation and presentation of current occupational information.

In order to develop a more effective program for vocational guidance in the schools, the National Manpower Council recommends that:

1. State and local governments and boards of education recognize that the provision of essential educational and vocational guidance services is a major responsibility of secondary education by increasing substantially and rapidly the funds and staff available for guidance and counseling purposes

2. School officials use their guidance and counseling staff primarily for vocational guidance purposes and, when expanded resources of staff and funds permit, also for counseling students with personal adjustment problems

3. School officials make vocational guidance available no later than the ninth year and have it continue throughout the high school course, and that they assign to the classroom teacher major responsibility for helping the student to make sound educational and occupational decisions

4. School officials take the lead in their communities to assure a vigorous cooperative effort, in which industry, business, labor, government, the armed services, and civic groups participate, to provide occupational information and other types of assistance essential for effective vocational guidance.

PROVIDING MORE EQUAL OPPORTUNITIES

To restrict opportunities for education and training on the basis of an individual's race, religion, ethnic origin, or sex violates American ideals. It also wastes the potential abilities of a significant proportion of our total population, and thereby prevents the full development and effective utilization of the nation's manpower resources. In recent years, major advances have been scored in reducing or entirely removing artificial barriers that limit the opportunities of members of minority groups to acquire a sound education or to secure training for employment as skilled workers. These gains have come about as a result of such diverse reasons as the quickening of the American conscience, the manpower needs of the armed services, and the maintenance of high levels of employment. Various voluntary groups, as well as several state and city governments and the Federal government, have taken the lead in breaking down artificial barriers to education and employment.

The greater the demand on the nation's available manpower resources, the more willing we have been to modify and even abandon traditional practices which place certain minority groups, particularly Negroes and Spanish-speaking Americans, in the position of second-class citizens with respect to training and employment. Where employers and unions, together with community leaders, have acted forthrightly and consistently to insure equal opportunities for employment, the resultant change in employment policy has worked out well. Where the Federal government has been vigorous in invoking its authority to require its officials and the employers working for it under contract not to discriminate against job applicants and employees because of race, creed, or national origin, traditional prejudices have been overcome.

In spite of the advances toward greater equality of opportunity, Negroes are poorly represented in most skilled and technical occupations. They continue to be barred from training and jobs that lead to skilled and technical work, especially in the South but also in other regions. In many parts of the country they are still excluded from apprenticeship training programs. Despite the strong stand against discriminatory practices taken by many national and international unions, some local unions continue to bar Negroes from membership, and, as a result, from gaining access to skilled jobs.

Overt discriminatory practices are not the only reason why the opportunities to acquire essential skills are not equal for all individuals. The basic education that a person receives, the information at his disposal when he plans his career, and the employment openings available to him all strongly affect his opportunities to become a skilled worker or technician. Consequently, communities that tolerate poor elementary and secondary schools and fail to provide adequate vocational guidance place major obstacles in the way of many of their citizens who seek to acquire skill.

In order to provide more equal opportunities for all individuals to acquire skill, the National Manpower Council recommends that:

1. All employers hire and promote employees and all unions admit individuals to membership without regard to their race, creed, color, national origin, or sex

2. Employers and unions and the Joint Apprenticeship Councils and Committees eliminate the practice, wherever it exists, of barring individuals from admission to apprenticeship programs because of their race or national origin

3. The President insure that the heads of Federal departments and agencies eliminate discrimination based on race, creed, color, national origin, or sex wherever it remains in Federal employment; and that the full authority of the Federal government be used to prevent such discrimination in all work performed for it under contract.

IMPROVING TRAINING FACILITIES AND METHODS

The facilities and methods used in the training of skilled and technical manpower must be constantly adjusted to changes taking place in the economy, technology, and education. There is a tendency for training systems to continue the practices of yesterday, rather than to adjust both what is taught and the methods of teaching to present and future needs. The more rapid the changes that are taking place in the larger society, the more dangerous and costly it is for training systems to remain rooted in outmoded practices.

Although some apprenticeship programs are kept under review jointly by employers and trade unions, there are others in which the content of instruction or the length of the training time has not been brought into alignment with technological and economic advances. A few states, notably New York and California, have undertaken comprehensive surveys of the present and expected demand for various types of skilled and technical manpower and have used this information in planning the development of vocational or technical programs in high schools, community and junior colleges, and technical institutes. In order to ascertain and remedy such deficiencies in training facilities as may exist, many more states and communities must undertake systematic surveys of this type, which should also cover the adequacy of programs for adult vocational education in the public schools.

Because so large a proportion of our workers acquire their skills on the job, employers have a major responsibility for the development of the nation's skilled and technical manpower. On-the-job training is always closely geared to immediate production needs, but many industrialists are coming to recognize the contribution that broader training can make to developing a more flexible work force. Workers who possess a high degree of versatility help to reduce labor costs and increase productivity. By providing different types of job assignments for their employees, employers can add to the versatility of their work force. Moreover, they can do more than they are now doing to make training a major responsibility of every supervisor and to help supervisory personnel discharge their training responsibility effectively.

Some employers have already recognized the advantages that can be secured by instituting formal training programs for selected groups of workers. Many more could establish such programs either within the plant, or by utilizing resources in the outside community. Every employer has an obligation to provide information to his employees at least about the opportunities for training within the firm and to help in disseminating information about the facilities for vocational education available in the community.

The armed forces are confronted with unique training problems in that most men serve for a short period of time — in the case of the Army mostly for only two years and in the other services largely for three or four. This means that a very large and continuing effort must be made by the armed services to train new men in a wide range of specialties so that complex military weapons and equipment can be effectively operated. To the extent that the armed forces can secure re-enlistments, especially of men who have had specialist training, they will be able to reduce their training burden and improve their skilled and technical manpower. However, the armed forces have been in a poor position to encourage re-enlistments because most men prefer the conditions of civilian employment. Reasonable adjustments in pay scales and service benefits for the core group of technicians, specialists, and noncommissioned officers would probably be paid for by savings in training brought about by less turnover.

Because so many men serve for such a short period of time, the educational preparation that men have before they come on active duty is particularly important. If every serviceman had the advantage of a good secondary education, the task of providing specialized training in the armed services would be simplified, and many individuals would derive greater benefits from available training opportunities.

The training burden of the armed services might also be reduced if they could make greater use of civilian training facilities and personnel. In operating their large training establishments, the armed services encounter difficulty in securing adequate teaching staffs. Although the armed forces will have to continue to do most of their own training, it is important to determine the full extent to which they could rely to advantage on civilian resources.

In order to improve the facilities and methods used to train skilled workers and technicians, the National Manpower Council recommends that:

1. Unions and employers and the Joint Apprenticeship Councils and Committees review regularly the content and length of training time of apprenticeship programs in order to insure their efficiency and effectiveness

2. Employers seek to provide greater opportunities for their employees to acquire increased skills through a planned

system of varied job assignments, broader training on and off the job, and increasing the training competence of their supervisory staffs

3. State and city governments undertake comprehensive surveys to determine whether existing training facilities are adequate to meet the requirements for skilled and technical manpower

4. The Congress, by adjusting pay and other service benefits, enable the armed forces to reduce excessive turnover and to encourage re-enlistment, so as to retain a larger core group of qualified technicians, specialists, and noncommissioned officers

5. The Secretary of Defense direct the Secretaries of the Army, Navy, and Air Force to utilize, wherever appropriate, the facilities and personnel available in the civilian community in meeting the training requirements of the services.

INCREASING KNOWLEDGE ABOUT MANPOWER

In recent years important additions have been made to the body of knowledge about our manpower resources. Yet the study of human resources is relatively new, and we are still far from possessing the relevant information and the broad understanding upon which sound policy should be based. Of the great variety of significant problems in the manpower field, several relating specifically to skilled and technical workers invite intensive inquiry.

The National Manpower Council recommends that:

1. The universities and foundations encourage and support research to increase our knowledge about manpower resources with particular reference to the complex process of occupational choice; the types of information essential for effective vocational guidance; the role of skilled and technical manpower in economic development; the impact of governmental policies upon the supply of skilled man-

power resources; and the relation between how people are trained and their subsequent work performance

2. The Secretary of Defense direct the Secretaries of the Army, Navy, and Air Force to evaluate the varied experiences of the services with training and make their significant findings and their new methods available for civilian use

3. The President direct the appropriate agencies of the government to provide periodic and comprehensive appraisals of the country's available resources of skilled and technical workers and to seek improvements in the methods of estimating future manpower requirements.

PART TWO

Facts and Issues
about Skilled Manpower

PREPARED BY THE RESEARCH STAFF

ELI GINZBERG, Director of Research
HENRY DAVID, Executive Secretary

DALE L. HIESTAND
BERNARD ROSHCO
ROBERT W. SMUTS

JAMES K. ANDERSON
DOUGLAS W. BRAY

CHAPTER I

Skill and Economic Development

WORLD WAR II, the partial mobilization after the outbreak of hostilities in Korea in 1950, and the necessity of being prepared for the eventuality of full mobilization have made Americans more aware than ever of the importance of an adequate supply of skilled workers and technicians. Greater public attention has been given to scientific and professional personnel, but the nation's resources of other kinds of highly trained manpower have not been ignored. The training and effective utilization of skilled and technical manpower have concerned industry, labor organizations, and government for some time. These problems have been the subjects of special study by nongovernmental bodies, as well as by the Office of Defense Mobilization, the Department of Labor, and the armed services.

Long before World War II, the nation had, at times, been deeply concerned with the more highly skilled segments of the nation's working force and with training methods. Interest in the skills of foremen and other supervisory personnel, resulting from shortages of skilled workers during World War I, carried over into the 1920's. The growing interest in technological unemployment during this decade led to a consideration of the effect of rapid and continuous technological change upon the skilled labor force of the nation. During the depression years of the 1930's, the waste of the abilities of highly trained workers and the possibility that the country might have a permanent surplus of skilled labor were regarded as major problems.

EARLIER CONCERN WITH SKILLED MANPOWER

It would be misleading, however, to convey the impression that Americans have been concerned with their resources of skilled manpower only in periods of crisis. The importance of skilled workers for the growth of individual enterprises and for the expansion of the economy as a whole could not be ignored. Early in the nineteenth century, European visitors to the United States repeatedly commented on the skill, the ingenuity, and the inventiveness displayed by Americans of all classes and occupations. At the same time, they noted that the lack of an adequate labor supply was a key economic problem.

During the early years of the American factory system, skilled mechanics, as well as experienced managers and machinery, were at a premium. Advertisements cited the fact that skilled immigrant workers made certain commodities as proof of their superior quality. Other nations have also depended upon imported skilled labor in order to develop certain industries. But in the United States, immigrant labor, because of its volume and the skills it supplied, has been a massive and perhaps unique influence.

A list of the fields in which European skilled workers played important roles would be a catalogue of American economic activities. A substantial proportion of the immigrants from Western Europe during the nineteenth century were skilled. Labor and skills from the United Kingdom, as R. T. Berthoff's recent *British Immigrants in Industrial America* shows in detail, played a decisive part in the growth of America's textile, heavy metals, and mining industries, and contributed to the development of many others. The immigrant tide from Eastern and Southern Europe late in the nineteenth and early in the twentieth centuries also brought many skilled workers to the United States. Even today, in spite of the severe restrictions on immigration, workers from other lands continue to enrich the nation's skilled manpower resources.

By the last decade of the nineteenth century, the United States was not only the leading producer of agricultural goods, it was also first among the industrial nations of the world. Other important causes were, of course, responsible for the rapid economic growth; but it would not have been possible without the constant flow of capital and labor from the old world. Nor would it have occurred without the ready application of scientific and technological knowledge, largely European in origin, and the consequent widespread introduction of labor-saving and labor-displacing machines and techniques. The relative scarcity of labor, particularly of skilled labor, and an entrepreneurial mentality that was not dismayed by innovation and risk stimulated improvements in technology at a rapid rate.

SKILL IMPROVEMENT THROUGH EDUCATION

The dependence of America's economic development upon the skills of its labor force was apparent early in its history. Before the Civil War, efforts were made to lift the skill level of the working force by increasing the opportunities and facilities for education of a vocational character. Beginning in the 1820's, a number of institutes, founded for the purpose of teaching "the sciences associated with the mechanic arts," became the nation's first technical schools. The movement for the extension of publicly supported compulsory education aimed at making not only better citizens and more intelligent and cultured individuals, but also more effective and productive workers.

The Morrill Act of 1862 was designed to encourage the establishment of state colleges that would teach "such branches of learning as are related to agriculture and the mechanic arts," as well as other subjects, in order "to promote the liberal and practical education of the industrial classes." The Federal acts of 1887 and 1890, which created the agricultural experiment stations connected with the land-grant colleges, also provided for instruction in both "the mechanic arts" and agriculture.

Meanwhile, courses of a vocational nature had been introduced into the public schools. At the same time several institutions for training in industrial design were founded, including the Lowell School of Practical Design, the School of Industrial Art in Philadelphia, and the Rhode Island School of Design. During the last two decades of the nineteenth century, instruction in manual training took firm root in the public school systems of the nation.

Trade schools of various kinds, some publicly supported, had also been established by the end of the nineteenth century. Industrial, philanthropic, and social reform groups founded schools designed to equip youngsters with a trade in as short a time as possible. The establishment of trade schools was encouraged by the relatively small number of apprentices and a growing knowledge of the industrial training facilities in European countries, especially Germany. The textile trade schools, which were recognized as outstanding institutions, were modeled upon those of Germany.

Both philanthropic and practical motives were behind the founding of a number of trade and technical schools during the 1880's and 1890's. Among these were the New York Trade School; the Pratt Institute in Brooklyn; the Evening Trades School of St. George's Protestant Episcopal Church in New York, which grew out of a boys' club; the Williamson Free School of Mechanical Trades, near Philadelphia; San Francisco's California School of Mechanic Arts; the Baron de Hirsch Trade School in New York, designed to provide Jewish youth with an opportunity for industrial training; and the Massachusetts Charitable Mechanic Association Trade School, which was as much concerned with increasing the supply of skilled mechanics as with the more general purpose of giving "American boys an opportunity to learn a trade."

The founding of trade schools, as well as demands for vocational instruction in the public schools, showed a lively interest in the state of industrial education and training. So did the Congressional action which directed the Commissioner of Labor to investigate and report on the industrial and technical school systems of the United States and other countries. The resulting report, published in 1892, was followed by a second, ten years later, describing in detail the existing means for the education and training of skilled workers.

In the 1902 report, Commissioner of Labor Carroll D. Wright observed that, "Manufacturers everywhere are turning to the subject of industrial education, no longer with any question as to its value, but merely as to the best means and methods." The depression of the 1890's had intensified interest in foreign markets and prompted a search for the reasons for Germany's growing success as an exporter of manufactured goods. It was widely believed that a major cause of this success was the superior training provided by Germany's technical and trade schools. Some Americans wondered whether the United States would not have to pay dearly for having failed to develop a national system of industrial education.

VOCATIONAL EDUCATION IN THE HIGH SCHOOL

The founding of the National Society for the Promotion of Industrial Education in 1906 reflected the dissatisfaction felt in industrial, business, and educational circles over the facilities available for training skilled workers. The Society's purposes were, in part, "to bring to public attention the importance of industrial education as a factor in the industrial development of the United States" and "to promote the establishment of institutions for industrial training." At its first meeting, Nicholas Murray Butler suggested that Americans were not "giving the attention we should to the development of the knowledge, the skill, and the artistic element in our everyday labor," and others asserted that a lack of properly trained workers was handicapping industry.

Informed industrialists, according to Frederick Perry Fish, then president of American Telephone and Telegraph Company, "know that we do not have the skilled mechanics of a former generation," which explained why a number of large companies had set up apprenticeship schools and other training programs. Another leading figure in the business world argued that "superior handicraft" had never enabled Americans to sell "an important consignment of goods in the world market," while the reverse was true in the case of Germany. Support for expanding the role of the public schools in industrial training came from President Theodore Roosevelt, in a speech in 1907, which also stressed the advantage superior skilled labor gave to other manufacturing nations. "What the American workingman has to fear," he said, "is the competition of the highly skilled workingmen of the countries of greatest efficiency."

It will be seen later that industrial and occupational instruction was both a cause and a consequence of the expansion in secondary schooling during the earlier decades of the century. At the same time old problems in occupational choice and guidance took on new meaning and new devices were fashioned for their solution. The vocational guidance movement in the United States was born at the close of the first decade of the century. There was a growing willingness to have the high schools offer specialized vocational courses of instruction and thus directly prepare boys and girls for certain occupations. This point of view prepared the ground for the Smith-Hughes Act of 1917, a measure which established the system of Federal aid for vocational education in the public high schools. With this legislation the broad movement to create additional means for the training of skilled workers reached a new stage.

A combination of circumstances lay behind the attempt to fashion new training facilities within the growing high school system. Changes in technology had profoundly affected traditional ways of learning skilled trades as well as the occupations themselves. As a training institution, apprenticeship was moribund. The new trade schools, moreover, were serving a relatively small number of students. The slight training efforts made by employers were directed largely to teaching workers how to perform specialized and limited tasks. Many of the skilled workers still coming into the United States from foreign lands were products of formal training systems — apprenticeships, technical institutes, trade and vocational schools. By contrast, the United States appeared to lack an adequate, national system of training.

Today, the development of skilled workers in the United States takes place mostly outside of formal training programs and through processes which appear to be "natural," rather than consciously directed and planned. The acquisition of essential skills through work experience, observation and imitation, occasional instruction on the job, changing jobs, and upgrading also occurred earlier in the century. But the actual role of these ways of becoming a skilled worker was not perceived. Yet there was a general belief in the economic as well as the other values of education and in the contribution of the public school system to the development of a skilled labor force. When it was felt that the facilities for training were seriously deficient, it seemed reasonable to use the growing institution of the secondary school in developing new formal systems of training.

DEVELOPMENT OF MODERN OCCUPATIONS

The central fact implicit in the various attempts in the United States to improve the means for training skilled workers during the nineteenth and twentieth centuries is the change in the nature of the occupations required by a developing economy. Transformations in the work man does and, consequently, in his skills and occupations, mirror the division of labor and specialization of function that characterize the development of modern economic life. Some measure of specialization of function and, consequently, of skill — a word which originally meant "a distinction"— is found in all known societies in all parts of the world. Intensive specialization in economic activity, however, is a distinguishing feature of the history of the Western world during the last three centuries.

In antiquity and in the medieval period, for example, few functions were differentiated and the number of specific handicraft skills was small. Many of the latter, moreover, were associated with slave or otherwise unfree labor. Later in the medieval period, the organization of free craftsmen into guilds reflected advances already made in handicraft skills and also contributed to their further development. The number of craft guilds provides some indication of the extent of specialization in industrial production. Florence, a leading center of industry, had twenty-one guilds at the opening of the fourteenth century but not all the specialized crafts were separately organized. Three gradations of craftsmen were distinguished by the guilds: apprentice, journeyman, and master. The first term still describes the worker who is learning essential skills under a contractual relationship with his employer. The second, in many trades, still identifies the highly trained, versatile, skilled worker.

That complex of developments beginning in the seventeenth century called the Industrial Revolution was made possible by, and resulted in, division of labor and specialization of function. The growth of scientific knowledge and of technology, together with the emergence of the factory system of production, radically altered the economic life first of the Western world and then of other parts of the globe. This transformation was accompanied by the appearance of many new skills and trades. Occupations proliferated and altered. In these developments, the manufacturing industries, with their greater potentiality for division of labor, played a particularly forceful role. The grouping of kinds of labor into such categories as skilled, semi-skilled, and unskilled was primarily a result of factory production.

The effect of division of labor is readily seen in the growing variety of jobs, but this is only one aspect of specialization. The other, not so easily discerned, is interdependence. As the number of separate and specific duties or tasks performed by workers multiplied, new integrating functions of an entrepreneurial and managerial nature also came into existence.

Some idea of the occupational revolution which has occurred in the course of a few centuries may be derived from the fact that there are between thirty and forty thousand different kinds of jobs in the United States today. Depending upon how jobs are classified and grouped, the number of separate occupations in existence may be counted not only in the hundreds, but in the thousands. Since as many as three or four thousand separate occupations can be identified under certain classification systems, the more than 400 described in the U. S. Department of Labor's *Occupational Outlook Handbook* may be said to constitute a small proportion of the total number now existing. Today, the Census returns indicate the existence of thirty or more professional occupations, not counting the professional specialties in the social and physical sciences. As late as the close of the eighteenth century, only three professional occupations were recognized — divinity, law, and medicine. In contrast to the handful of skilled occupations in existence prior to the Industrial Revolution, there are now four or five hundred classified as skilled.

OCCUPATIONAL AND SKILL CLASSIFICATION

It has already been indicated that the broader occupational categories into which different kinds of work are classified depend upon the criteria used. Those generally employed are: the actual operations involved in performing work tasks; the nature of the training required for proficient performance; the earnings derived from the work; and the social prestige attached to it. The completion of a program of formal higher education and training and the existence of a professional society are used as standards to determine whether a given field is a professional occupation. The size of an occupational group can be substantially affected by the criterion used. If graduation from an engineering school is used to determine the number of engineers, the result is almost 20 percent — roughly 100,000 — below that reported by the Census, which bases its count on other considerations.

Classifications of kinds of work in terms of level of skill also depend upon which criteria are used. The basic rule employed is simple: the greater the preparation and training required, the more skilled the occupation. Its application to specific cases, however, raises countless problems. The skills required for the varied functions of an advanced society form a continuum, and the unskilled, semi-skilled, and skilled categories of occupations and workers represent artificial divisions. The boundary lines separating one grouping from another are of necessity arbitrary. There is, consequently, always ground for legitimate dispute over placing some workers under one heading rather than another.

History and convention may dictate the skill description of an occupation. Many workers in mining continue to be regarded as unskilled or semi-skilled because of the nature of the work they did years ago, which frequently has little resemblance to what they do today. The machinist's occupation is traditionally viewed as skilled. A study by the U.S. Bureau of Labor Statistics indicates, however, that on the basis of the functions they actually perform, perhaps the majority of those who call themselves machinists in reporting to the Census could be described as semi-skilled. Modern farming requires a high degree of technical knowledge, managerial ability, and competence in the maintenance and repair of machinery and equipment, in addition to more traditional agricultural skills. Yet it is not classified as a skilled occupation.

The problems involved in deciding whether a group of workers belong to one occupational or skill category rather than another have high practical significance. An adequate understanding of the manifold facets of the skill and occupational structure of the nation's work force is essential if sound public policies are to be developed.

The name of an occupation may contribute to its prestige and thus may influence its appeal as a field of work to young people thinking about their future vocations. When, as in the United States, white collar occupations are frequently more highly valued than "blue collar" work, some may be attracted to a field primarily because those in it are called "technicians," rather than skilled workers. The name given to an occupation may affect judgments on the adequacy of the training facilities available. For example, technicians are sometimes defined as workers whose training takes the form of one, two, or more years of post-high school study in technical institutes or in junior or four year colleges. Using this definition, it could be argued that the facilities existing in the United States for training technicians are inadequate.

Occupational and skill classification systems have a bearing on wage rate determination, and they have posed difficult problems for the National Labor Relations Board. In ruling on issues of union representation and bargaining units, the Board has had to decide whether certain groups of workers whose training is of a professional nature should be given professional status in view of the actual work functions they perform; or, whether certain technicians should be separated from or classed with "production" or clerical workers. Many arbitration cases under collective bargaining contracts involve questions of skill classification. Finally, the problem of occupational grouping is also involved in many union jurisdictional disputes.

IDENTIFYING SKILLED WORKERS

The fact that old handicraft trades have long been designated as skilled does not mean there is an absolute, permanent standard for judging what work is skilled and what is not. On the contrary, the concept of skilled work is culturally determined and is a relative one. Changes in technology, in forms of economic organization, and in educational levels within a society alter the view of what kinds of work are skilled. On the other hand, work held to be skilled in one society may be regarded as semi-skilled in another. Such cultural factors as the degree of education and of exposure to the processes and products of an advanced technology affect the skill value assigned to certain kinds of work. The Census of Soviet Russia in 1926 classified as skilled a number of occupations, including automobile, truck, and tractor driver, which were counted as semi-skilled in the United States.

The rule of thumb which is followed in grading work according to skill level — the greater the preparation and training, the more skilled the work — underlines the relative nature of skill. The criterion of training provides a starting point for specifying the attributes which differentiate skilled workers from others. Their training extends over fairly long periods of time. Its purpose is to equip workers with a cluster of distinctive abilities essential for certain tasks and competence in work performance. The combination of distinctive abilities and competence may be regarded as a kind of personal capital possessed by the skilled worker. The minimum formal schooling and experiences available to the population at large do not suffice for the acquisition of this personal capital. Because special training is necessary to develop the distinctive abilities and competence in performance, they are found in relatively few members of the labor force.

These general attributes are reflected in the terms used to describe the peculiar and valued qualities of skilled workers. Skilled workers are spoken of as being versatile, adaptable, and resourceful; as being able to carry responsibilities, to make independent decisions, to meet new situations and challenges, and to teach others; as understanding the significance and relationships of the tasks they perform. These terms suggest a mastery in a field of work attainable only through special effort and long experience.

Their relatively small numbers and the investment in training of one form or another which they have to make give skilled workers a strategic position in the economy which is generally reflected in their earnings and social prestige. The supply of skilled workers cannot be significantly increased overnight. They cannot be replaced by workers possessing only more common and more limited skills unless significant adjustments are made in technology and work functions.

"Considering the glibness with which workmen are pigeonholed as 'skilled,' 'semi-skilled' and 'laborers' in many industries," observed Anna Bezanson more than three decades ago, "it is surprising to find very little definition of what constitutes skill, or lack of skill."

Every existing definition of the skilled worker is an invitation to interminable debate. A skilled worker may be tentatively described as a person who can competently perform tasks which require significantly differentiated abilities developed through specialized training over an extended period of time. But this statement is only the beginning of a definition. Many members of the work force to whom it applies are distinguished by other characteristics sufficiently important to justify a different classification. The nature of the training required or the functions they perform warrant the exclusion from the skilled worker category of at least the following groups: professional workers and scientists; the owners and managers of business enterprises, agricultural as well as nonagricultural; and government officials.

Two crucial points remain to be made about the characteristic form and the time of training of skilled workers. In the first place, training may be acquired in one or more of three ways — through formal instruction, more or less informal training, and work experience. No one training system, therefore, can be used as a standard for determining whether a group of workers is skilled or not. Training through apprenticeship is critical for some skilled trades, but it would be pointless to maintain that it is the only form of training suitable for developing skilled workers.

Second, it is necessary to stipulate a minimum period of requisite training for acquiring the distinctive abilities and competence associated with skilled work. This is a source of difficulty. Any minimum time that is set may be open to question in specific instances. What constitutes the amount and content of training essential for the performance of particular functions has been inadequately studied. Such data as exist point to the conclusion that even with very intensive training most skilled workers cannot be developed in much less than two years. A shorter time is probably sufficient for some workers whose essential skills are acquired through formal instruction in post-high school institutions. Most apprenticeship programs, however, are four years long. The criterion of minimum training time bars from the skilled worker category two groups of workers: those whose skills are of a general character and are widely distributed throughout the working population, such as the ability to read and write and to handle simple arithmetical processes; and those whose particular skills can be developed in a relatively short time — from a matter of days up to a year or even more.

When all these considerations are taken into account, eight or nine million persons in the United States today may be counted as skilled workers. Thus, there is only one skilled worker for every seven or eight members of the nation's civilian work force, which now numbers about 64 million. Most groups of skilled workers are not impressive by weight of numbers alone, and the whole skilled worker segment of the country's total manpower is relatively small. No single skilled occupation matches the size of the teaching profession, and many skilled trades have fewer members than such professional occupations as engineering, law, and medicine.

The Census does not use the designation "skilled workers," but workers whom it reports under the heading "craftsmen, foremen, and kindred workers" are commonly regarded as skilled. In Census terms, this combined grouping represents the skilled worker component of the nation's work force. "Craftsmen, foremen, and kindred workers" totaled almost eight million in 1950, and now come to almost nine. The bulk of these workers meet the criteria here presented — distinctive abilities, competence in performance, and length of training. For reasons already suggested, which will be treated more fully in the following chapter, not all of those reported as "craftsmen" by the Census warrant the designation skilled workers. Nor do all of those classified as "foremen and kindred workers."

On the other hand, an undetermined number of the workers placed in other categories by the Census do possess the key features which distinguish skilled workers. The increasing numbers in these other categories point up the relative decline in importance of the segment of the work force employed in construction and manufacturing, the fields with which skilled workers have traditionally been associated. The Census headings of "clerical and kindred workers," "sales workers," and "service workers" represent broad functional, rather than occupational, categories. Some of the workers in each of them have the abilities, competence, and training which distinguish skilled workers, and they should be counted as such. Unfortunately, the occupational data available do not enable one to indicate their number.

There is still another group of workers, the size of which is much more accurately known, which the Census does not classify with "craftsmen, foremen, and kindred workers." This is the group called "technical workers." Most of its members can be properly counted with the skilled worker component of the labor force.

TECHNICIANS

There are today about 400,000 "technical workers" or technicians, such as draftsmen, surveyors, engineering aides, testing technicians, laboratory assistants, and a variety of medical and dental technicians. They are frequently described as semi- or subprofessional workers. For many of them, formal education after high school graduation is the required form of training. In a number of technical occupations there are societies similar to those in the professional fields which set standards of competence and training. Moreover, provisions for the licensing of technicians in the medical and health fields, radio and television broadcasting, and the aviation industry are becoming increasingly common.

Most technicians perform tasks which either were at one time, or still continue to be, within the range of the functions of professional personnel. Many of them work in a direct, supporting capacity to professional persons and scientists. The qualities peculiar to technicians are said to rest upon a combination or blend of two elements: some of the theoretical knowledge associated with a profession, and skills which are manual or involve the use of instruments. Many experts separate technical workers from the skilled group and locate the technician midway "between the skilled person and the professional person in the developmental structure of American jobs, in his work performance, and in his educational attainment."

There are good reasons for regarding technicians not only as a separate group, but also as a part of the skilled manpower segment of the work force. The functions of most technicians are related to and directly support the work of professional personnel; the same observation may be made about skilled workers. Divisions of labor and specialization render the functions of all types of workers supportive and interdependent.

The use of the term technician rather than skilled worker does not necessarily reflect significant differences in the nature of their skills. It is more likely to indicate the influence of certain institutional factors. These are the positive values assigned to white collar and professional status in American society; the type of training now associated with preparation for technicians' jobs; and the relative newness of most technician occupations. The growing practice of designating certain groups of workers as technicians grows partly out of a preference on the part of many people for work that is "mental" and "clean" rather than "manual" and "dirty." Actually, many technicians do work primarily with their hands and get them dirty in the process. It need hardly be added that much of the work performed by skilled labor is mental in character.

Formal instruction in post-high school institutions is heavily relied upon to train technicians. But many technicians also develop their skills through work experience and informal training. Vocational instruction in technical institutes and community or junior colleges — one of the evidences of the long-term trend in the United States toward more and more education — encourages the use of the term technician in connection with the occupations taught in these institutions.

The Census still presents relatively little information on workers in different technician occupations. Most technician occupations can be traced to recent applications of scientific and technological knowledge to the production of goods and services, which have altered the content of older bodies of skills or created new ones. This has also happened to machinists, tool and die makers, electricians, and other skilled workers to whom the term technician is not applied. In the case of older and well-established trades, even substantial changes in required skills are not likely to be accompanied by changes in name.

On the other hand, there are instances where the term technician has come into use primarily because of a new way of organizing work processes in an enterprise, the appearance of a new department, or a change in wage scales. Many workers now called technicians perform very much the same functions they did in the past, when they were called "testers." Until recently almost all medical and dental services were provided by professionals. In these fields technicians are a new group that came into being because of new knowledge and techniques and largely in response to the growing demand for medical and dental services. Were this demand met by professional personnel alone, the cost of health services would be much greater.

Skilled workers, like technicians, have theoretical knowledge as well as competence in manual skills and the use of instruments. The difference between the two is likely to reside in the extent to which the skilled worker's theoretical knowledge is acquired practically and is implicit in the tasks he performs, while the technician's is usually explicitly acquired through formal instruction. This contrast points up the fact that new occupations cannot rely on traditional ways of learning and doing and resort, therefore, to teaching their theoretical content in systematic and formal fashion. The theoretical knowledge of older occupations, where the change in essential skills takes place more or less gradually, is likely to be obscured by learning methods which emphasize observation and practice.

TECHNOLOGICAL CHANGE AND SKILLED WORKERS

Science and technology have brought new skills and occupations into existence. Yet their so-called "destructive" effects upon skilled labor and upon the spirit and intelligence of workers have received primary attention since the close of the eighteenth century. It is not difficult to understand why. Among the most obvious and immediate consequences of the earlier stages of the Industrial Revolution was the displacement of skilled handicraft workers by factory operatives, many of whom were women and children, who were taught relatively quickly to perform narrowly specialized and routine tasks. The painful adjustments forced upon handicraft workers in a specific industry by introducing labor- and skill-saving methods are far more readily perceived than increases in the demand for skills that occurred elsewhere in the economy as a result of the introduction of new production methods.

The factory employee's work has long been contrasted to disadvantage with an idealized version of the work of the traditional handicraftsman. The latter's work is represented as varied, interesting, and creative in character because he produced a commodity from start to finish. This view does not recognize the degree of specialization in handicraft production by the eighteenth century, the routinized and repetitive character of much skilled handwork, and the relatively small number of commodities made entirely by the same craftsman.

Lewis Mumford's remark in his *Technics and Civilization* that "the castration of skills" was one of the basic "requirements of the factory system" represents the still dominant conception of the impact of technological change and the factory upon skilled labor. Much the same view appears in Professor W. Lloyd Warner's summing up of the changes which have taken place in skilled work: "The vertical hierarchy of skilled jobs has become a horizontal layer of low-skilled ones. Each of the skilled jobs has been divided into a number of simple, low-skilled ones and machines are performing most of the actions necessary for each job." Taking the American shoe industry as a case in point, he writes that the "virtue, prestige, and respect" given to craftworkers of the past by skills acquired through apprenticeship no longer exist because "the machines" have destroyed "the skill hierarchy that dominated their occupation."

The contention that skilled trades have been fragmented, reduced in importance, or rendered obsolete by changes in technology is, of course, valid. But it is also one-sided and misleading. In spite of the revolution in technology, the skilled handicraft worker still remains important in production, repair, and other fields, although he may now use powered tools on new materials to perform functions which did not exist in the past. More important, an advancing technology creates higher skill requirements and new kinds of skilled workers.

Mechanization and other innovations in technology have destroyed certain handicraft skills, but they have not prevented the growth of the skilled component of the work force in the United States or in other industrialized countries. The Census data are inadequate and they are weighted in favor of older skilled occupations, but they provide sufficient evidence to show that the impact of technology upon skill is not primarily destructive. It will be seen in greater detail in the next chapter that from 1870 to 1920 the skilled group — consisting of those classified as "craftsmen, foremen, and kindred workers" — grew at a more rapid rate than the total work force. During the next two decades, these groups increased in size less rapidly than the total work force. Then the situation was again reversed between 1940 and 1950. In 1950, "craftsmen, foremen, and kindred workers" represented almost 14 percent of the total labor force, compared to 11.6 percent ten years earlier.

Complex interactions take place between technological change and skilled manpower resources and requirements. Technological change is a continuing process, and at any given time the skills available in the work force may accelerate or retard it. At the same time, technological innovations may raise or depress the skill levels required by different industries. The diverse consequences for skilled labor of technological advances outlined by Dr. Harry Jerome two decades ago in *Mechanization and Industry* still holds.

Where the mechanization of a process involves the substitution of a processing machine directly for the handicraftsman, it is probable that the typical effect, even after allowing for indirect as well as direct effects, is a net decrease in the grade of skill required. . . .

The transition to mechanical processing does not always affect the level of skill adversely. If the displaced manual methods require only semi-skilled or even common labor, then mechanization tends to raise the proportion of skilled workmen. . . .

Also if operations which have already been reduced to progressive assembly or progressive processing advance to a more highly mechanized stage where mechanical devices displace some of the workers along the assembly line, the change is likely to reduce the number of semi-skilled operatives and tends, on the whole, to increase the demand for skilled workers and trained technicians in the construction and training departments.

Much remains to be learned about the long-run consequences of modern technology for skilled labor in specific industries, for the skilled worker component of the nation's work force, and for the skill characteristics of the working population as a whole. What is known warrants the broad generalization that the net effect of advances in technology is to increase rather than reduce the over-all demand for skills. Within modern, developing economies, the proportion of skilled workers in the work force seems to remain fairly stable over long periods of time. It must be borne in mind, however, that the general skill level in such economies rises over time and that the base against which skilled workers are differentiated also rises.

An advancing technology reduces and eliminates the need for certain kinds of skilled workers. But it also requires more and new types of skilled labor to plan and make the models of the increasingly complex machines it creates, and to produce, service, control, and maintain them. This is the testimony of the past. It throws some light on what is likely to transpire in the future, as the potentialities of existing scientific and technological knowledge are realized and as fully automatic systems for producing goods and carrying on business functions come into existence. Even the most optimistic of those who speculate on the implications of what is called "automation" do not expect the advent of wholly self-directing and self-tending machines tomorrow, or to find them in all fields of economic activity even in the remote future.

From today's vantage point, the automatic factory of the future promises to displace the semi-skilled operative — the machine-tender whose work is narrowly specialized and more or less routine — in much the same way that earlier changes in technology adversely affected the handicraftsman, and to give added significance to the skilled and technical labor needed for production, maintenance, and repair of the new automatic machinery. One forecast of the manpower results of automation sees the appearance of a new type of "artisans" who will be "skilled adjuster-builders."

HUMAN RESOURCES AND ECONOMIC DEVELOPMENT

The measure of economic development is found in continuing increases in the per capita production of goods and services. In attempts to explain this process, the size of the labor supply and its skill characteristics are acknowledged to be key factors. Adam Smith centered attention upon the critical importance of the human resource factor to the productive capacity of a people in asserting, "Whatever be the soil, climate, or extent of territory of any particular nation, the abundance or scantiness of its annual supply [of goods], must, *in that particular situation* depend upon two circumstances" — the proportion of its people engaged in useful occupations and their skill.

The extent to which a society's resources of skilled manpower are assumed to play a major role in economic development is reflected in the efforts of "underdeveloped" areas to modernize their economies. It is well known that a necessary first step toward this goal is a rise in the skill level of the working population and the training of essential groups of skilled and technical workers. One of the sixteen measures a group of experts assembled by the United Nations urged upon nonindustrialized countries seeking to develop their economies reads: "Prepare a program of education and research showing its goals and its proposed expenditures for some such period as five years; and showing separately what is proposed for agricultural services, for industrial training, and for the training of scientists and administrators. . . ."

There is universal agreement that the quantitative and qualitative characteristics of a country's labor supply have a vital bearing upon its economic development. However, neither the nature of the influences which the human resources factor exerts upon economic development nor the specific roles played by skilled manpower have been carefully analyzed. Nevertheless, several statements about the role of skilled manpower can be made with safety. It is clear that the lack of skilled workers can impede economic expansion, and that technological advances depend as much upon the availability of skilled and technical labor as upon the contributions of scientists and professionally trained workers. There is also evidence that comprehending the meaning of the tasks on which they are engaged makes it possible for skilled workers to introduce improvements in technology.

Underdeveloped societies cannot realize the potentialities of an existing technology if they do not have the requisite kinds of skilled workers. So-called advanced societies, on the other hand, are always under some pressure to facilitate the acquisition of the new orders of skills needed by a changing technology or run the risk of retarding their economic growth.

The experiences of the United States and other countries drive home the point that adequate and balanced resources of skilled manpower are essential to produce the goods and services required for a high standard of living and continued economic growth. Moreover, it is known that individual enterprises decide for or against expansion, the location of a plant, or the entrance into a new field of production at least in part in terms of the availability of certain kinds of skilled labor. In Walter P. Chrysler's account of his opposition, when he was with the General Motors Corporation, to the building of a frame-making plant by Buick, the difficulty of finding the "talent" and the "mechanics" which the venture would require occupies a prominent place. Unfortunately, comprehensive studies still remain to be made of the weight given to the availability of skilled manpower in policy decisions of this kind. It should be added that such investigations require dealing with imponderables and with a number of inter-dependent factors. The weight given to manpower considerations will always be related to possible adjustments in technology and to their cost.

In seeking to grasp the causes of economic development, econ-omists have stressed a number of factors including savings and capital formation, the organization of the market, legal and politi-cal institutions, entrepreneurial mentality and behavior, the state of scientific and technological knowledge, income distribution, and physical resources, as well as population growth and skill or ability. Broadly speaking, as Dr. Wilbert E. Moore observes, in the work done in the field of economic development "the subtler aspects of labor supply have been largely neglected. This neglect has arisen in part from an exclusive quantitative, demographic approach to manpower or 'labor force,' in part from a naive view of economic motivation."

Problems relating to the total supply of labor — its composition in terms of age, sex, and occupation; its mobility and growth; and the proportion of available labor actively employed — have been the subjects of increasing inquiry. Stimulated by the concern with technological displacement and unemployment, intensive investi-gations have been made of the impact of greater productive effi-ciency upon labor requirements. The effects of such factors as wage rates and the attitudes of workers toward mechanization have also been studied. The significance of structural changes in fields of employment and in occupations, which accompany eco-nomic growth and productivity, has been recognized. The part played by literacy and the educational level of the mass of the population in productive efficiency has been investigated. A con-siderable body of experience is now available on the strategic use of small numbers of highly trained personnel and the part they can play in accelerating economic change in underdeveloped areas.

A comprehensive attack upon the role of skilled manpower in economic development, however, still remains to be formulated

CHAPTER II

Trends in Skilled and Technical Manpower

THE MOST important conclusion emerging from the occupational data and the experience gained during the last fifteen years is that at any given time the number of skilled workers is determined principally by the demand for goods and services and by the existing technology, which determines how goods are produced. When the demands for skilled workers go up, the number of skilled workers increases through expanded training programs and movement of semi-skilled workers into skilled occupations. When the demand for skilled workers either does not increase or goes down, training programs are curtailed and fewer semi-skilled workers enter skilled occupations.

An adequate, over-all forecast of the number of workers required in the various individual skilled occupations has never been made. An accurate forecast of this sort requires detailed examination of trends in the demand for goods and services and in methods of production, and of the effect of both these factors on the demand for manpower. Technological changes and demands for goods and services, moreover, are in turn influenced and modified by the nature of existing skills and by the available supply of skilled workers. Although these factors are interdependent, it is still true that the number of workers in any skilled occupation tends to adjust relatively rapidly to the demand for them. The number of workers in most skilled occupations can increase considerably within a year, and substantially within a few years. If the demand for skilled workers is temporarily greater than the forthcoming supply, an effective increase in the supply of essential skilled worker services frequently can be secured by redividing work functions. Workers who have lesser skills or who are more quickly trained can assume less demanding functions, while skilled workers concentrate on the more difficult phases of the work.

The available data not only provide few guides to what may be expected in the future, but also throw limited light on what has happened in the past. Statistics on the labor force, employment, and occupations in the United States are abundant and detailed. Systematic thought and investigation of the relationships between skill and economic development, however, have lagged far behind the collection of data. This is reflected in turn in the character of the data, which provide an inadequate basis for understanding changes in the nature and importance of particular skilled occupations and of skilled work in general.

OCCUPATIONAL DISTINCTIONS

The basic source of data on skilled workers and technicians in this country is the U. S. Bureau of the Census. Census reports are based on a detailed enumeration of the total population every ten years and, in recent years, on surveys of representative samples of the total population which provide very general occupational estimates every three months. Workers have been classified according to a variety of criteria. The early occupational statistics of the Bureau of the Census usually classified workers according to the industries in which they were employed. As the economy expanded and different industries and occupations emerged, the Census gradually added distinctions based on function, social status, and technology.

Early attempts to develop skill classifications were stimulated largely by concern with the changing social and economic position of the individual workers, rather than by concern with the adequacy of manpower resources to meet the needs of an expanding economy. This interest in the changing position of the individual worker led to a basic distinction between "white-collar" workers on the one hand, and "blue-collar," or "manual," workers on the other. The standards for making this distinction and for classifying workers within either division were not always clear.

Within the white-collar group, workers have been distinguished primarily according to whether they filled professional, proprietary, managerial, clerical, or sales functions. The blue-collar workers were broadly distinguished according to whether they worked in handicraft or similar occupations; in the highly mechanized industries where a high degree of specialization prevails; or in service, menial, and unspecialized occupations.

While these classifications may be broadly correlated with skill, each group contains workers at almost all levels of skill. The Census counts those whom it considers "craftsmen, foremen, and kindred workers" in one occupational group, which in 1950 contained 8.2 million workers. The Census at one time developed a "skilled worker" classification, which was made up largely of "craftsmen, foremen, and kindred workers." The Census no longer presents figures for skilled workers as a group. Craftsmen, foremen, and kindred workers have continued to be designated as skilled workers by many others, however, who overlook the fact that workers in other types of employment also possess significant skills. As Chapter I noted, technicians comprise one large group, most of whom can be properly counted with the skilled worker component of the labor force. In the 1950 Census, 375,000 technicians were listed among the "professional, technical, and kindred workers."

In collecting information about the occupational skills of the population in a highly dynamic economy, the desirability of greater theoretical clarity must always be balanced by considerations of operational efficiency and the availability of funds. Over the decades the Census has sought to adjust its categories to take account of the major changes in the economy that affect the category of skilled manpower.

Still other adjustments would provide a sharper picture of the skilled segment. Currently, some individuals with a job title that falls within the skilled category are not in fact truly skilled. Other sizable groups of individuals, primarily in the expanding operative, clerical, and service occupations, are not currently classified as skilled but warrant such a designation on the basis of their abilities, experience, training, work, and income.

JOB TITLES AND ACTUAL SKILLS

Job titles do not always reflect levels of skill largely because, as the economy, the technology, and the society change, the characteristics of jobs, the skills of many workers, and the social status of many occupations also change. The Census is not concerned exclusively with occupational data. Census occupational classifications are based on only a few of the many varied questions asked a worker or some member of his family by enumerators with relatively little training. To the worker or even his employer, the job title which is given to the census taker often implies a different level of skill than it does to the occupational specialist.

While the organization of work functions is constantly changing, job titles which are meaningful in terms of the newer job structure develop only gradually. Usually, a machinist is considered to be a worker who uses various machine and hand tools to shape metallic objects according to blueprints or written specifications. He must frequently devise his own procedures. He must know how various metals, machines, and tools operate under different speeds, temperatures, and stresses. If functions in a machine shop are specialized, some machinists may be assigned to specific machines. Their broad training and experience enable them to perform a wide variety of tasks at this machine. Workers with little training may also be assigned to a single machine, but their work will be routine. In the same shop, some of the all-round machinists may continue to work at many different machines.

Despite their varying functions and different levels of skill, all of these workers may be called "machinists." Or, workers assigned to one machine may be called "machine tool specialists," "machine tool operators," or "machine tool operatives." To different employers and occupational specialists, each of these titles may signify different levels of skill.

The same job title may be used for entirely different kinds of work, or entirely different titles may be used for the same work. A skilled cabinetmaker employs many different hand and machine tools to cut, shape, and assemble furniture, using a variety of woods, joints, paints and varnishes, etc. A skilled welder uses a variety of techniques and tools to fuse metals together. A worker who routinely fuses panels for metal cabinets in an electric welding machine may be reported as a welder, a cabinetmaker, or an electric spot welding machine operator.

Many skilled workers acquire their distinctive abilities gradually through informal training or experience as they move from one job to another. At what stage such workers should be called skilled presents a problem. The title "carpenter" may designate workers at many skill levels, ranging from those who are able to work from blueprints in fashioning a complicated structure to those who are handymen using only a saw and hammer or those who are carpenters' helpers. Handymen and helpers may or may not be skilled, but many who are not will subsequently become skilled.

Those reported as technicians include workers who differ greatly in terms of skill levels. Some reported as draftsmen have considerable responsibilities as engineers' assistants, but others are tracers who copy the work of more skilled draftsmen. A laboratory analyst may be a high school graduate with one chemistry course and a few weeks of on-the-job training fitting him for routine tests, or he may be a graduate of a technical institute. On the other hand, many skilled laboratory analysts have not had extensive formal training.

It was suggested in Chapter I that the possession of a minimum of two years specialized training, or the equivalent in experience, could be used as a rule of thumb in deciding who is a skilled or technical worker. The dominant group in a field, however, usually is the standard for this judgment. While a two-year apprenticeship is standard in some skilled occupations, a machine specialist with two years of training may be called semi-skilled, for the standard machinist apprenticeship lasts four years. In medical occupations, where physicians are the standard for comparison, the Census reports medical technologists, physical therapists, and occupational therapists as medical technicians. Yet, like professional personnel, many entering these occupations now receive a bachelor's degree and specialized postgraduate training. All the schools of occupational therapy approved by the American Medical Association and most approved schools for physical therapists and medical technologists now either require a bachelor's degree for admission or grant a degree after a program which usually runs five years. Whether workers should be classified as professionals or as technicians on the basis of their education or of the functions they actually fill on the job constitutes a separate question.

The Census classifies foremen in the same group with craftsmen, but it is not clear whether they should be considered skilled, technical, or otherwise. Foremen might be excluded from the skilled group on the ground that they have management functions. Many foremen, however, must have experience as skilled workers, and others must have become familiar with the technology of their units through broad experience or training. On the basis of their skills and technical knowledge, if not of their functions, foremen can be considered skilled manpower.

SKILL IN OTHER THAN THE TRADITIONAL FIELDS

The tendency of occupational data to reflect conventional distinctions rather than actual differences in skills or training is illustrated by the fact that the Census lists 400,000 registered nurses by the common title, "professional nurse." In recent years many nurses have received bachelor's or advanced degrees. The vast majority, however, have only three years of training beyond high school, no more than many persons conventionally classified as skilled workers or technicians. Practical nurses have been used increasingly as aides to physicians and professional nurses, but practical nurses are listed by the Census as service workers, a category often viewed as unskilled. Many hospital attendants, barbers, beauticians, cooks, firemen, and law enforcement officers, who are also reported as service workers, might be considered skilled because of their distinctive abilities and training.

Many of the more able clerical and sales workers might also be called technical or skilled. A calculating machine operator in a business office is classified as a clerical worker. If employed in an engineering laboratory, he might be given a technician title. Many clerical and sales workers in the medical, legal, scientific, engineering, real estate, and financial fields must acquire substantial distinctive skills, sometimes in special schools, and might well be viewed as skilled or technical workers.

While workers reported as "operatives" are usually semi-skilled, many could be counted as skilled workers. In several occupations workers in the operative category receive higher average incomes, according to the Census, than those in the craftsman and foreman group. These include railroad brakemen and switchmen; street, subway, and elevated railway motormen; power station operators; and welders and flame cutters. Many of these workers undoubtedly deserve to be called skilled in terms of their training and functions as well as their earnings. Many skilled workers are counted as "operatives" because the majority of workers with similar titles are semi-skilled. This is especially true where their skills have little relationship to the traditional handicrafts, but consist, rather, of a mastery of certain processes in a special industry. Many operatives in oil, chemical, or metals processing, for instance, have abilities which are acquired only through several years of training and experience. Even assembly-line workers include utility workers who can step into any position in a given department, assemblers of major subunits, and final adjustors, for all of whom experience in a wide range of jobs in their departments is necessary.

While most persons who work on farms are either owners, managers, operators of rented farms, or unpaid family workers, nearly 1.5 million wage workers employed on farms in 1950 were counted as laborers by the Census. Many of these workers, however, have significant skills. In recruiting farm hands, it is frequently necessary to insist on certain types of experience with particular kinds of machinery, crops, or animals.

SKILLED AND TECHNICAL OCCUPATIONS IN 1950

Occupational specialists must compromise among feasibility, purity of concept, and convention. The Census figures on skilled occupations are the only large body of broadly comparable data covering a long period of time. Although the Census data on the technician, craftsman, and foreman occupations are subject to qualifications, they can be used to indicate the broad outlines of the nation's skilled manpower resources. Table 1 shows the

Table 1. Craftsmen, Foremen, Kindred Workers, and Technicians, 1950 (Thousands)

	Male	Female
Craftsmen, foremen, and kindred workers		
Mechanics and repairmen	1,746	22
Carpenters	980	5
Foremen, n.e.c.	784	69
Machinists	525	9
Painters, construction and maintenance	422	9
Electricians	322	2
Plumbers and pipefitters	294	2
Stationary engineers	217	1
Linemen and servicemen, telegraph, telephone, and power	211	5
Brickmasons, stonemasons, and tile setters	175	1
Compositors and typesetters	167	11
Toolmakers, diemakers, and setters	156	1
Tinsmiths, coppersmiths, and sheet metal workers	128	1
Excavating, grading, and road machinery operators	111	1
Bakers	110	15

	Male	Female
Inspectors, n.e.c.	107	8
Cranemen, derrickmen, and hoistmen	106	1
Cabinet makers	75	1
Locomotive engineers	73	a
Tailors and tailoresses	69	17
Plasterers	64	1
Molders, metal	63	1
Millwrights	60	a
Upholsterers	58	5
Shoemakers and repairers, except factory	56	2
Locomotive firemen	56	a
Structural metal workers	55	a
Other specified metal industry occupations	206	3
Other specified light industry occupations	179	22
Other specified construction occupations	119	4
Other specified printing occupations	110	23
Unclassified craftsmen and kindred workers	102	2
Total craftsmen, foremen, and kindred workers	7,908	245

Technicians

	Male	Female
Draftsmen	116	9
Technicians, testing	60	17
Technicians, medical and dental	34	44
Surveyors	25	1
Technicians, n.e.c.	23	4
Radio operators	15	2
Dietitians and nutritionists	1	21
Total technicians	275	98
Total technicians, craftsmen, and foremen	8,183	343

n.e.c. = not elsewhere classified.
a Less than 500
Source: Bureau of the Census

number of workers reported in various technical, craftsman, and foreman occupations in 1950. These represent the major portion of the nation's skilled manpower resources. Any discussion of skilled manpower inevitably concentrates on these groups.

This table shows clearly that while there are a great number of skilled occupations, most skilled workers are employed in only a few of them. Over half of those reported as craftsmen, foremen, and technicians work in 5 occupational groups: mechanics and repairmen, carpenters, foremen, machinists, and construction and maintenance painters. Over two thirds are employed in 10 occupations. The Census reports list about 80 smaller occupations, none containing more than 2 percent of the total.

A recent survey of craftsmen, foremen, and kindred workers in six major cities provides some indication of the extent to which the figures in Table 1 include workers who are not skilled. Census techniques were used, but the questions were put directly to the worker rather than some other member of the family, which probably resulted in more accurate reporting. Nevertheless, when the reported occupational titles were checked against wages received, previous training or experience, and other information, it was concluded that 10 percent of the respondents whose titles were in the craftsman or foreman categories did not belong in these categories.

Information collected by other governmental agencies on employment in various industries sometimes provides check points for comparison with Census reports, except for depression years when many workmen are employed at jobs below their capacity. The estimates of other agencies are based on the records of employers, which provide better indications of the skill level of individual workers. The job titles given by employers, however, do not always clearly indicate skill, and the actual duties of workers must also be checked in many instances.

The Bureau of Labor Statistics, in the course of wage surveys in particular industries, has prepared some occupational estimates. For instance, in 1950, a year of moderately high employment, the Census reported 150,000 tool and die makers, while the BLS figures indicated there were about 100,000. The Census reported about 525,000 machinists. The BLS reported only 165,000 all-round machinists and about 470,000 machine tool operators, and stated that a "majority" of machine tool operators are semi-skilled. Reports by the Interstate Commerce Commission on employment in railroads suggest that the Census data overstate the number of locomotive engineers by 30 percent, but both sources agree substantially on the number of firemen.

The data for comparison with the Census reports are only fragmentary. The overstatement in the Census data varies among occupations, and in a few cases the Census reports fewer workers in an occupation than are reported by some other sources. Some experts have held that, on an over-all basis, as many as 90 percent of those reported as craftsmen, foremen, and kindred workers are skilled, while others have suggested that the correct proportion is as low as 50 percent. The available evidence suggests, however, that probably about 80 percent of the total shown in Table 1 are skilled workers or technicians. This would indicate a national total in 1950 of just under 7 million skilled workers among the craftsmen, foremen, and kindred workers and in the listed technician occupations.

There seems to be no reliable basis for estimating the number of skilled workers reported in operative, clerical, sales, service, farming, and other occupations. They probably number at least as many as are erroneously included in the craftsman, foreman, and technician occupations. The best judgment indicates that the skilled manpower segment of the labor force now totals at least 8 or 9 million workers.

SELECTED CHARACTERISTICS OF SKILLED WORKERS AND TECHNICIANS

Most skilled workers have certain common characteristics in addition to their skills and work. The typical skilled worker is a white male, slightly older than other males in the labor force, and possesses an average amount of education. There are wide variations among skilled occupations, however, and the race, sex, age, and educational characteristics of the skilled labor force have changed and will continue to change.

Women have always constituted a very small proportion of skilled workers, accounting for only 2 percent or less as late as 1940. In that year, however, women were 18 percent of all technicians. By 1950 three percent of all craftsmen and foremen and

25 percent of technicians were women. Most women in skilled and technical occupations are employed as foremen (primarily in nondurable manufacturing), medical and dental technicians, testing technicians, tailoresses, repair mechanics, or printing workers.

Relatively few Negroes have been employed as skilled workers or technicians and almost all are men. Negro men were 2.6 percent of all craftsmen and foremen in 1940. They increased to 3.6 percent by 1944 and have been about 4 percent during recent years. About 9 percent of all male workers are Negroes. Approximately 4 percent of medical and dental technicians are Negroes but there are very few Negroes in other technician occupations. Most skilled Negroes are employed in the South, where most Negro workers live.

Negroes are usually found in skilled occupations in which work is arduous, or dirty, or where long-term employment prospects are not good. Negroes have also maintained an important position in some building trades in the South since before the Civil War. Negro men are employed in only four skilled groups in greater proportion than they are in the labor force as a whole: metal molders; plasterers and cement finishers; masons, tile setters, and stonecutters; and shoemakers and repairers. Other occupations where large numbers or a significant proportion of Negroes are employed include auto mechanics; carpenters; painters and paperhangers; cranemen, hoistmen, and construction machinery operators; bakers; blacksmiths; locomotive firemen; and tailors. Relatively few Negroes are employed in some building trades, in printing or the metal trades, in most other skilled factory occupations, or as foremen.

Skilled workers are slightly older than other workers. Until 1940, the average age of craftsmen and foremen increased each decade. Between 1940 and 1950, however, as the skilled labor force grew rapidly, many young workers entered. In 1950, craftsmen and foremen averaged 41 years, compared to 40 years for all male workers.

The occupations which grew rapidly in recent decades, such as the technician occupations, radio and television mechanics and repairmen, and telegraph, telephone, and power linemen and servicemen attracted the largest number of young workers and have the lowest average age. Few young workers have entered occupations in which employment has been declining, such as locomotive engineers, tailors, blacksmiths, and shoe repairers. The advanced age of most engineers is also due to the fact that long service as a fireman is a requirement for entering the occupation.

The skilled labor force includes relatively few workers who have had either very limited or very extensive education. The typical skilled worker has from eight to twelve years of formal schooling. Whether skilled or not, younger workers, as a group, have completed more education than older workers, reflecting the general rise in schooling. In recent years, about half the young people entering the skilled occupations have completed high school. The average educational level is usually lower in those skilled occupations which include a high proportion of older workers, Negroes, or, in some instances, Southern white workers.

Technicians usually have more schooling than skilled workers. This is partly because most technicians are young, partly because training in technical schools is counted as education, while apprenticeship or on-the-job training is not, and partly because of the higher level of general education among entrants to technical work. In 1950, more than 70 percent of the workers in each of the technician occupations reported by the Census had completed high school.

The changing characteristics of skilled manpower reflect the continuing interaction among demands for goods and services, the technology, and the available manpower resources, conditioned by many social and cultural factors — all of which are constantly changing. As the technology and the pattern of demands for goods and services change, new occupations appear and old ones grow or decline in importance. These changes in the occupational structure are clearly reflected in the age and educational characteristics of the workers in many skilled occupations. Recent increases in the employment of women and Negroes as skilled workers and technicians reflect the high demand for skilled manpower in recent years as well as changing social attitudes.

LONG-TERM TRENDS

In spite of the difficulties of using job titles as indications of skill, long-run changes in the employment of skilled workers can be indicated in general terms. The skilled worker group, alone of all major occupational categories, has shown no consistent tendency to increase or decrease as a proportion of the labor force over the past half century. During this period, there has been a steady decline in the proportion of the labor force employed in farm work and as unskilled workers. The proportion of workers in professional, clerical, sales, and semi-skilled occupations increased markedly and the proportion in managerial occupations increased slightly.

The proportion of all workers employed as skilled workers has moved irregularly between about 10 and 15 percent of the labor force. The fragmentary Census data available indicate that the proportion in skilled work increased from 1870 to 1910. The number and proportion of workers in skilled occupations at Census dates between 1910 and 1950 were as follows:

Table 2. Skilled Workers and Foremen, 1910-1950

Year	Number in Thousands	Percent of Labor Force
1910	4,364	11.7
1920	5,571	13.5
1930	6,283	12.9
1940	6,105	11.7
1950	8,153[a]	13.8

[a] Craftsmen, foremen, and kindred workers in 1950.
Source: Bureau of the Census

Sample statistics since 1946 indicate that the proportion of all workers who are employed in skilled occupations varies with changes in the general level of employment. The tendency for both absolute and relative employment in skilled jobs to change together with changes in total employment apparently occurs because most skilled jobs are in the manufacturing and construction industries, in which employment fluctuates more widely than it does in most other segments of the economy. Part of the decade to decade fluctuations in the proportion of skilled workers is probably the result of differences in the over-all employment level in various census years.

Several changes in employment in specific technical and skilled occupations between 1910 and 1950 are worth noting. Employment in a number of occupations increased much faster than the total population. These include telephone, telegraph, and power linemen; tool and die makers; decorators; roofers; and excavating, grading, and road machinery operators. A number of occupations which are new or did not appear separately in earlier Census reports have increased rapidly in recent years. Among them are foremen, the various technician occupations, construction machinery operators, opticians, heat treaters, and airplane, radio, office machine, and auto mechanics and repairmen.

Occupations in which employment has not increased as rapidly as total employment include stationary engineers, tailors, furriers, millers, and stonecutters. A number of other occupations increased rapidly during the earlier decades following 1910 but have since lagged. These include machinists; railroad engineers, firemen, and mechanics; boilermakers; jewelers and engravers; and paperhangers.

The emergence of many new skilled occupations and irregularities in the growth of some older occupations indicate that mere projection of long-run trends in numbers is not very useful in seeking to anticipate future developments. For this purpose, a more detailed evaluation of recent changes is somewhat better.

SKILLED OCCUPATIONS DURING WORLD WAR II

World War II led to great increases in employment in many industries, especially in manufacturing and construction, although, as the armed forces expanded, employment in some industries fell below the levels reached in 1942-43. To meet rapidly growing demands, many skilled worker training programs were established early in the war, and the scale of existing programs was increased sharply. Workers who had gained some familiarity with elements of skilled work as semi-skilled workers, or as helpers to skilled workers, were promoted to skilled work after relatively brief training.

The resulting increase in the number of skilled workers did not meet the increased demand. Major changes in the division of work functions and the assignment of workers became necessary, although the specific techniques of production were frequently changed very little.

Increases in the scale of operations both permitted and required greater specialization in many lines of work. The tasks of skilled workers were broken down and assigned to a group of workers, each of whom had only limited training. Large groups of semi-skilled workers were built up around cadres of skilled workers. Many skilled workers were shifted from production to supervisory or pre-production jobs. As tool and die makers, set-up men, and lay-out men they concentrated on the essential skilled worker functions of making, adjusting, and repairing machines and equipment and of preparing machines and materials for particular operations. Actual production was then carried out by semi-skilled workers.

Many skilled jobs which consist of highly complex, interrelated tasks could not be easily subdivided. This was true of many kinds of tool and die making, pattern and model making, drafting and designing, and repair operations. Even in these occupations, however, some less demanding tasks were assigned to less skilled workers, who worked under close supervision. For instance, a toolmaking team might consist of a skilled toolmaker with three or four skilled machinists and semi-skilled machine operators under his direct supervision. The toolmaker was responsible for organizing and supervising the work and for the final precision operations.

Increases in the employment of semi-skilled and skilled workers and foremen were accompanied by greatly expanded industrial training activities. The greater part of this training was sponsored by employers, either in special classes or on the job. The Federal government also sponsored and paid for large-scale training programs. Those for semi-skilled workers used the facilities and staffs of vocational high schools. As the demand for manpower increased, most of these programs were transferred from schools to factories, and publicly paid teachers were used to train production workers in classes and on the job. Federal apprenticeship training officials assisted in the expansion of programs designed to prepare experienced workers for promotion to more highly skilled positions. The government also sponsored a large increase in training programs for foremen, with particular emphasis on training foremen in methods of training the greatly increased numbers of semi-skilled workers.

Increased demand for professional services led to the assignment of technicians to many tasks usually performed by professional workers. This in turn led to increases in the demand for technicians. Again, specialization was sometimes possible because operations were on a larger scale. The Federal government supported a major training program in colleges and universities. The program provided brief, intensive training for persons with some related education or experience. In many cases, professionals drew upon clerical, service, and maintenance workers around them or were permitted to hire workers with some related education or experience. Many technicians received little systematic training, but were taught the elements of their jobs as particular operations or problems occurred.

These procedures were not without their penalties. In efforts to maintain quality production, the number of supervisors and inspectors was greatly increased, often without full success. In some cases, quality was deliberately sacrificed or the design of products changed so that they could be made adequately by the workers available. To avoid the need for training versatile workers, or for retraining workers with narrow skills, major changes in products or techniques of production were avoided. In some instances, none of these measures sufficed and production was held up for lack of needed skills. Nevertheless, the war demonstrated that large increases in output could be achieved by extensive reassignment of work functions and large increases in the scale of training for workers at all skill levels.

During World War II, the number of women and Negroes employed in skilled and technical work increased substantially, and many private and public training facilities were opened to them. The growth of opportunities for women and Negroes, however, was much greater in some occupations and communities than in others. Postwar gains in the employment of these groups in skilled and technical work suggest that, in spite of the urgent needs of war production and sweeping changes in work assignments, the skills and abilities of the nation's manpower resources were not utilized to the fullest extent in World War II.

SKILLED OCCUPATIONS DURING THE KOREAN WAR

The experience in World War II was paralleled in part during the limited mobilization for the Korean war. Because the demands for manpower were not so great, however, there was no over-all manpower shortage. Consequently, it is easier to perceive the impact of efforts to increase defense production upon the skilled and technical occupations which are of critical importance in a mobilization period. The occupations which were most affected are shown by the list of critical occupations issued by the Labor Department in cooperation with the Departments of Defense and Commerce and the Office of Defense Mobilization. The list was designed to assist local draft boards and the Defense Department in considering requests for occupational deferment or delays in the call to active duty for reservists and members of the National Guard. It included shortage or potential shortage occupations which are indispensable to essential industries or activities and which require at least two years of training or experience for satisfactory performance.

The critical technical and skilled occupations numbered about 40 in all and fell mainly into six broad classifications: the aircraft industry; the communications equipment industry; shipbuilding, repair, and operation; metal mining and manufacturing; oil production and refining; and assistants to professionals and scientists. Workers in a few critical occupations, such as maintenance mechanics, were employed in many industries. Clearly, the list represented in large part the peculiar demands of mobilization. Some occupations which had been declining in absolute or relative size proved critical for mobilization. These included blacksmiths, metalmolders, boilermakers, machinists, and pattern and model makers. Metal miners, who are not ordinarily considered skilled, were also on the list.

In contrast to the long-run peacetime expansion of the service industries, the critical occupations during this partial mobilization were found in extractive and manufacturing industries. On the other hand, the increasing employment of professional and supporting technical personnel was reinforced by the nature of modern technology in civilian and military activities. The differences between long-run trends in demand for skilled manpower and the mobilization demands emphasizes the earlier suggestion that the demand for skilled manpower at any given time depends in large part on the national level of demand for specific goods and services.

CHANGES AMONG SKILLED OCCUPATIONS, 1940-1950

Many of the changes in skilled and technical employment during World War II continued into the postwar period, but many other influences were at work. This is indicated by an examination of the figures in Table 3, which shows the percentage changes from 1940 to 1950 in the number of workers reported by the Census in the technical and skilled occupations. It must be emphasized that, for the most part, the figures indicate changes in the number of workers reported as employed in the several technical and skilled occupations, rather than changes in the number of workers who are skilled. Because unemployment was substantial in 1940, many skilled workers may have been employed at jobs outside their crafts.

Some 2.2 million of a reported increase of 2.5 million in the skilled labor force fell into three broad classifications: construction

Table 3. Ranking of Technical and Skilled Occupations, by Percent Change in Employment, 1940-1950

Technicians	*Percent Change*
Technicians, n.e.c.	173.0
Radio operators	160.5
Technicians, medical, dental, and testing	125.6
Average, all technicians	102.0
Surveyors	89.8
Draftsmen	67.8
Skilled Occupations	
Mechanics and repairmen, airplane	174.2
Mechanics and repairmen, n.e.c.	139.5
Cranemen, hoistmen, and construction machinery operators	105.5
Linemen and servicemen, telegraph, telephone, and power	97.9
Cement and concrete finishers	96.8
Roofers and slaters	87.0
Brickmasons, stonemasons, and tilesetters	85.9
Mechanics and repairmen, automobile	74.2
Heat treaters, annealers, and temperers	74.1
Opticians, lens grinders, and polishers	72.7
Carpenters	67.6
Electricians	64.5
Plumbers and pipefitters	64.0
Foremen, n.e.c.	62.3

Occupation	Percent Change
Toolmakers, and die makers and setters	62.1
Plasterers	61.0
Upholsterers	60.8
Piano and organ tuners and repairmen	60.0
Decorators and window dressers	59.0
Tinsmiths, coppersmiths, and sheet metal workers	58.6
Glaziers	54.7
Average, all craftsmen and foremen	50.9
Structural metal workers	49.5
Pressmen and plate printers	49.3
Electrotypers and stereotypers	47.4
Millwrights	46.1
Cabinetmakers	44.8
Jewelers, watchmakers, goldsmiths, and silversmiths	42.5
Photoengravers and lithographers	35.9
Loom fixers	35.2
Boilermakers	30.9
Pattern and model makers, except paper	28.3
Inspectors, n.e.c.	24.8
Locomotive firemen	23.5
Painters, construction and maintenance	23.4
Engravers, except photoengravers	22.1
Inspectors, scalers and graders, log and lumber	18.8
Stationary engineers	17.7
Motion picture projectionists	16.8
Locomotive engineers	14.7
Mechanics and repairmen, railroad and car shop	14.6
Machinists, including job-setters, metal	11.7
Compositors and typesetters	9.1
Rollers and roll hands, metal	6.3
Bakers	−1.9
Stonecutters and stonecarvers	−4.4
Shoemakers and repairers, except factory	−7.0
Furriers	−13.4
Molders, metal	−17.2
Paperhangers	−17.6
Tailors and tailoresses	−22.9
Blacksmiths, forgemen and hammermen	−29.1
Millers, grain, flour, feed, etc.	−34.9

n.e.c. = not elsewhere classified.
Source: Based on data from U. S. Bureau of the Census

trades (about 1 million), mechanics and repairmen (nearly 1 million), and foremen (over 0.3 million). A large and perhaps increasing proportion of those in the so-called construction trades also perform repair or maintenance functions in manufacturing, utilities, mercantile establishments, etc. Many telegraph, telephone, and power linemen and servicemen, the one other group which reported a sizeable increase (more than 100,000), also perform repair functions. The rapid increase between 1940 and 1950 in the employment of skilled workers in repair work is evident.

The technician groups all increased by considerable percentages, although their absolute numbers are still not large. The total increased by less than 180,000 between 1940 and 1950.

Several groups of occupations did not increase as fast as the average, or actually decreased. The printing trades and skilled railroad occupations lagged considerably. The railroads have not shared proportionately in the general growth of the transportation industry. The printing industry has been making greater use of lithographic and related processes which require relatively fewer skilled workers than letterpress printing. Several foundry and mill occupations increased slightly or not at all as mechanization and different metal handling techniques permitted increased reliance on semi-skilled workers. Several specialty custom and service trades such as tailors, furriers, shoe repairers, bakers, and skilled workers in precious stones and metals increased less than most skilled trades, or declined, because of shifts in both production methods and consumption patterns. Changes in public tastes also led to a decline over the decade in the number of stone cutters and carvers and paperhangers, even though most other construction trades grew rapidly.

CHANGES IN EMPLOYMENT BY INDUSTRIES, 1940-1950

The impact on the skilled labor force of changes in the pattern of demand and production, in the technology, and in the availability of workers in various occupations is also illuminated by changes in employment in different industries.

The rapidly increasing use of machinery and complex equipment, not only in manufacturing, but also in various service and distributive industries and in the home and office, has led to a growing demand for many kinds of skilled workers for installation, repair, and service. This development is reflected by the increase in the employment of skilled workers in every major sector of the economy between 1940 and 1950. Employment of skilled workers grew rapidly even in industries which employ relatively few skilled workers, such as transportation, communication, public utilities, wholesale and retail trade, business and personal services, mining, and agriculture.

Only in the construction industry were skilled workers a smaller proportion of the total in 1950 than in 1940, and even here the relative decline was slight. Because of the rapid growth of the industry, the number of skilled workers in construction increased substantially, and in 1950 the industry employed one fourth of all skilled workers.

Manufacturing, with 37 percent of all skilled workers and foremen in 1950, remains the largest employer of skilled manpower. Both employment of skilled workers and foremen and total employment in manufacturing increased about 40 percent between 1940 and 1950. In several major manufacturing industries, however, employment of skilled workers and foremen did not increase as rapidly as total employment. The relative decline in employment of skilled workers in printing has been noted. Tremendous expansion in output by the motor vehicle, aircraft, and apparel industries was accomplished by greatly increasing the numbers of assemblers and other semi-skilled operatives, with less than proportionate increases in foremen and skilled workers. In nonelectrical machinery manufacturing, increased use of automatic production machinery and changes in the organization of work also permitted greater reliance on semi-skilled operatives.

In a number of other manufacturing industries, however, the introduction of more automatic machinery led to increased employment of skilled workers. The most striking case is tobacco manufacturing, where improvements in cigarette machines and further mechanization in cigar manufacturing permitted increased production with a 10 percent reduction in total employment. Employment of skilled workers, largely for equipment maintenance and service, increased almost one third. Continuous processes in chemicals, mechanical handling devices and larger, higher speed machines in paper and pulp manufacturing, and machinery improvements in textiles led to faster increases in skilled worker employment than in total employment. Experience in the rubber, leather, and the stone, clay, and glass products industries was similar.

THE FUTURE DEMAND FOR SKILLED WORKERS

This analysis of past trends in employment does not permit more than very modest conclusions. The skilled group is made up of a great number of diverse occupations in many different lines of enterprise. Their growth, decline, and change are subject to a wide variety of different influences which can be subsumed under the headings of changes in demand for goods and services and changes in the technology. Knowledge of how these forces have affected skilled manpower in the past is limited. One can only trace, and not very precisely, their net effect on the numbers of workers in the various occupations.

Little work has been done on future trends in skilled occupations. The Bureau of Labor Statistics is responsible for most of what has been done, largely in connection with its *Occupational Outlook Handbook*. These forecasts are helpful to young workers seeking information about career prospects, but they cover only certain occupations and do not constitute a systematic forecast of skilled employment. A. J. Jaffe and R. O. Carleton of Columbia University have undertaken the only other major work on occupational projection, but their studies were methodological and were concerned with the factors influencing the supply of workers, once demand for them is stipulated.

To forecast adequately changes in the skilled occupational structure is an extremely complex and difficult task. It requires, first, a forecast of the level of demand for goods and services in each industry and for each sector of the economy. Preliminary estimates of changes in the employment of different kinds of skilled workers in each industry can then be made by assuming that the number of workers in each occupation will change in direct proportion to anticipated changes in the demand for the industry's goods and services. Reasonably accurate forecasting, however, requires an additional step. Each industry must be analyzed in terms of the forces which influence its occupational structure, including changes in the level of production and employment, changes in the distribution of production and employment among the various firms, the availability of different types of manpower resources, and the impact of technological change.

For some time, the Bureau of Labor Statistics has been engaged in preliminary work on which systematic estimates of the future occupational structure can be based. It is nearing completion of only the first step, which is to refine Census data in order to arrive at an accurate estimate of the occupational composition of each industry in 1950. It has not yet attempted to estimate future demand and employment or changes in the occupational structure, except in a few industries. A comprehensive study is not likely to be done in the near future because of budgetary limitations.

An exploratory study by the Bureau of Labor Statistics of the manpower requirements in the nonferrous foundry industry under conditions of full mobilization indicates the extensive analysis which is necessary in order to assess the impact of changes in the demand for products. The Bureau considered only those occupations which require prolonged training. The analysis indicates that as demand for foundry products increases, changes in the occupational distribution within individual foundries depend on the type of metal used, casting technique, size of foundry, size of casting, extent of mechanization, end use of castings, and the size of production runs. With this many variables, the number of possible combinations is very large. Actually, the Bureau found that it could achieve satisfactory results by considering only five major combinations. This degree of detail seemed necessary to arrive at an estimated increase in total employment from 44,000 to 69,000 workers, with less than 5,000 of the increase in skilled and technical occupations.

Some industries, such as aircraft manufacturing, present even greater difficulties in forecasting occupational requirements. During World War II, completely different technologies were used by different aircraft manufacturers, depending on whether their prewar experience had been in aircraft or automobile manufacturing. On the other hand, there are many other industries in which the problem is easier because skilled workers are not so crucial, the proportion of skilled workers is smaller, or the industries themselves are less varied and depend on fewer crucial occupations.

Clearly, the task of forecasting occupational requirements for total mobilization is formidable, even though the demands for individual products can be fairly well stipulated. In normal times, the problem is greater, for the pattern and level of demands resulting from the operation of a free market are much more difficult to estimate. While the problem is simplified by stipulating full or nearly full employment, high levels of employment may be achieved under varying conditions of demand for goods and services. Some of the more important variables appear to be the demand for construction, military orders, other governmental purchases, business investment, and the changing pattern of consumer purchases.

THE INFLUENCE OF THE TECHNOLOGY AND THE LABOR SUPPLY

The nonferrous foundry study did not consider the effect of changes in the technology or the labor supply on the occupational structure. There has been little systematic thinking on how these aspects of the problem can be dealt with. Changes in technology are evolutionary. Each change is subject to many influences, including the diverse market conditions for the relevant economic factors and the character of the technology as it has developed in the past. At any one time many possible technological changes are on the horizon, but some of them will never be introduced. New production methods, processes, and machines are adopted only after their economic as well as their technical soundness has been tested.

Even if technological changes could be stipulated, their manpower implications would not be self-evident. Present knowledge of the relationship between technology and the occupational structure permits only the loosest kinds of generalizations. It has been pointed out that technological change reduces the importance of some occupations, and makes others more important. The introduction of machinery sometimes creates new types of skilled jobs. In other cases, skilled jobs are broken down into semi-skilled jobs. The old-style skilled workers may disappear or become supervisors. As final products change and as the individual steps in production are examined by engineers, the tasks of the semi-skilled workers will be altered. The specialized jobs may no longer be combinable into a recognized skilled occupation. Foremen may have less control over processes and serve mainly as general administrators instituting changes developed by engineers. Formerly, changes in particular production techniques might have been made, in part at least, by foremen and skilled workers. As they increase in importance, engineers may also lose some of their functions to technicians.

Even if the technology, the level of industrial activity, and other factors affecting demand for technicians and skilled workers could be adequately forecast, the influence of the supply of manpower would still have to be determined. The available supply of trained workers influences the way in which production is carried on and thus the future demand for workers. The use of technical and skilled workers rather than semi-skilled workers, or of particular kinds of skilled workers rather than other kinds, depends on the supply of these various types of workers. Machinists will not be used as members of a toolmaking team unless they are more readily available than toolmakers. The demand for technicians depends in part on the supply of professionals. An abundant supply of untrained workers may create an incentive for breaking down skilled jobs. The reluctance of workers to accept certain working conditions may encourage the development of new machines. To complicate the matter, the supply of skilled workers is essentially local rather than national, so that the influence of the labor supply on future demands for skilled manpower will vary from community to community.

GENERAL TRENDS IN THE ECONOMY

Although adequate estimates of future changes in the demands for technical and skilled workers are not now possible, several relevant economic developments may be discerned, and their general consequences foreseen.

Capital equipment per worker is at a very high level and apparently will continue to increase. The use of machinery has spread to every industry, including business offices, commerce, and agriculture. The modern home contains more and more machinery and equipment, and the use of automobiles continues to increase.

At the same time, the economy is becoming more complex and interdependent. Within enterprises and between enterprises, a wide subdivision of tasks has evolved. The range of jobs, at the technical and skilled level, as well as other levels, has become broader. Local markets are more integrated with the national economy, with increased transfer of goods and services between communities.

The nature of goods and services produced has changed considerably. There has been a relative movement away from extractive industries. In recent decades, the proportion of the labor force employed in manufacturing has shown no marked tendency to increase or decrease, but many experts expect that it will decline as the service industries continue to expand rapidly. Within the service areas, domestic and similar services, such as restaurants and hotels, barber and beauty shops, laundry and dry cleaning establishments, and repair and maintenance were originally of greatest importance. Later, employment in transport, commerce, communications, finance, and administration expanded. The latest shift is the growth in relative importance of those services aimed directly at the promotion of individual, social, and economic development, including medical care, education, research, and recreation.

The economy has been subjected recently to greatly increased military claims on output and manpower. Apparently, there will be no drastic reductions in military needs in the near future.

Whether the proportion of the labor force employed in construction will be larger or smaller in the future is problematical, but it is unlikely that employment in the construction industry will increase as rapidly as it did between 1940 and 1950.

IMPLICATIONS OF THE GENERAL TRENDS

These general trends in the economy have a number of implications for technical and skilled manpower. The greatly increased capital investment per worker increases the risks of using workers with limited training. This has been evident for some time in many fields and is now becoming apparent even in agriculture.

The increasing use of machinery will raise the demand for skilled workers for installation and maintenance purposes, and in some cases to control or operate the new equipment. Although much industrial machinery can be handled by semi-skilled workers, in the long run the demand for skilled repair and service workers has increased as the use of machinery has increased. The costs of having equipment temporarily out of production make it urgent that repair operations be performed rapidly and that breakdowns be prevented. This is especially true in such highly integrated operations as steel mills, where any lengthy interruption can ruin a whole production run. On the other hand, some repair functions are now handled by rapid replacement of entire units. Damaged parts are then repaired at leisure. Moreover, where repair operations are on a large scale, assembly line methods are often possible. Although these tendencies may limit the demand for skilled repair and service workers, the over-all demand for them will probably continue to grow.

The trend toward using skilled workers in the developmental and pre-production stages of industrial operations, rather than in actual production of the final product, will probably continue. These functions are filled by engineers' assistants, designers, set-up and lay-out men, and makers of tools, jigs, dies, templates, patterns, models, and cores. Increasing employment of foremen, scheduling clerks, production technicians, inspectors, trouble shooters, and utilitymen to compensate for the lack of flexibility of semi-skilled workers may also be expected to continue. It is in the pre-production and supporting functions that the importance of the role of technicians and skilled workers as a connecting link between professional and scientific workers and production workers is most clear.

The increased complexity of the economy and society have been accompanied by a great increase in the importance of transportation. Motor and air transport have become increasingly important, but railroads have not kept pace. Communication functions have expanded even more rapidly. The growth of telecommunications and record keeping has contributed to the demand for electronic technicians, linemen, clerical workers, etc. Machinery and electronic devices may tend to increase the need for electronic and other types of skilled workers, and to decrease the need for clerical workers, but clerical employment will probably continue to grow for some time.

While quality is both difficult to define and control in service operations, there is considerable room for improvement in the quality of work done in many service fields. This will depend in part on the production of a larger number of better trained skilled service workers. As the national income rises, the growing demand for medical, educational, research, and other professional services will probably lead to increased demands for technicians in these fields.

Continued high demand for goods and services for military purposes will probably support the demand for many of the critical occupations mentioned earlier, which include assistants to professional and scientific personnel and technical as well as skilled workers in aircraft manufacturing and operation, metal mining and manufacturing, and oil production and refining. The demand for maritime and shipyard workers is not likely to be high unless the United States becomes involved in another major war.

ADJUSTMENTS TO CHANGING DEMANDS

In the absence of specific numerical forecasts, what can be said about how changes in the demand for skilled workers — resulting from changes in the demand for goods and services and in the technology — will be met?

In the first place, a wide range of adjustments can be made at any time to restore the balance between the demand for and the supply of skilled workers. The labor force contains personnel with a wide range of competence. As the nature of a firm's demand changes, it has considerable leeway to reassign functions. This may involve either large or small changes for any worker or group of workers. The cumulative effect of even small shifts in the functions of professional, managerial, technical, skilled, and other personnel may often be sufficient to meet changing manpower needs.

Second, it is very easy to overestimate the impact of technological change during relatively short periods of time. As noted earlier, many changes are always on the horizon. But some are only ideas, and many are feasible technically but not economically. In any case, major technological changes are usually the result of a series of smaller changes which can often be assimilated readily as they occur.

Third, the technology and the product can both be adjusted to the manpower resources available. Certain things are not done because they would place too much strain on the available manpower resources. Persistent manufacturing errors or repair difficulties resulting from lack of workers with adequate skills may be overcome by changes in product design.

Finally, and perhaps most important, because of the nature of the process through which workers become skilled, the supply of technical and skilled personnel may be altered markedly in relatively short periods of time. Chapters VIII and IX show that training for technical and skilled work is remarkably responsive to changes in the demand. There are always a large number of workers in the process of being trained whose training can be accelerated or redirected to some extent. Moreover, most skilled workers are not trained in formal programs. They usually advance to the skilled level through a series of promotions or through successive changes of jobs, each of which add to their skill. If demand in some areas increases, opportunities for promotion and for working where skills can be picked up also increase. If demand is low, the flow of workers through the structure of jobs to the skilled level is considerably retarded. The fact that training of skilled and technical workers responds quite readily to changes in demand is one of the reasons why forecasts of the technical and skilled work force are so difficult. At the same time, it reduces the urgency of specific forecasts in so far as national manpower problems are concerned.

On the other hand, it is difficult to meet drastic increases in demand for skilled manpower such as occur during mobilization. There are also some occupations which are not readily responsive to the market. Where training programs are highly formal and training facilities cannot be quickly expanded, as in some technician fields, rapid adjustments in the supply of workers are difficult to accomplish. Many technicians in each of the various technician occupations, however, acquire their skills informally. Where the individual tasks of skilled workers are complexly interrelated, as they are for some mechanics and tool, die, pattern, and model makers, the extent to which functions can be shifted from one group to another is limited, but in many cases, still substantial.

Although there are many ways through which the supply of and the demand for skilled and technical workers are brought into line, the present difficulties in anticipating future needs are a serious handicap. Individuals, companies, government agencies, and labor unions are constantly making decisions based on uncertain estimates of future needs for skilled workers. Individuals could make sounder career plans; companies, unions, and educational institutions could plan their training programs better; and the entire economy would be better off if future lines of development could be clarified.

In the face of rapid changes in the economy and uncertainty as to the effects of these changes, the need for workers who can shift functions and readily acquire new skills is evident. Since new technologies can only be introduced as fast as the necessary manpower is trained, it is important that workers have a broad foundation of basic knowledge and skills together with attitudes which will facilitate their learning new tasks as the need and opportunity arise.

CHAPTER III

Education and Training of Workers: An Employer Appraisal

What qualities do employers look for in hiring young people who may become skilled workers or technicians? To what extent do they find what they seek? What do they think the schools could do to provide more young people with the desired qualities? The National Manpower Council put these and similar questions before small groups of executives in four metropolitan areas — Chicago, Detroit, San Francisco, and Atlanta.[1]

The fifty-six conference participants were all high-level executives directly involved in the recruitment, selection, and training of workers. Wide agreement marked their responses to the questions asked by the Council, but some sharply contradictory opinions as well as significant differences in emphasis did appear. Both the viewpoints expressed and the degree of unanimity voiced should be evaluated in the light of the firms represented.

These included a variety of enterprises differing in occupational characteristics and size, among them, a brokerage house, a steel mill, a retail department store, a shipping line, an automobile manufacturer, and several public utilities and pharmaceutical houses. Nevertheless, they did not constitute anything like a comprehensive sample of American enterprises. Large companies, heavy manufacturing, and highly technical industries dominated, and small concerns and the construction and service fields were

[1] Descriptions of these and other conferences held by the Council in connection with the present study, together with lists of conference participants, appear in the Preface and Acknowledgments.

underrepresented. Moreover, conferences conducted in other metropolitan areas with different industrial patterns, labor market conditions, and educational facilities would undoubtedly have produced somewhat different findings.

The participants agreed overwhelmingly on one principal conclusion. When hiring young workers for positions below the professional level, they are far more concerned with general qualifications than with specific aptitudes or skills. Proper attitudes, general intelligence, and good ability in reading, writing, speaking, and arithmetic are valued far above specific training. It was also clear, however, that the application of this general rule is modified by the condition of the local labor market, the location of the company, the particular industry involved, and the size of the firm. Thus it is quite likely that if the building trades had been more fully represented, greater emphasis would have been placed on specific skills acquired through apprenticeship training. It is also possible that the presence of more representatives from medium and small enterprises would have resulted in less emphasis on the importance of attitudes and basic abilities. Small companies, lacking intensive training programs of their own and with limited job openings, could be expected to show far more concern with specific aptitudes and skills in hiring new workers.

Another caution to be kept in mind in interpreting the viewpoints of the conference participants was stressed by the participants themselves. Company practice, they pointed out, may differ substantially from company principles. Companies which set good attitudes and general abilities as qualifications for employment are also aware of the difficulty of determining the presence or absence of the attitudes and abilities they seek, Hence, when examining job applicants, they tend to fall back on specific training and prior experience, which are easy to evaluate.

DEFINITIONS OF TECHNICIANS AND SKILLED WORKERS

The emphasis on general qualifications and the failure to demand specific attributes in younger workers were due in part to uncertainty as to who is a skilled worker. It was agreed that neither common usage nor job titles can be relied upon for useful distinctions. Some participants felt that it is possible to distinguish clearly between skilled and technical workers, for the first rely mainly on manual ability and the latter on theoretical knowledge. They reasoned as follows: The skilled worker has a wide range of abilities which enable him to perform a variety of tasks without close supervision. The technician's narrow training confines him to work as the direct assistant of a professional. The skilled worker receives his training in the shop, while the technician usually has one to three years of formal training after high school. The former is often a union member while the latter is usually not. The skilled man is a production or maintenance worker, while the technician is often engaged in design or development work.

Other participants maintained, however, that these distinctions often disappear in practice. They pointed out that the tool and die maker — who is the archetype of the skilled worker — often has more intelligence and more theoretical knowledge than many who are generally considered technicians. Like the technician, he is frequently employed in design and development work. The draftsman, usually regarded as a technician, does more work with his hands than many skilled workers. Moreover, many technicians are trained on the job rather than in school.

Some conference members even asserted that no general definitions and distinctions are possible, and that efforts to go beyond the description of the aptitudes, functions, and training required for specific jobs lead only to meaningless generalities. All that is needed, they said, is to know what aptitudes and training are required for a given job, regardless of its name. On the other hand, some urged that clear and improved definitions are essential to identify accurately occupations in which there are shortages of personnel and to clarify the application of Federal collective bargaining legislation to different categories of workers.

It has already been indicated that most large companies do not look for specific skills or technical knowledge in hiring young workers. Most of the workers who ultimately become skilled initially hold simple beginners' jobs. They move into jobs classified as skilled on the basis of performance, desire and ability to exploit the training opportunities at hand, and seniority. Consequently, employers are interested in motivation and attitudes more than in specialized skills, in general intelligence more than in specific aptitudes. In a large organization there is always room someplace for a conscientious workman, whatever his particular qualities. As one conferee from a large company put it: "Give us a man with the right physique and attitudes, and we'll find work for him." Large industrial firms have found it relatively easy to adapt the worker to the job through training, and to adapt the job to the worker through supervisory practices and by breaking down complex jobs into many simple jobs.

The motivation and attitudes of young workers received more attention than any other qualification for employment. The attitudes sought were identified as pride in workmanship; interest in the work and in a long-term career with the firm, and in self-development or personal progress; a sense of responsibility; and an ability to adjust to work regulations and to get along with others.

While attitudes were always regarded as important per se, employers emphasized that their particular significance depends upon the kind of position which has to be filled. Obviously, for a job requiring specific major skills, training and experience are stressed, and the fact that an applicant has made a large investment in acquiring such skills is also likely to be regarded as evidence that he has the proper attitudes. The inherent limitations of the means necessarily used to judge the attitudes of job applicants were readily admitted. Generally, employers rely on written references, evaluations made in personal interviews, and scholastic records.

Most Northern employers felt that their employees, especially newly hired young workers, are seriously deficient in the desired attitudes. Representatives of retailing concerns were especially critical, reporting that they have great difficulty in finding employees with a sense of responsibility and willingness to serve the customer properly. This was attributed, in part, to the fact that so many retail employees are young women who regard their jobs as temporary, merely filling the time between graduation from school and marriage. Poor attitudes are manifested in disinterest in the work, refusal to accept responsibility or promotion, and absenteeism and tardiness, all of which require additional expenditures for supervision. These shortcomings, it was also noted, are partly balanced by the fact that young women get along better with customers and adjust more easily to new situations, probably because they are not strongly involved in their work.

Some employers felt that there has been a marked deterioration in recent years in worker attitudes. It was contended that workers are no longer governed by internal standards of work; that they display less of the old-time willingness to please the boss; that cooperation is no longer spontaneous. The difficulty lies not in getting people to work hard in the physical sense — for machines have made this unnecessary — but in application to the job.

A number of explanations were offered for the alleged decline in worker motivation. Some blamed the schools for no longer stressing discipline, the teaching of fundamentals, scholastic achievement, and respect for work. Inadequate supervision at home, the fact that many mothers are employed, and the decline of family life were also cited. Not only do many young workers come to employment with poor attitudes, it was asserted, but these attitudes may be re-enforced by their experiences on the job. Unionization may reduce the effectiveness of economic incentives by guaranteeing the same reward to the indolent as to the conscientious. Seniority provisions and uniform wage scales may prevent management from adequately rewarding the outstanding worker.

Poor attitudes, however, were not traced solely to the short-comings of parents, schools, and unions. Many conference participants emphasized the importance of changes in the work situation. Full employment, they believed, gives the worker less reason to fear loss of his job and more choice in how he works. The greater job pride ascribed to workers in the past, they held, should be viewed rather as a mark of job insecurity, which has since been reduced by full employment, unions, and unemployment insurance. Shorter working hours have given the worker more leisure and other interests outside of his work. Management practices and technological advances were also held to be partly responsible for the growth of undesirable attitudes. When the skilled worker sees his job broken down, simplified, and performed by people with little training he can no longer take pride in it. Supervision and leadership can do much more than they have to develop pride in work and better worker morale. Management, it was repeatedly asserted, is often slow in putting into effect tested knowledge about motivation and attitudes.

A few participants refused to accept the view that the attitudes of workers have deteriorated. They maintained that there is no reliable evidence showing that workers applied themselves more intensively in the past. Several stated that the good attitudes they seek very often appear among young workers who have been out of school several years, who have had a chance to try out different jobs, and are married and have acquired family responsibilities. One executive later wrote that he thought the conference in which he had participated had placed too much stress on the decline of motivation. After talking to his supervisors, he concluded that today's young workers are "different," but that they make excellent employees when supervisors learn to understand and handle them properly. It was also suggested that part of the difficulty encountered in dealing with young workers is a product of the common management belief that men do not know anything until they are past thirty. This results in underutilizing those between eighteen and thirty, which in turn encourages feelings of dissatisfaction among young employees.

Employers in the South also emphasized the importance of attitudes, but, unlike their Northern counterparts, had few complaints on this score. They agreed that the South is amply endowed with bright, willing, and potentially able workers who can be readily trained for factory work. Several spoke of the greater willingness to work and interest in self-development found among workers with farming experience as compared to those coming from urban areas.

In spite of the dominant view that many young workers lack the ambition to invest substantially in acquiring skills, there was no feeling that employers are faced with a shortage of young people able and willing to undertake training for responsible positions. Even companies with very low hiring standards had no difficulty filling their training quotas from among their young workers.

The educational background of young workers ranked in importance next to attitudes in the judgment of the conference participants. Overwhelmingly, they were less concerned with the applicant's course of study than they were with his possession of a high school diploma and a good scholastic record. Except in the South, most participants indicated that their companies are reluctant to hire young people who are not high school graduates. Since, in most Northern cities, such a high proportion of high school students now graduate, the young man or woman who does not is regarded with suspicion.

More specifically, the completion of high school with a good record is regarded as an indication of basic intelligence, good motivation, and ability to absorb training. These qualifications were held to be especially important for jobs which offer opportunities for training and promotion. The increasing complexity of machines and processes and the need for frequent retraining because of changes in production methods underline the need for qualities reflected in successful completion of high school. In this connection, some fear was expressed that frustration is encouraged by placing highly intelligent high school graduates in purely routine jobs.

Southern employers were much less insistent upon high school graduation, not because of indifference to its advantages, but because fewer graduates are available for industrial employment. They called attention to the difficulty and expense of including in company training programs basic subjects which most young workers in the North had studied in school. One Southern executive stated that when his plant was established, only 3 percent of the available workers had gone to high school. Technician positions for which at least high school graduation would be required in other regions of the country were often filled in the South by men who had not gone beyond elementary school.

In so far as employers were concerned with what their new employees had studied, as well as with how well they had done in school, they were again less interested in specific industrial skills than they were in the ability to do arithmetic, spell, read with understanding, and communicate accurately. For some jobs, employers also looked for basic training in mathematics and science. The emphasis which Southern employers placed on the need for a sound high school background in these subjects reflects the growing importance of the chemical, electronics, petroleum, synthetic textile, and other highly technical industries in that region.

SELECTION, TRAINING, AND UTILIZATION

The standards actually applied by employers in hiring new workers vary considerably with the state of the labor market. Educational requirements, test scores, and other qualifications for employment are raised or lowered depending on the abundance or scarcity of applicants with the desired qualities. One conference participant remarked that employers who can pick and choose are fortunate, for, he said, he has "had to hire anyone able to get to the office" for the past thirteen years. Some companies, on the other hand, do not relax their standards below a certain point, no matter how badly they need employees. Instead, they resort to overtime or intensify their efforts to improve the utilization of their work force.

Conference participants recognized that their preoccupation with attitudes, basic knowledge, and other very general qualities was partly a reflection of tight labor market situations. The point was made that when a young applicant with specific training is equal in other respects to one without such preparation, the former is hired. In recent years, however, applicants with good specific training, as well as good motivation, high intelligence, and good educational background have been relatively scarce.

Past experience in transforming highly skilled, multi-operation jobs into a series of jobs handled by workers of lesser skill was taken to justify the conviction that specific skills and aptitudes are of secondary importance. Employers have learned that workers can be trained for many tasks in much less time than had formerly been thought possible. One employer reported that during World War II, when he was short of operators for earth-moving machinery, he was supplied by error with "machine operators" who turned out to be needle-trades machine operators. A relatively short training program, however, turned them into excellent operators of heavy earth-moving machinery.

All participants agreed that there is a definite limit on the adjustments possible through job breakdown and brief, narrowly specialized training. In almost all fields there is a small core of highly skilled workers — tool and die makers, truly skilled machinists, master tailors, millwrights, master masons — who are absolutely essential for continued operation and whose training approaches that of professional personnel in length and intensity. When such workers are needed quickly they can be obtained only by scouring the labor market and stealing them from other employers. Recently one large company literally found it necessary to canvass the world to find 480 tool and die makers for an emergency retooling project.

Northern employers recognized the critical role filled by such workers and believed that it would be good to train more of them.

Yet they did not feel that there are serious shortages of highly skilled workers or technicians. Southern employers, on the other hand, were concerned with shortages of skilled workers and especially of technicians. They complained about the necessity of importing them from the North, of undertaking expensive training programs to turn inexperienced men into versatile mechanics, and of related problems involving the selection and training of supervisors.

One Southern industrialist said that in the South there is today no real choice between hiring "the man with experience or . . . the man with good common sense and ability to learn . . . we have to have experience . . . After you get a fairly good nucleus you can look to a youngster who can be trained and who has the aptitude even if he doesn't have experience." This suggests that employers in the North can afford to stress general ability and favorable attitudes above specific skills because they can take for granted the existence of a substantial group of skilled, experienced workmen. Comments from Southern participants also suggest that specific training and experience are much more important in new and rapidly growing enterprises than they are in old, established companies. Much of the concern expressed with shortages came from men who were involved in organizing new plants. Several participants from older organizations, which already possessed a core group of skilled and experienced men, indicated that they were not severely pressed by shortages.

In both North and South, some companies normally secure skilled workers by "stealing" them from others. In the North, on the other hand, many firms refuse to hire skilled craftsmen from the outside, except in case of emergency, preferring to train their workers themselves. Similar variations in methods of obtaining technicians were noted. Some companies select their most intelligent young workers for on-the-job training, partly because of difficulties in obtaining school-trained technicians. Others, who train most of their skilled employees themselves, make an exception in the case of technicians and seek men with school and military training. One company had formerly hired men with bachelors' and masters' degrees for technician positions. Because many became discontented with the lack of opportunity for advancement, the firm now plans to hire men without college training. Other companies, however, fill their technician openings with professionally trained personnel who, having demonstrated their competence, may be advanced to professional jobs.

Employers know what general qualities they are looking for, but they are frequently troubled by the methods they use to identify the young workers who possess these qualities. Different hiring practices, based on different standards, are often equally successful. It was even contended that personnel men could operate fairly well if they merely closed their eyes and made a random choice among applicants. This position was defended on two grounds: the high adaptability of most persons and the selection function exercised by job applicants themselves, most of whom have enough insight to present themselves for jobs which they are more or less qualified to fill.

Some companies, however, have developed fairly elaborate selection procedures. One firm believes it has succeeded in excluding most applicants who are likely to quit after a short period by taking into account such factors as completion of education, age, IQ, mechanical aptitude test results, marital status, and total job experience. While a great deal of psychological testing is carried on, many employers expressed doubts about its value. They noted that test score standards are frequently lowered when not enough applicants meet the established score, and that those responsible for hiring often fail to rely on or make proper use of the tests. Some participants were afraid, on the other hand, that too heavy reliance is often placed on test results of uncertain validity.

Because it is difficult to assess attitudinal factors in advance, some companies have come to depend upon a variety of quite specific criteria, even though their bias is to apply very general standards of motivation and ability. Test results, specific training, and prior experience are often relied upon, both in hiring and in selecting men for training and promotion. The tendency to over-value formal scientific and engineering training in selecting employees for supervisory positions was singled out as an important reason for poor utilization of capable men who have not had such training.

Even though most employers seemed well satisfied with the ability of industry to meet its needs for skilled people through training programs, it was also maintained that not enough thought or money has been devoted to industrial training. The point was repeatedly made that much of what passes for on-the-job training is no more than learning through unsupervised experience. There was testimony that many supervisors regard training as a nuisance which should be allowed to interfere with production only when absolutely necessary. It was also charged that industry tends to regard training as a means of filling specific openings and not of providing opportunities for the continuing development of the capacities of individuals. Several executives argued that industry has done an unusually poor job of training skilled men to be super-visors, and that much supervisory training is too brief and inten-sive. On the other hand, it was suggested that many industrial training programs run longer than necessary because they are poorly organized and controlled.

Conference participants noted that reliance on job breakdown, intensive training, and increased supervision to meet requirements for skilled workers involves costs which are often poorly appraised. In some firms job simplification has been carried so far as to be uneconomical, necessitating a reversal of the process and the re-combination of jobs. The use of inadequately trained men may impose inordinate demands on the time and attention of super-visors or require an increase in their number. Lack of sufficiently trained technicians often leads to using scientists and engineers for work which men with less training could perform.

Many employers expressed concern that job-security and seniority provisions in union contracts give unions a major share in the selection, training, and promotion of workers to skilled and supervisory positions. Yet most of them did not regard union participation in these functions as a serious obstacle to efficient operation. Seniority, it was said, "can kill you, if you don't watch out, by providing people not qualified for promotion," but it was also observed that seniority has served the useful purpose of forcing management to devote more attention to the initial selection and subsequent training of potential skilled workers and supervisors. The point was made that firms which complacently accepted the strict application of seniority rules during and after World War II, without bothering to make the necessary adjustments in selection and training policy, have since experienced certain difficulties. Seniority restrictions, it was also stressed, are not entirely the result of union demands; many companies, on their own initiative, follow seniority in making promotions.

Some employers described two requirements for living with a seniority system. It is necessary, first, to make sure that all employees who are placed on the first rung of the promotional ladder have the qualities necessary to occupy successfully some of the upper rungs. In this connection, the importance of selecting young workers with good attitudes, general intelligence, and sound training in the basic skills of communication and computation was reaffirmed. The second requirement is that all workers who are in line for promotion receive adequate training. This involves the provision not only of training opportunities, but also of adequate incentives, in terms of wages and working conditions, to insure that able employees apply for training. When these requirements are met, it was asserted, conflicts between management and the union are reduced, and the union shows greater flexibility in its response to specific management problems growing out of the application of seniority provisions.

At each of the conferences, the participants were asked in what respects requirements for young workers ten years in the future are likely to differ from those of today because of changes in products, processes, and technology. They were generally unwilling to venture specific estimates of the character of their future requirements. It was evident, also, that they were expecting the gradual extension of recent developments rather than radical departures.

Employers agreed almost unanimously that the demand for skilled and technical workers will continue to be high. They also agreed that higher levels of skill will be essential and that skilled workers will need more technical and theoretical training. The level of business was given slight weight as a factor determining the demand for skilled workers. When it was considered, it was assumed that the level of production and employment would remain high. There was no expression of concern over the possibility of future surpluses of skilled workers.

As one reason for their expectation of a continuing high demand for skilled workers, a few participants offered the judgment that the long-term trend toward subdivision of labor is now being reversed. For the most part, however, industry representatives stressed the manpower consequences of automatic factories, the peacetime use of atomic energy, increased expansion of the electronics and chemical industries, further increases in the complexity of precision machinery, and still other changes in technology.

There was no expectation that these developments will displace the skilled worker. On the contrary, it was contended that both the percentage of skilled workers and the levels of skill required will go up and that the unskilled worker is in much greater danger of displacement. Automatic machines will require highly skilled maintenance and repair men. Atomic generators will require maintenance men who are more skilled than at present. Many of today's electricians will have to learn electronics if they are to retain their skilled status. Pipefitters may have to learn hydraulics. A skilled worker who formerly measured with calipers and now uses a micrometer will soon have to learn to work to tolerances measured with light waves. It was predicted that there may be almost no place left for the unskilled industrial worker. Today, even a handtrucker must be able to interpret charts to see where supplies are needed.

It was also anticipated that the demand for skilled workers in nonmanufacturing industries will continue to expand rapidly. Agriculture is demanding fewer workers, but a constantly increasing proportion of skilled and technically trained men. The continuing rise in the standard of living and the increasing mechanization of the home and the office will lead to steadily rising needs for skilled service and repair workers.

The difficulty of foreseeing the nature and consequences of future shifts in the skill composition of the labor force was stressed. No one was prepared to forecast what would happen to the economy, or to the labor force as a whole, if the number of technicians or of versatile, highly trained, skilled workers were substantially increased. Although existing ratios between various types of workers — engineers and technicians, or technicians and skilled workers — are frequently discussed, it was pointed out that no one really knows what they mean or what would happen if they were changed. The complex interdependence of different skills is illustrated by the fact that during World War II the attraction of high pay in war industries led to shortages of garbage collectors and laundry workers which, in turn, interfered with production in some war plants.

The conferees were agreed, in any case, that the future will continue to bring constant changes in processes, machines, and job requirements. Consequently, training and retraining will constitute an even more important task than at present. Employers, however, were no more worried about future training problems than they were about meeting their current needs for skilled workers. The most important requirement for workers at every level, they said, will be their willingness to accept change. If this quality is present and if industry accepts its obligation to find jobs for men displaced by new developments, the retraining tasks will not be difficult. Recognition of the likelihood of constant change in job content led to suggestions for some sort of basic training which would help the worker to adapt to the requirements of many different jobs. The nature of such basic training, however, was not specified.

THE SECONDARY SCHOOLS AND THE QUALITIES OF WORKERS

Comments on education were focused on ways in which the high schools can produce graduates with the qualities that past experience has led industry to regard as essential. There was little disposition to recommend changes in secondary education to anticipate different future requirements. This, of course, reflects the strong interest in certain very general qualities in young workers and the fact that most participants could not see how these requirements would be likely to change.

Judgments on how well the high schools are meeting the needs of industry were extremely mixed. Complaints centered about the failure of the schools to provide adequate training in fundamentals — reading, writing, speaking, arithmetic — and to inculcate self-discipline, responsibility, and other desirable attitudes. Generally, those participants who were most critical of the attitudes and abilities of young people applying for employment were disposed to place the blame for their shortcomings upon their education and to hold that the nation's schools have been going downhill. One participant noted that his company's training program was moving gradually backward to make up for training which the schools no longer provide.

On the other hand, many participants declared that the schools were doing a good job, certainly as good as could be expected in view of the handicaps under which they have been operating. Some maintained that today's high school graduates are better prepared for employment than those of the past and that the adverse judgments of secondary education are frequently based on the exception rather than the rule. A retailing executive reported: "At Christmas time we double our staff, usually from high schools and junior colleges. Right after Christmas we had half-a-dozen managers raising hell about people who couldn't write or figure. Analysis showed that out of some 2,000 hired, maybe twenty-five were deficient and it was those the whole organization heard and talked about, and not about the others, who did a good job. This is typical of how we judge our secondary institutions."

Differences in judgment undoubtedly reflected differences in school systems, as well as in standards of evaluation. Participants in the San Francisco conference, for instance, spoke well of the California schools. Southern employers, on the other hand, were highly critical of the quality as well as the quantity of Southern secondary education. Even high school graduates, they said, are poorly prepared in reading, writing, arithmetic, and elementary science. The high proportion of applicants who fail to qualify for apprenticeship training was cited as objective evidence of these deficiencies. It was also asserted that far too many students take business courses in Southern high schools, not only because they think in terms of white collar employment, but also because business courses are regarded as easier. In addition, the basic academic subjects are badly taught because salaries are too low to attract good teachers, and school officials do not appreciate their importance.

Employers who were highly critical of the quality of high school graduates recognized that the schools alone were not to blame. It was pointed out that the spread of high school education has probably resulted in some reduction in the average ability of the total student body, and that lack of financial support and interest by the community — business included — were responsible for many of the difficulties encountered by the schools.

The participants agreed emphatically that the high schools should devote themselves to better teaching of fundamentals and to instilling attitudes of ambition, responsibility, and adaptability, rather than to specialized training for work. "All anybody can hope to get out of the high schools," said one executive, "is a constant flow of people capable of learning and motivated to go on and learn, plus some understanding of the system in which they have to live."

The educational recommendations of the conference participants may be divided into two related groups: those dealing with subject matter and those dealing with the general goals of secondary education. As far as subject matter is concerned, there was overwhelming agreement that the major need is for better training in reading, writing, and arithmetic. While the major responsibility for these skills lies with the elementary schools, it was asserted, the secondary schools have neglected to provide for their continuous development. Many were also convinced that, in view of the increasing complexity of the technology, the high schools should provide more and better training in mathematics and the sciences. There was some disagreement, however, over how advanced such training should be, and, on balance, training in mathematics and science was made secondary to sound education in the three R's. Participants held that the schools should resist pressures to add new subjects to the curriculum, such as automobile driving, psychology, and community relations. There was no objection to such courses in themselves, but it was urged that they should not be allowed to divert the schools from their primary mission.

In addition to emphasizing the formation of proper attitudes, the participants placed high value on having the schools achieve several other goals. These included the development of thoughtful, well-informed citizens; teaching students to recognize, analyze, and solve problems rationally; inculcating a creative approach and the ability to innovate and to adapt to change; giving students sound study habits and the desire to make learning a lifelong process. The participants left no doubt that they valued these goals far above any specific skills the schools might teach, and they felt, generally, that the schools had not been particularly successful in achieving them.

The strong emphasis of the conferences on the importance of basic abilities and good attitudes might seem to suggest that most of the participants were actively opposed to vocational education. This conclusion would not be warranted.[2] A few employers were definitely opposed on various grounds, some because they had had unfortunate experiences with the graduates of poor schools. At the opposite extreme, several reported that they were favorably impressed by graduates of vocational schools whom they had hired and would seek more. A majority of the conferees, however, seemed more or less indifferent to vocational education. When considering secondary education, they did not think primarily of vocational schools. They had no objection to vocational education, provided skill training was not allowed to interfere with other more important objectives. A number of conferees spoke very favorably about evening vocational courses for retraining or extending the skills of adult workers, but few believed that full-time vocational schools were important for the maintenance of an adequate supply of skilled workers or that they should be assigned a primary role in secondary education.

Vocational guidance in the public schools was strongly criticized. Conference participants reported that many young high school graduates hired by industry would be good management material if they had been advised in high school to continue their education. Nevertheless, it was said, most school guidance personnel seem well qualified to give advice about higher education, but know little about employment opportunities in industry. Students are thus left in ignorance about the opportunities open to skilled workers and technicians. Many employers, especially in the South, were concerned over what they regarded as the overvaluation of white collar jobs by parents, teachers, and students. The guidance problem is intensified in the South because industry is new in many localities, and teachers, parents, and young people are entirely ignorant of the nature of industrial employment.

[2] See Chapter VII for a more detailed treatment of attitudes toward vocational education.

Because workers are not able themselves to select jobs for which they are qualified, the selection and training problems of industry are intensified.

In discussing the shortcomings of vocational guidance, the participants pointed out that business has done relatively little to see to it that teachers, guidance officers, and students receive reliable information about employment opportunities. If the high schools are not doing an adequate job in the guidance field, said one, it is largely because "business is too obsessed with its own problems to get together with the schools."

BUSINESS AND THE SECONDARY SCHOOLS

In spite of many differences in emphasis and detail, the conference participants were substantially agreed that the high schools should turn out young people who can read, write, spell, compute, and communicate with others. In addition to these basic skills, they wanted young people with the ability to recognize and tackle problems intelligently, to think creatively, to absorb training, to study on their own, and to get along with other people. Finally, they wanted young people to possess the proper attitudes, including a sense of responsibility, willingness to work, ambition to advance, and perhaps most important, a state of mind which welcomes and adapts readily to change.

Some of the participants were highly critical of the schools for not achieving these goals more fully. Others believed that the schools have done at least as good a job as could be expected considering the size of the task and the limited resources made available to the schools. Almost unanimously, however, they agreed that in one respect or another, the schools are not doing a good enough job. They readily admitted that a large part of the blame must be placed on the failure of business and the community at large to take sufficient interest in and provide sufficient support for the schools. Although they were anxious to help the schools to do a better job in the future, it was clear that they had given little attention to the question of what specific steps should be taken to achieve this end. Educational methods and curricula received virtually no consideration at the conferences, and there was little argument over the relative merits of vocational and general education, so long as the basic goals were always placed first.

In short, although the goals of the high schools were derived by the conference participants from the general qualities they want young workers to have, there was no pleading for specialized training at public expense to meet the particular needs of industry. The participants, moreover, were quite willing to leave the task of translating these goals to the experts in education.

CHAPTER IV

The Armed Forces and Skilled Manpower

Traditionally, Americans have shown little interest in their armed forces. Throughout their history they have opposed the maintenance of large numbers of men under arms. The Army has always been forced to get on with very little in peacetime and the Navy has been treated only slightly better. When a major war broke out, as in 1917 and again in 1941, the nation made a maximum effort to build up its military strength in the shortest possible time. With the return of peace, the pressures for speedy demobilization were great, and in 1918 they led to the almost complete disintegration of the armed services.

In 1945, although these pressures were again strong and partially effective, they did not have this extreme consequence. During the nine years since the end of World War II, Congress has granted huge sums for defense. Except for the short period from April, 1947 to June, 1948, it has authorized the use of compulsory Selective Service to supplement enlistments in order to insure that the armed forces receive all the men they are authorized to have. In short, there has been a major change in Congressional behavior which has given the armed forces a continuing importance which they held earlier only in times of full-scale war, though this is not to say that the armed forces have considered the appropriations fully adequate for the missions assigned to them.

THE ARMED FORCES IN AMERICAN LIFE TODAY

Federal expenditures for the current fiscal year are about $66 billion. Of this amount, almost $45 billion, or just under 70 percent, is devoted to "national security." Over $10 billion is spent on the pay and support of military personnel on active duty. Ever since World War II the armed services have been the largest single employer in the country. Slightly more than 3 million men, nearly 7 percent of the 44 million males in the labor force, are now on active duty. The armed services also employ directly over a million American civilians and many thousands of indigenous personnel at foreign bases. At least two of every three young men in the country, at current induction and enlistment rates, will spend two or more years on active duty in one of the services.

A recent study by the Selective Service System found that, of the males born in 1930 and 1931, 62 percent had completed military service or were currently in the armed forces or their reserve components; and an additional 3 to 5 percent would probably enter service as soon as they completed the education or training for which they were deferred. Another estimate indicates that of all young men reaching eighteen in 1954, almost three out of four will eventually enter service.

In spite of the public's anticipation of future "push-button warfare," it still has a strong tendency to think of the man in service primarily as a rifleman in an infantry squad. As Korea so forcefully demonstrated, the foot soldier is far from obsolete. Nevertheless, the military technology now being developed requires for efficient maintenance and operation a level of training and skill far beyond that demanded of the rifleman of World War II. The armed services are now spending about $1.7 billion annually on research and development. Although some projects will fail and others will yield only small improvements, an effort of this magnitude is certain to transform, and to keep transforming, our basic military technology.

This emerging technology is still too new for the armed services themselves, much less the general public, to appreciate its full manpower implications. Recently Air Force leaders have emphasized one aspect of these implications by pointing out that they expect to lose about 200,000 trained enlisted men during the coming year. The Air Force estimates that it spends about $4,400 in training and maintaining an airman during his first year of service, the period in which most of his technical training is completed. This financial and training investment represents only part of the total outlay of money, time, and skill the Air Force invests in a trained airman. In addition to formal training, the airman receives informal training and work experience — whose cost is not easily calculated — which, after four years, has greatly increased his skills and degree of competence.

The difficulty faced by the services in meeting their growing needs for skilled and technically trained men is enormously compounded by the fact that most of their men are in service for only a short time. Turnover is also high in industry, but workers who leave after a short spell of employment are mostly young people in whom industry has made no great investment. A large proportion of the skilled men in the armed forces, however, leave after one term of two to four years, a substantial part of which is spent in training. If industry had to cope with a similar training and turnover problem, the entire structure of the American economy would be different. No one has ever calculated the total cost of training in the current military establishment, but it must represent a very large part of the more than $10 billion devoted annually to the pay and support of active duty personnel.

In a period of partial mobilization like the present, the armed forces have several missions to perform. First, they must maintain sufficient strength to back the nation's foreign policies, which include discouraging a potential enemy from attacking. Second, the military establishment has a training mission, not only to provide it with the skills it needs currently, but also to prepare young men in the ways of warfare so that they can be mobilized and used quickly if major hostilities break out. Finally, the armed forces must provide the basis for quick mobilization of the nation's full strength at any moment.

In carrying out each of these missions, moreover, the armed forces must look forward to the possibility that the present international tensions will last for decades. Consequently, the actions of the armed services must be evaluated in terms of their long-run impact on the total strength of the nation, the health of its economy, and the quality of its manpower.

In view of the size of Federal expenditures for defense, the fact that most young men will spend at least two years in the armed services, and the increasing requirements of the services for men with skill or the potentiality to acquire skill, the training and utilization of skilled and technical manpower in the services have not only narrow military importance but broad national significance.

MANPOWER AVAILABILITY

The characteristics of men now entering the services are quite different from those of men who serve during a period of full mobilization. During World War II, men were inducted up to the age of thirty-seven, and, for a time, even up to forty-four. Consequently, the services received many skilled workers with ten to twenty years of experience. At present, only a few men over twenty-six are eligible for induction and most of those entering service are much younger.

In the Air Force, four out of ten men with less than a year of service are under nineteen; seven out of ten are below twenty; and nine out of ten are under twenty-one. Men entering the Army are only slightly older. Almost 50 percent in the two lowest pay grades — mainly first-year men — are twenty or younger, and seven out of ten are not more than twenty-one. Since many of these young men remained in school until they were at least eighteen, they have had, at most, one or two years of work experience. In the United States, most skilled workers are developed through a prolonged combination of work-experience and informal training. Thus, very few men enter the services with a skill that can be used immediately. The Air Force estimates that not more than one in twenty has an immediately usable skill.

Lacking men with developed skills, the armed forces must make the most of those who are capable of being trained to fill the growing number of skilled and technical positions. Hiring standards in private industry depend largely on the state of the local labor market, but even in periods of labor shortages, industry never hires all the men that appear at the gate. To a considerable extent, the armed forces operate in a similar manner. During World War II, and especially in 1943 when the manpower pool became very shallow, the armed forces reduced their selection standards and accepted many men with poor educational backgrounds and with physical, and, to some extent, emotional disabilities. Recently, the manpower pool has been more than adequate to supply the services with the numbers they require. The services therefore would like to keep their standards as high as possible, on the theory that the men inducted would make better soldiers and would be less expensive to train.

The desire of the armed services to be as selective as possible is in conflict with the attitude of Congress and the public at large. The law which authorizes compulsory service is entitled the Universal Military Training and Service Act, and there is widespread feeling that it requires the services not to reject as unsuitable large numbers of men. Congress has objected particularly to the rejection of men who meet requirements in every respect except their mental test score, which, in fact, reflects the amount of formal schooling they have received as well as their innate intelligence. Congress feels that formal education is not a relevant standard for selecting future servicemen. The services, on the other hand, are concerned with finding men for specialist training courses and for leadership courses for noncommissioned officers. They know that success in such training depends to a considerable degree on prior education.

The armed forces divide men into five classes on the basis of mental scores. Classes I and II, which include about 30 percent of all men in service, are considered above average. Class III is considered average; class IV below average. At present, the armed forces are trying to avoid taking any men in class V, but a few get by. Practically none of those in class V and, at best, possibly 10 percent of those in class IV can succeed in training for skilled or technical assignments. The armed forces, therefore, must find the men to train for the wide range of skills they need, as well as the men who must be trained as noncommissioned officers, from among classes I, II, and III.

During World War II, a man's score on the Army General Classification Test was the main criterion of his ability to absorb training in the Army. Since the end of the war, each service has developed more refined instruments, including tests for specific aptitudes as well as for general ability to learn. A man whose score is relatively low on the present Armed Forces Qualification Test may score quite high on the test for mechanical aptitude. Under the old system, he would not have been eligible for technical training, but under the present system he may be assigned to training in a mechanical specialty. This change in selection methods results in a 20 percent gain in the number who can be selected for technical training. The services use substantially similar systems, basing selection for training on combinations of scores, including scores on verbal, arithmetical, clerical, and mechanical aptitude tests.

The crucial importance of the quality of the manpower available to the armed services is underlined by two facts: the services can give skilled and technical training only to the men in the upper three mental groups; total requirements for skilled and technical manpower and for noncommissioned officers amount to about half the enlisted personnel in the services.

TECHNICAL AND SKILL TRAINING IN THE ARMED FORCES

Each of the services provides every new man with basic military training, which includes instruction in the use and care of small arms, military courtesy and discipline, and other knowledge deemed essential for all men in the service. Some men then receive further training in purely military skills, such as machine-gunner. Others are trained for skilled or technical occupations common to both the services and civilian life, such as airplane mechanic or X-ray technician. If a man is learning a fighting skill, much of his training is devoted to exercises aimed at making him proficient in working in close harmony with others, first in small, and then in larger groups. Training for skilled or technical specialties is more likely to be individual in nature, but if the man is eventually to be assigned in support of a fighting arm, he must still be trained to operate as a member of a unit. The Navy trains individuals in both fighting and support skills. At sea the naval vessel must be self-sufficient, and, with living space exceedingly limited, men must be versatile.

The Army recognizes about 5,000 distinct duty positions (for example, welder's helper, welder, etc., which indicate the different levels of competence required in different duty positions) which it groups into about 450 military occupational specialties. It provides formal training in order to qualify men for assignment to many of these 450 specialties. More than 50 are designated as "long lead-time specialties," which require the completion of a formal course of at least sixteen weeks.

Men drafted into the Army are required to serve for two years, but some of this time is spent in transit, in basic training, or on leave, and some men are separated slightly before their term of service is completed because it does not pay to reassign them. Consequently, sixteen weeks of technical training represent about one fourth of the effective time a draftee must spend in the Army. As far as possible, therefore, the Army has sought to make enlistment for an additional year a prerequisite for assignment to long training courses. The size of the Army's investment in training these specialists is indicated by the fact that nearly 20 percent of the enlisted men complete formal courses of at least sixteen weeks.

The Air Force designates ninety "hard-core" specialties which require long training periods, though not all of this training is done in school. Some of it may be on-the-job training. About one third of all new men receive training which qualifies them for one of these specialties. The Navy has set up apprenticeship programs in twelve occupational groups which lead to assignment in one of sixty-two major job fields. The Navy estimates that about 6 percent of its total enlisted strength is in training, exclusive of recruit and officer training, at any one time. About four out of every ten Navy enlisted personnel receive some formal school instruction.

It is not possible to determine precisely the numbers of men in each of the services who can be designated as skilled or technical personnel. In times of full-scale war, when the services are expanding rapidly, they tend to break down each skilled job into a number of more easily learned jobs so that they can train men as rapidly as possible. This, of course, is just what industry does when expanding rapidly. On the other hand, when new men are coming in less rapidly, as in times of partial mobilization or of peace, there is a tendency, particularly in the Navy, to provide more rounded training which prepares skilled and technical personnel for a much wider range of responsibilities.

Perhaps half the men entering all the services receive some type of technical training. Of these, again perhaps half are given extended school and on-the-job instruction. This prepares them for work in such skilled or technical fields as the following: aircraft maintenance engineering, automotive repair, communications, electronics, explosives disposal, fire control, foreign languages, internal communications, jet mechanics, office machine repair, photography, printing, sonar, weather observation.

As in civilian life, there is no single process through which men acquire skill in the armed services. Although the services make more use of formal school training than does industry, much skill acquisition is the result of both formal and informal on-the-job training. The Navy and Air Force use centrally administered proficiency tests to determine when a man is qualified for advancement up the skill ladder. In some cases, he first has to qualify by taking a locally administered performance test.

All three services generally rely on formal schools to provide the first elements of skill, and then use on-the-job training for advanced specialization. The Air Force has five levels in its career structure: helper, apprentice, specialist, supervisor-technician, and warrant officer or superintendent. Most formal school training in the Air Force is used to advance helpers to the apprentice level. Supervisors and technicians, however, may attend an advanced school besides receiving on-the-job training. Less than 10 percent of all entering airmen receive advanced formal technical training.

The Army has three principal skill levels: apprentice, journeyman, and supervisor. Formal school training is used primarily to advance a soldier from apprentice to journeyman. Usually, he becomes a supervisor only after a specified period of on-the-job training. The range of the Army's schooling system is indicated by the fact that it operates thirty-five different schools which offer over 500 different courses. More than two thirds of all Army enlisted personnel receive some formal training in one of these schools.

The services have found that when it is necessary to provide similar training for a large number of men it is definitely quicker to use school training. On the other hand, they recognize that school is not as effective as on-the-job training for certain purposes, especially the teaching of advanced skills. Each of the services uses schools when the introduction of new equipment or methods produces an immediate need for a substantial number of men trained in new skills. Thus the Air Force sets up a special school or mobile training unit when it must retrain skilled men, whose experience has been gained on one kind of aircraft, to provide them with the knowledge to maintain and repair a new model.

TURNOVER AND TRAINING

The rapid turnover of personnel, as has been seen, adds greatly to the training problems of the armed services. The Army has the most difficult turnover problem. Most of its men are inducted through Selective Service for a two-year term of duty, and less than one out of ten of the selectees who are eligible to enlist for a second term currently do so. The Air Force and the Navy have been relying exclusively on volunteers, most of whom enlist for four years. Only three out of ten, however, re-enlist for another term of service. With the majority of men serving for only two or four years, it is exceedingly difficult for the armed services to determine how much and what kinds of training will contribute most effectively to the performance of both their immediate and their long-range missions.

Industry also faces a turnover problem. It is always possible that a worker will quit after a company has made an expensive investment in prolonged, formal training for him. Experience has shown, however, that the more a company invests in a man's training, the more likely he is to remain, for the simple reason that his training increases his opportunities for advancement within the company. The armed forces, on the other hand, know that most of their men are certain to leave at the end of their first term of service. In short, making a large investment in the prolonged, formal training of an individual is always a gamble, but it is a far better gamble for industry than for the services.

Moreover, because turnover among highly skilled workers is relatively low in industry, companies rarely face the problem of training large numbers of skilled workers quickly. This is one reason why most skilled workers are not produced through formal training programs. For the most part, industry can afford to wait while skilled workers emerge as the product of a long process of experience and informal learning. If the worker quits at any point in this process, the company loses little, for the man has been working and producing all the while he has been learning.

The services, on the other hand, have to take men who will remain for a very few years and train them quickly enough to use them in skilled positions for a reasonable period before they leave. To save time, the services rely on formally organized school training to a greater extent than does industry. School training saves time, but it is costly in terms of military service, for neither the student nor the instructor is performing immediately useful work. The Air Force, however, has found on-the-job training to be costly and time consuming because an adequate number of qualified instructors for this type of training is not available. Frequently, the manning table makes no provision for an instructor to do this way is, however, small.

In order to cut training time still further, the services have tended to train men in rather narrow fields of specialization. This, too, is a procedure which saves time but raises some other costs. There is considerably less flexibility for necessary rotation and reassignment when men have been trained in very narrow specialties. There are also more direct costs. The Army has estimated, for instance, that three narrowly trained men are used for certain tasks in connection with guided missiles which could be handled as well by one broadly trained soldier.

Each of the services is constantly re-evaluating its training in order to eliminate waste time. The Army in particular has sought to keep its training schedules flexible so that men who learn quickly can complete their training and be assigned to a duty position earlier. Curricula are constantly reviewed to be sure that nothing is taught which is not essential for performance on the job. Both the Navy and the Air Force recently eliminated a considerable amount of training in basic mathematics and science. Instead, they are seeking to teach only the particular applications of these subjects that are necessary in a given assignment. The refinement of curricula in order to secure greater efficiency in teaching, however, is very difficult. Little is known about how teaching or not teaching particular elements of a subject affects performance in a given job.

The training problems of the services have been intensified not only by high turnover, but also by rapid engineering improvements which have often been introduced without due consideration of their manpower implications. It has not always been understood that the advantages of more efficient equipment may be canceled by the costs of the longer training necessary to produce men who can operate and maintain it. Recently, however, the services have become more aware of this problem and have sought to weigh the gains from technological improvement against the additional manpower problems arising from operating and maintaining the new equipment.

Unfortunately, some of the efforts of the services to cope with turnover problems by adjusting training methods have probably compounded, rather than reduced, the basic problem of high turnover. By narrowing the type of training they provide, the armed forces minimize one of the attractions of military service. If men found that, by serving for two or three terms, they could acquire excellent training useful in civilian employment, they might be more willing to re-enlist. Moreover, in order to facilitate training, the services have usually preferred to train men in the upper two mental test-score groups. These, however, are the men most likely to have definite plans for a civilian career and most difficult to interest in a second term of service. The armed forces have begun to recognize this fact and are now seeking to build interest in military careers among capable men in class III by giving them the opportunity for extensive technical training. For example, the Air Force has found that slow learners from modest family backgrounds, who frequently have modest occupational goals, can often be trained in highly skilled jobs — if adjustments are made in the training program. Such men will re-enlist in greater numbers than enlisted men who are faster learners and may come from more affluent families. At the same time, the Air Force must utilize its most intelligent recruits for certain electronic and other highly skilled work, fully realizing that, in most instances, it will lose its training investment at the termination of the airmen's enlistments.

The services are unable to use monetary incentives to the same extent that industry does to attract and hold men with specialized skills. All men in the same grade receive the same base pay, and Congress limits the number of men in each grade. Consequently, the services find it impossible to make many of the higher grades available to men in their first period of service. Failure to secure advancement in grade and pay makes capable men reluctant to remain in service when they know they could do much better in civilian life.

It is not possible to acquire skill, and surely not possible to acquire a high level of skill, unless one is motivated to do so and puts forth real effort. But it is very difficult for men to put forth maximum effort unless they can relate their expenditure of effort to some future advantage to themselves. In times of war there are other motives for serving, and there are always some men who will do their best regardless of circumstances. But in a period of partial mobilization like the present, with no active front, the majority of men in service cannot be expected to work their hardest if they have no intention of remaining, if they cannot anticipate substantial promotion while in service, and if they are learning little they can use directly in civilian employment.

High personnel turnover creates one more training problem that should be mentioned. Each of the services hires some civilian instructors and sends some of its men to civilian schools which are under contract to conduct classes for servicemen. Most of the elaborate training program of the services, however, is conducted within the military and with military teachers. Individuals possessing both the ability and the desire to teach are scarce. It is not surprising, therefore, that the military finds it difficult to attract and hold competent instructors. The services no longer maintain that technical proficiency in a subject is the sole requirement for teaching it. Each service requires its instructors to pass a course in teaching methods. The Navy stresses volunteering for teaching duty as a means of securing not only technically qualified, but also highly motivated, teaching personnel. Because such an assignment entails three years of shore duty, it is much sought. Yet instructors continue to leave the services for the same reasons as other highly trained personnel.

Classroom and correspondence courses in many nonmilitary subjects are offered the serviceman through the United States Armed Forces Institute (USAFI). As of July, 1954, 268,000 en-

listed men and 21,000 officers were enrolled in various USAFI
courses. Although many men use these courses to secure high
school and college credits, approximately 30 percent of the men
enroll in "technical" as distinct from academic courses. The technical courses in auto mechanics and electronics draw the most
students. More than one fourth of the men in technical courses
have indicated that they enrolled to prepare for civilian careers.
Since only one man in fifteen completes the technical course he
is enrolled in, the number prepared for civilian employment in
this way is, however, small.

THE ADVANTAGES OF CAREER PERSONNEL

The manifold difficulties that the armed services encounter in
trying to perform their missions with such a large number of short-
term men have not prevented them from performing their functions
effectively. Nevertheless, they could undoubtedly perform their
several missions still more effectively, and at a lower cost, if they
could operate with a larger proportion of career personnel and
therefore with a smaller burden of training.

The Army could make spectacular savings if it could increase substantially the number of four-year men and reduce the
number of two-year selectees. Increasing the number of four-year
men who re-enlist, at least for one additional term, would lead to
further important gains. A two-year man who receives four months
of specialized training probably does not give more than sixteen
months of effective performance when allowance is made for such
things as basic training, travel time, and leave. On the other
hand, four months of training is only a small part of a four- or eight-
year term of service. The Army must train at least four two-year
men for a total of at least sixteen months in lieu of one man who
enlists for four years, receives four months of training, and re-
enlists once.

Increasing the number of career personnel would also permit
some reduction in total manpower requirements. With men obli-
gated to serve for only two years, the Army must break down its

jobs so that, for example, it can train three men for four months each, rather than one man for a year. This is necessary in order to get a reasonable return in work from the training investment. In some cases, however, the total work of the three men could be performed by one man with a year of training — if the one man were willing to remain long enough to justify such lengthy training.

The career man is likely to be a better as well as a less expensive skilled worker. Skill and technical competence depend heavily on both experience and motivation. The career man with long experience will know the job better. He is also likely to want to do it better because he thinks of the armed services as at least a temporary career rather than as a period of compulsory service to be completed as quickly and easily as possible. There is no precise information on the cost to the services of poor work in the operation and maintenance of equipment. To take one example, however, there is a widespread impression among well-informed people that many of the losses of military aircraft are caused by poor operation and maintenance resulting primarily from inadequate skill and poor motivation.

It is clearly a matter of national importance to consider the incentive and reward systems now in effect, and to see what can be done to encourage a larger number of young persons to make at least a temporary career in the military. The last session of Congress belatedly recognized this need by raising the re-enlistment bonus, by providing funds for military housing, and by providing for medical care for dependents. It thus began, at least, to rectify the damage done previously when Congresses sought to economize by cutting the perquisites of servicemen.

THE ARMED FORCES AND THE NATION

There is a deep-seated tendency in all military establishments to solve their own problems in their own ways. In large measure this attitude is shaped by experience. The military has found that, at least in most democracies, the public is fickle and is also likely to be ignorant of its highly specialized needs. The gap between military and civilian concerns and outlook is very great. Moreover, the flexibility of American society and its rapidly increasing economic wealth have made it possible to superimpose a tremendous military effort without precipitating great debates over the most efficient ways of integrating the military effort with established institutions, particularly the schools and industry.

This superimposed military system, however, has been exercising important influences on the ways of life and, in particular, on the training and skills of the nation's manpower. It is now clear that, for the indefinite future, most young men will spend at least two years in the armed forces. The men who pass through the military are civilians before they become soldiers and civilians again after they have been soldiers. It is therefore essential to explore the significant areas in which the related efforts of the civilian and military sectors of American life may be better coordinated.

One of these areas has already been considered in detail, but only from the viewpoint of its military implications. The heavy reliance that the armed forces are forced to place upon short-term men also has serious consequences for the civilian labor force and for the individual who passes through the services. If his training is narrow and if he can be used only in assignments commensurate with his training, his period of service is largely a waste in terms of his own career development, important as it may be as a contribution to national security. Obviously, on the other hand, a man who has the good fortune to acquire a major skill in the armed services can benefit for the rest of his life from his military training. The contribution of this training to the skills of individuals is important for society as well. The broader and more fundamental the training which men receive in the armed services, the greater is the contribution of the services to the pool of skills available to the community at large.

Even though the services have necessarily concentrated on narrow training, there is evidence that they are significantly affecting both the subsequent careers of young men and the nation's supply of skills. Many employers place heavy reliance on service-trained veterans in filling technical positions, especially in the electronics field. A study made in 1952 by the University of Minnesota found that one veteran out of five was making at least some use of his military training in civilian employment. A study by the Department of Agriculture of the employment of Korean veterans found that the general, and particularly the technical, training which men from farms received while in service greatly facilitated their relocation in urban areas after their discharge from service.

The elaborate training offered by the armed forces opens up areas of training and work experience to many who, in civilian life, would be barred from such training and work because of discriminatory practices. Some men, of course, are so severely handicapped by lack of proper education and training prior to their entering service that they cannot be given technical training. The fact that military training in many cases provides the impetus for new and higher occupational goals underlines its importance for men from depressed farm areas, for Negroes, and for others who do not have equal access to civilian training opportunities. If the services can contribute this much under present circumstances, it is clear that they could do far more to advance the skills of individuals and of the labor force if more men stayed in service long enough to justify the substantial investment necessary to provide them with broad training.

The age distribution of apprentices clearly indicates that few young men of eighteen are entering apprenticeship today. Most men complete their military training and service before beginning apprenticeship. Because of GI benefits, many who would not otherwise have continued their education or training have attended schools of all types. Many veterans will not be able or will not want to continue in the same field in which they received military training when they enter a civilian training program. Nevertheless, the extent to which civilian training can benefit from foundations laid during military service obviously depends on the breadth and depth of military training.

So far this chapter has evaluated military training in terms of its contributions to the current operations of the services, to the subsequent careers of individuals, and to the skills of the nation's labor force. There is still another relevant standard. One of the major missions of the armed services is to train people in peacetime so that they can be readily mobilized in times of war. Therefore, military training must also be judged in terms of its value in helping to establish and maintain an effective reserve force. By its very nature, an effective reserve system requires intimate coordination between the military and the civilian sectors of national life.

Many competent observers, however, have been pointing out that the nation does not now have an effective reserve system. President Eisenhower has declared that "We have failed miserably to maintain that strong, ready military reserve in which we have believed or professed belief for 150 years. Now at long last we must build such a reserve. And we must maintain it. Wishful thinking and political timidity must no longer bar a program so absolutely essential to our defense."

Among the most difficult problems that the country will face in building an effective reserve force will be those involved in keeping alive the specialized skills that men have acquired in the military when they return to civilian life. Unless these skills are preserved, the reserves cannot be quickly mobilized and effectively used in case of national emergency.

The American labor force is conspicuous for its mobility. Many men change occupations a number of times. There have been no comprehensive studies of the post-service employment of men who acquired specialized skills in the military, but one study indicates that a substantial number of veterans fail to make even limited use of their armed services technical training in civilian employment. The civilian work of some reservists is so close to their reserve assignment that they will require little or no additional specialized training. Others will require considerable special training during their reserve service if they are to function effectively when needed.

It is clear, in any case, that an effective and economical reserve system will depend in large measure on the successful coordination of military and civilian training and experience.

Better coordination of military and civilian education and training involves adjustments, not only in military training, but also in the schooling of young men before they enter the military. Chapter X points out that many young persons fail to take full advantage of their opportunities in high school because they do not know how to relate their studies to the types of responsibilities and opportunities that will confront them when they go to work. Certainly most high school students are not aware of how their schooling might affect their opportunities when they enter service, or how their opportunities in service might affect their plans for future education and work.

Recently the armed forces have emphasized the importance of a high school education for men entering service. The occupational handbook of the Navy states that "while no specific amount of education is demanded for joining the Navy, it is obvious that a good education will contribute to the effectiveness of those who work in a vast technical organization which demands trained men to operate its units afloat, ashore, under the sea and in the air." The Army and Air Force have also stressed the importance of completing high school. It has been seen that selection for technical training in the services is based largely on test scores which, in part, reflect the prior education of the individual. If more parents, teachers, and young people realized this, fewer young men might quit school before entering service.

The armed forces have been willing to state how much education they want young men to have, but they have been reluctant to take a position on the kinds of schooling they consider desirable. They recognize that the high schools of the country cannot and should not be turned into vocational schools preparing young men for the armed services. On the other hand, there is undoubtedly ample scope for modifications in secondary education which would ease the training problems of the armed forces without interfering with the more basic goals of the high schools. Training in industry, as well as the military, would be easier if students graduated with better preparation in mathematics and the sciences.

The services are, however, less desirous of obtaining men with detailed knowledge of specific subject matter, or even with specific job skills, than they are of securing young men who have acquired proficiency in reading, writing, and computing, good study and work habits, the facility of adapting one's self to varying situations, and an understanding of the responsibilities of American citizenship. Interestingly, industry usually stresses the same factors.

Civilian schools might reduce the training problems of the armed forces in still another way. It has been seen that one of the most serious training problems of the armed forces is to find and hold effective teachers. It has been suggested that the services might obtain better training at lower cost if they made somewhat fuller use of civilian instructors and training facilities.

One of the most important considerations in seeking to coordinate civilian and military training is the timing of entrance into military service. The law and Selective Service regulations provide for deferment of students so that the services may receive the benefit of their schooling and that their education not be interrupted. Although similar provisions also apply to apprentices, they are seldom invoked. As has been seen, most young men complete military service before beginning apprenticeship.

Great Britain and Canada have each taken different approaches to the problem of articulating apprenticeship and military training. In England, all apprentices complete apprenticeship before military service and are then individually assigned to appropriate military positions. In Canada, some young men who are inducted into service are placed in a reserve status and assigned to civilian training programs where they are trained at government expense before being called to active duty. These approaches are feasible in Great Britain and Canada because of different civilian institutions and military procedures. Better coordination of military training and apprenticeship in this country could be achieved more easily through increased use of existing deferment regulations.

Some experts who are familiar with skilled and technical training in the armed forces believe that the services have developed training methods which might well be emulated by civilian industry. The services have been forced to cope with a training problem larger and more pressing than any ever faced by a private concern. Their solutions, moreover, have been developed in an environment which facilitates controlled experiment and the measurement and comparison of results. It would be surprising, therefore, if they had not learned some important lessons, particularly in the area of organizing and using formal classes for rapid instruction in fundamentals. Unfortunately, however, the gap between military and civilian life has made it difficult for industry to profit from the experience of the services, and vice versa.

Compulsory military service has begun to alter significantly the education and development of the nation's human resources, particularly its skilled manpower. Better knowledge of the relations between military and civilian training and experience is required to permit the design of more effective ways of utilizing the total training facilities and human resources of the country.

CHAPTER V

Secondary Education
and Preparation for Work

W HAT IS the purpose of secondary education? An attempt
to answer this question is implicit in every current dispute over
our public educational system. This is true whether the speaker
bewails the alleged inability of contemporary students to write,
read, or mind their manners; whether he insists that more education for all is the surest way to cure the world's ills; whether he
protests that too many people are getting too much education; or
whether he calls for larger appropriations for school buildings and
teachers' salaries. No matter what his point of view, he bases his
arguments and his judgments on his concept — frequently un-
stated and unexamined — of what our educational system should
accomplish.

Lack of agreement on what should be the purpose of education
is not a new phenomenon. Aristotle wrote:

All people do not agree in those things they would have a child taught,
both with respect to improvement in virtue and a happy life; nor is it
clear whether the object of it should be to improve the reason or rectify
the morals.

Just as education's purposes have been disputed, dire fore-
bodings have similarly been voiced regarding the educational
achievements of the young. Some of those who critically compare
the present with the good old days, when solid learning was sup-
posedly pounded into their own heads, would be taken aback by
a New York *Sun* editorial of 1902:

When we were mere boys, boys had to do a little work in schools. They were not coaxed; they were hammered. Spelling, writing, and arithmetic were not electives; and you had to learn. In these more fortunate times, elementary education has become in many places a sort of vaudeville show. The child must be kept amused and learns what he pleases.

Complaints about the effectiveness of the schools were chronic at the opening of the century — a period now often cited as a standard for comparison — and even much earlier. Such criticism, however, has been valuable. It is doubtful whether many of the significant accomplishments of American public education would have been possible if critics of the schools had not stimulated self-examination and change. It is important, therefore, to remember that education has been recurrently subjected to critical inspection and that the current educational controversies have long histories. Today, however, they take place within a new setting distinguished by the tremendous expansion in secondary education which has taken place during the past half-century.

HOW THE SCHOOLS PREPARE FOR WORK

Before a decision can be made as to who should be educated and how, it must be decided why students should be educated — that is, the purpose or purposes of education. A review of the educational literature or an examination of any school system's curriculum reveals at once that education has a variety of purposes. Nevertheless, whatever else they do, the secondary schools are a major institution for preparing the youth of the nation, in different ways and with varying degrees of success, for work.

Training in the professions — medicine and law, for example — could once be acquired informally through a form of apprenticeship. Now, for scientists and professional personnel, high school graduation is the prerequisite for an extended period of education and training in institutions of higher education.

Skilled and technical work is evolving comparable though lesser requirements. Many technicians are trained in technical institutes and junior colleges, which usually require high school graduation for admission. Most apprenticeship programs require high school graduation of young applicants. Many employers will not hire young workers who have not graduated from high school.

Preparation for work is a need common to all students. Certain knowledge, skills, and attitudes must be acquired both by those who go on to the most advanced university education and those who will have no additional formal training after graduation from high school. Consequently, the type of high school preparation required by different students cannot be determined solely by differentiating between those for whom high school is or is not considered "terminal."

Secondary education is not really terminal for many students. Even those who do not go on to junior colleges or to regular four-year colleges may attend technical institutes or adult education classes, enter apprenticeship, take on-the-job training, or study through correspondence courses. For all who will seek some form of advanced education or training, the necessity for learning does not end with the high school diploma. They all need, to a greater or lesser extent, a common foundation in high school.

A consideration of secondary education as preparation for work is dictated by this study's central concern — the adequacy and the quality of the nation's resources of skilled workers and technicians. Preparation for work, moreover, is one function of the schools on which all agree. It thus offers a valuable vantage point from which to analyze current educational issues and to develop criteria for assessing educational curricula and methods.

Preparation for work is not conceived of here as specific vocational training; it may be achieved through a wide variety of different subjects and by different methods. Preparation for work is not the sole purpose of education and there is no necessary conflict between it and other essential purposes. In addition, it is an intrinsic part of other goals, such as the inculcation of good citizenship.

The basic set of common skills is the ability to read with comprehension, to communicate understandably — both orally and in writing — and to use arithmetical processes accurately. The foundation for these basic skills is supposed to be laid in the elementary school, but for some students, the high school may find it necessary to use remedial techniques to bring them up to a minimum standard. For the others, the high school seeks to augment these skills. Since a high school education establishes the basis of eligibility for and adaptability to subsequent education and training and is increasingly required for desirable employment, the high schools would do their students a disservice if they failed to provide as much academic training in these skills as students could absorb.

Another set of skills required by all students lies in the area of work habits. These, too, are provided both deliberately and indirectly by the schools. The school environment exposes youngsters to conditions and experiences comparable, in a number of important ways, to those which they will encounter when they go to work. The school enforces a regular schedule by setting hours of arrival and attendance; assigns tasks that must be completed; rewards diligence, responsibility, and ability; corrects carelessness and ineptness; encourages ambition. Of all the cultural institutions a youngster encounters — his family, the church, his peer group — the demands made by the school come closest to those made by an employer. Because the school's manner of operation resembles the employment situation, it can be viewed as a training and preliminary testing ground in the work habits and methods, motivations, and attitudes that will be considered desirable when the student seeks employment.

Completion of high school as a prerequisite for even noncollegiate training is an increasingly common requirement for two broad reasons. First, the applicant who has completed the high school program with satisfactory grades is considered to have acquired the basic skills and knowledge most employers consider desirable in young workers who are potential trainees. The second reason is that high school graduation is considered an indication of a youngster's commitment to his own development and, therefore, his willingness to undertake further training. Large firms, especially, place particularly heavy emphasis on the young worker's attitudes toward work even more than on his specific aptitudes and his high school courses.

The young man or woman with a satisfactory school record is felt to have shown at least fundamental ability to complete a task and accept work discipline. With the enormous expansion in high school enrollment, most employers look dubiously at the young job applicant who has not availed himself of this opportunity for education. He is usually considered inadequately prepared for work, both academically and psychologically — and more particularly, for the training through which he can become a skilled worker.

It is one thing to point out that there are certain needs common to all students to which the high school must respond in order to fulfill its responsibilities. It is another to determine how this obligation can be met most effectively with today's large and diverse high school population. What methods and curricula are to be employed? At what point should the schools begin differentiating their offerings in order to meet the particular needs of different segments of the student population?

THE GROWTH OF SECONDARY EDUCATION

The United States is the only country where high school education has been made freely available to those not seeking college preparation. School-leaving age laws have, in fact, made at least some high school education virtually compulsory for most youngsters. In Western Europe general education for those who will become workers — skilled or not — usually stops at fourteen or fifteen. The same holds true in Australia and the situation is similar in New Zealand. Only in this country has it been considered desirable to extend secondary education to everyone who wants it — and frequently to many who do not.

Equal educational opportunity is part of the nation's social philosophy. The United States has a tradition of faith in the beneficent value of expanding popular education. Working class parents have viewed education as the means by which their children could achieve social and economic advancement.

In addition, economic factors have influenced the expansion of secondary education. A crucial factor is that only this country could afford it. Because of the extensive use of machinery and the increase in worker productivity, our economy could afford to let part of the labor supply remain unused. The spread of urbanization and industrialization; the development of mechanized farming; the decline in the agricultural population and the reduced demand for unskilled farm labor — all these changes made it possible for boys and girls to spend what used to be working years in school.

When the major depression of the early 1930's struck, economic pressures to prolong schooling became more immediate. With millions of unemployed, youngsters seeking work would only add to the surplus labor supply. The unions wanted to keep them out of the labor market. One way of doing this was by raising the school-leaving age and providing additional school facilities.

The pressures exerted in response to the unemployment problem probably were more effectual than school-leaving age laws in lengthening the period of secondary education for many students. Today, school-leaving age laws are still flexible enough in most states to allow students under 16 to leave school in case of family need, if they are employed, and if they have completed the eighth grade. Twenty-two states allow children to leave school at 14 and have no general restrictions on child labor above this age. The laxity of these laws was demonstrated during World War II, when many students left high school to take jobs.

Secondary education is now generally considered to begin with the seventh grade, the beginning of junior high school, and continues through the twelfth grade. In some communities, secondary education is often considered to last through the fourteenth grade, the end of junior college.

The traditional division of public schooling in this country has been eight years of elementary school and four years of high school.

In recent years the trend in secondary education has been away from the four-year high school toward a system that includes some form of junior high school. The biggest growth has been among junior-senior high schools, which span a five- or six-year period. The next largest growth has been among the separately organized junior high schools. The new three-year senior high schools, as distinct from "regular" four-year high schools, constitute the smallest group of secondary schools. But in recent years the number of senior high schools and their enrollment has been growing rapidly. Currently the annual cost of running the public high schools is probably more than $1.75 billion.

In 1952, with a total of 7,688,919 daytime students enrolled in 23,746 public secondary schools, the enrollment in the different types of schools was as follows:

1,526,998 students were in the 3,227 junior high schools.

1,528,006 students were in the 1,760 senior high schools.

1,937,210 students were in the 10,168 regular high schools.

2,696,707 students were in the 8,591 junior-senior high schools.

The following figures prepared by the Office of Education illustrate how secondary education has expanded in this country:

The number of students enrolled in the last four years of the public high schools rose from 202,963 in 1890 to 5,695,514 in 1952.

In 1890, 3.8 percent of the fourteen-seventeen year olds were enrolled in the eighth through twelfth grades. In 1952, the figure was 65.3 percent.

In 1890, 3.5 percent of the seventeen year olds graduated from high school. In 1949-50, 59 percent graduated.

With the nation committed to making at least some secondary education available to practically the entire teen-age population, and with a national birth rate that in recent years has remained at record highs, the secondary school population will continue to expand enormously. High school enrollment in 1960, it has been predicted, will be more than nine million; by 1965, it is expected to reach twelve million. For some regions of the country — the South particularly — the cost of expanding secondary education will be disproportionately high. The South is faced with a particularly acute expansion problem because its present level of secondary education is far below the national average. Two other difficulties that add to the problem are the high rural birth rate and the realization of desegregation.

About 80 percent of the country's fourteen-seventeen year olds acquire some secondary school education. Not counting the South, the percentage would be even higher. In the South, only 65 percent of the white, and 45 percent of the Negro, youngsters are attending high school. The Southern Regional Education Board estimates that by 1967-68, 71 percent of the whites and 64 percent of the Negroes will attend high school.

The effort required to provide the present percentage of the expanding high school age group with schools — and, in the case of the South, to catch up with the rest of the country's current standards — cannot be minimized. The schools are not only trying to accommodate an increasing school population, but they are also trying constantly to bring an increased percentage of the total age group into the schools and to hold them in school longer.

The high school now must cope with many students who have not been motivated to learn — or lack the ability for further education — and do not wish to remain in high school. Compulsory education laws or inability to find employment because of their age force most of them to attend school until they are at least sixteen. The number of such low-ability or inadequately motivated students varies in different communities. In New York City, for example, it has been estimated that such students constitute 20 percent of those in the early years of high school.

Several decades ago, youngsters such as these would rarely have been admitted to high school. They may lack the fundamental ability in the Three R's that entitles them to graduate from elementary school. But the general introduction of a continuous promotion policy, which keeps students moving along with their own age group at a lower level of scholastic achievement, pushed them into high school. Now that the high schools have been forced to retain a substantial number of students who are recalcitrant or inept, or both, they must devote a great deal of attention to disciplinary problems.

In theory, continuous promotion is supposed to apply only so long as a student's achievements measure up to his abilities. In practice, continuous promotion too often produces cases like one reported in Washington, D. C. There, a fourteen-year-old juvenile delinquent, who had led a gang that terrorized his junior high school, had been promoted through elementary school although he was barely able to read. Not until he reached junior high school did he get the lessons in remedial reading that, it was believed, might have helped alleviate his behavior problems.

If the school is to perform effectively its function of preparation for work, the introduction of an ever-increasing percentage of the young population into high school will require more than enlarged school facilities. If educators are seeking the beneficial psychological effects continuous promotion is supposed to confer, remedial efforts will be needed for students retained in school and pushed too rapidly for their ability. Otherwise, as one observer pointed out, continuous promotion often creates frustrated, resentful academic failures who become delinquents. To educate them effectively and not detrimentally affect the education of other students, requires special provisions.

Such students usually need courses tailored to meet their needs and teachers specially trained to handle them. They probably need a school-work program and special vocational opportunities and guidance. Exactly how much education, and what kind of education, would be most worthwhile for such youngsters is a problem both educators and the community will need to consider in terms of these students themselves and of the total resources for education available in the community.

The expansion of secondary education has created a wide diversity in the functions demanded of the high school. Fifty years ago, 75 percent of those who graduated from high school went to college. Compared to today's student body, the students of that time were comparatively homogeneous in social background, intellectual ability, and scholastic purpose. The high school's purpose was college preparation; it attempted to discipline its students' minds through training in literature, languages, and mathematics.

Today, although the actual number of college entrants is close to record levels, a little less than 40 percent of high school graduates go on to college. Contemporary high school students are vastly diversified in social background, in intellectual ability, in their level of previous scholastic achievement, in their life goals, and, consequently, in their reasons for attending high school.

Another obstacle that makes it difficult to formulate common goals generally applicable to the high schools is the wide diversity in the standards and facilities of schools throughout the country. Some high schools have 5,000 students, others have 50; some send almost all their students on to college, others send almost none. Such differences in size and occupational goal also influence the variety of courses offered and the level of achievement demanded.

The continuing expansion of the secondary schools may obscure the need to define their purpose. By itself expansion will not solve the most fundamental problems of the secondary schools. The process of alleviating shortages of facilities may, however, postpone their consideration. The difficulties created by an expanding school system that does not clearly define its major purposes is illustrated by the problems secondary education faces today after half a century of extraordinary growth.

THE INFLUENCE OF VOCATIONAL EDUCATION

The rapid growth of the high school population during the past half-century compelled the high school to acquire other purposes than college preparation. But, at the same time, the introduction of vocational courses into secondary education in turn helped spur the remarkable expansion of the high schools. It seems safe to say that, to a large extent, the high school population and high school offerings expanded together, with each helping to spur the growth of the other.

In his study of *American Apprenticeship and Industrial Education*, published in 1921, Paul H. Douglas remarked that, "Perhaps the most important educational movement of the past decade has been that of industrial education." Beginning in the 1880's, there was a growing preoccupation in educational circles with the vocational or industrial content of the public school curriculum. This was reflected first in the introduction of manual training courses and schools and, later, in the appearance of specialized trade and industrial schools. Next it was manifested in the growth of vocational schools and in the expansion of vocational courses in the general high schools.

These innovations in the kinds of secondary schools and in the curricula offered indicate that, early in the century, a special effort was already being made to serve the vocational needs of high school students who did not plan to enter college. In addition, cooperative courses, consisting of alternate work and study periods, and continuation schooling for those who left school early, also were established in the public school system.

The widespread diffusion of vocationally directed courses and facilities throughout the general high schools is indicated by the fact that Federally reimbursed trade and industry vocational courses are today given in 2,000 high schools. Only 400 of these are vocational schools. The rest are general high schools. About 10,000 high schools have agricultural vocational courses. Over 85 percent of the public secondary schools have shop facilities.

Exact figures on the number of general high school students taking vocational courses of one kind or another are not available. Probably more than one million students in the general high schools take Federally supported courses in trade and industry, home economics, and vocational agriculture. At least as many study industrial courses outside of the Federal-state vocational program. More than 50 percent of the students in the general high schools are enrolled in at least one commercial course.

The available data thus indicates that the general high schools have assumed certain responsibilities in the area of vocational preparation. In fact, the larger part of all the vocational education offered by the secondary schools is provided by the general high schools. As the next chapter shows in detail, the growth of the vocational high school has been limited for a number of reasons. The general high school has thus acquired the task of educating a large body of students who will seek immediate employment or specific skill-training after they graduate. At the same time it retains its old function of preparing students for college entrance.

THE GOALS OF SECONDARY EDUCATION

At the same time that the high schools face the task of educating an enormously enlarged and highly variegated student body, they are supposed to assume the educative functions formerly performed by various other institutions. Thus the high school is often expected to train the student in personal relations and family living. It may try to teach the student how to swim, dance, drive, cook; it may try to make him into a hobbyist, a knowing consumer, an athlete. Not many schools aim at all these targets, but to offer instruction along these lines is frequently declared to be the duty and function of the high school. In any case, it is clear that in addition to its earlier preoccupation with formal learning, the school now frequently assumes many of the duties of the church, the family, and voluntary groups.

The public's differing, and often contradictory, views of what the school's functions should be are illustrated by a study conducted under the auspices of Harvard's Graduate School of Education. Interviews with 105 Massachusetts school superintendents during 1952-53 showed that they were subjected to the following contradictory demands:

50 percent were pressured to put more emphasis on the Three R's; 64 percent received demands that more courses and subjects be taught.

39 percent received protests against the introduction of new school services, such as guidance and health programs; 63 percent were urged to have the schools introduce such services.

40 percent faced demands from the community for less emphasis on athletics; 58 percent were under pressure to put more emphasis on athletics.

Many vocational or avocational courses—such as driver-training — have been added to the curriculum as the result of local demands. Often they have had no clear relationship to an all-embracing concept of the function of education. They have simply been instituted in response to what was considered a local need — which may sometimes be a sufficient reason.

A good part of curricular expansion, however, has grown out of a conscious attempt to broaden the scope of secondary education. This broadening has gone far beyond the introduction of traditional vocational courses. Many educators have maintained that the student body's many needs were not met solely by adding vocational courses to the older classical curriculum. They have also emphasized that the high school cannot be satisfied only to train students to enter college when most students do not plan to go to college. These educators have insisted that the school must expand its offerings to meet the highly varied needs of youth and to stimulate and explore their interests. They have advocated that the high school seek to give the student what has been described as "preparation for life."

Consequently, there have been introduced into the curriculum courses in personal relations, family living, consumer education. Preparation for life attempts to arouse the student's interest in learning by presenting school activities related to his outside interests and activities. It is concerned with the student's psychological adjustment and his ability to get along with others. It places as much importance on achieving personal adjustment as on amassing knowledge of subject matter. It stresses the need to diversify the curriculum in order to fill the needs, stimulate the interests, and discover the abilities of the diversified student body.

CRITICISMS OF SECONDARY EDUCATION

The critics of the contemporary educational trends inspired by these expanded concepts of the school's function claim that secondary education has virtually abandoned intellectual training. These critics, however, differ widely in the substance of their criticism.

One group, typically businessmen, maintains that high school graduates are applying for jobs without having mastered the fundamentals of spelling, penmanship, and arithmetic. They claim that many young men seeking admission to skill-training programs have not mastered basic mathematics sufficiently well to make them eligible without extensive prior training. These critics call on the schools to place greater emphasis on the fundamentals of computation and communication.

The other principal group of critics, for which the spokesmen are mainly faculty members of liberal arts colleges, makes a more sweeping attack on contemporary educational trends. They claim that the new curriculum based on preparation for life is stunting the mental growth of capable students. By neglecting to provide intensive intellectual training, many schools are said to be undermining such students' capacity to acquire advanced education.

Many of the critics of secondary education base their criticisms on the allegedly superior achievements of high school graduates a half-century or more ago. It would seem, therefore, that one way to judge the schools' effectiveness in preparation for work would be a comparison of the accomplishments of present-day students with those of the past.

Several difficulties block this effort. There are little comparative objective data. Most criticisms are based on limited personal experience or the culling of a few horrendous examples. Frequently, subject matter has changed, preventing a direct comparison. For example, cube root is no longer taught in arithmetic; the content of spelling lists has changed.

Even where there are comparative data, how is it to be evaluated? Can the 3.5 percent of the seventeen-year-old population who graduated from high school in 1890, most of whom prepared for college, be directly compared to the approximately 60 percent who graduate today — most of whom go directly into employment? The effort to arrive at comparisons illustrates the need to determine what we expect secondary education to accomplish today and for whom. Still, whatever comparisons can be made will illustrate the problems that must be solved.

The following is noted in a spelling text: "For years, teachers, principals, superintendents, and school boards everywhere have been wearied by the cry of businessmen: 'The boys you send us can't spell.' " This book was published in 1909. The Chicago Board of Education observed: "It is a common complaint among businessmen that the young people seeking employment are not well grounded in the fundamentals." This comment was made forty-five years ago. These remarks offer no positive comparison with the achievements of contemporary students, but it puts the matter into perspective to realize that complaints were chronic in "the good old days."

The meager evidence that is available allows the following conclusions: The best of the high school graduates are certainly as good — and probably better — than those of the past. Comparison of the test scores of average high school students with scores made on the same tests by students of thirty to one hundred years ago indicates comparatively equal achievement.

The National Education Association's Research Division sought data on comparative tests in city schools during the past thirty years. Few school systems could produce objective evidence showing whether the teaching of fundamentals was more effective now or in the past. In 1950 the NEA released a report entitled *The Three R's Hold Their Own at the Midcentury*. It concluded that there was "partial evidence . . . that in general present-day pupils are holding their own in achievement in the basic skills." It found reason to believe that "present-day pupils for the most part equal, and often excel, the achievements of pupils in similar grades in the past."

However, supporting the claim that at least certain standards have changed is the fact that fewer high school students now receive intensive training in science and mathematics. The importance of such training has been stressed by Dr. James Bryant Conant, former president of Harvard, in his *Education in a Divided World:*

Mathematics, of course, is of the first importance, and probably more talent is lost to the sciences pure and applied (including medicine) by the inadequacies of our schools in this field than in any other. . . . As both a former professor of chemistry and one who has heard evidence from colleagues in the other sciences concerned with freshmen from all over the United States, I venture to be dogmatic on (this) point. . . .

Many high school students cannot study mathematics beyond the freshman year because no advanced courses are offered. This is often due to a lack of properly prepared teachers. This situation exists, for example, in more than one fourth of all the high schools in Arkansas, and it is also found in many high schools in other states.

Exact figures are hard to secure, but informed estimates are that not only a smaller percentage, but actually a smaller total number, of students are now taking fairly demanding courses in physics and chemistry. Studies made in 1952 by the Office of Education found a decline in the number of students taking chemistry and physics as compared to 1947.

These figures bear upon the problem of preparation for work in several ways. Lacking the opportunity to take mathematics and science courses, many youngsters lose the chance to acquire and develop scientific and technical interests. Many who possess such interests lose the training opportunities that would make them eligible for collegiate training in science or advanced technical training in technical institutes. The inability to develop scientific interests and skills may either deflect them from going into skilled fields or hamper them if they should desire skill-training.

Many courses in science and mathematics have been dropped from school programs because it was claimed they were beyond the capacity of most students, or that most students were not interested in taking the courses, or that equivalent educational values could be derived from other courses or forms of training. The Harvard Committee, in its report on *General Education in a Free Society,* estimates that "probably little more than half the pupils enrolled in the ninth grade can derive genuine profit from substantial instruction in algebra or can be expected to master demonstrative geometry." It is, however, impossible to say what proportion of the present student body could successfully pursue more rigorous courses if there were changes in the quality of instruction and in student motivation.

Thus far, the problem has been attacked not simply by changing teaching methods to make subject matter more interesting, but by altering, and sometimes eliminating, subject matter. Instead of algebra and chemistry, for example, courses have been offered in "general mathematics," actually arithmetic, and "general science," in which students are taught about science rather than a science itself.

As requirements have been lowered to accommodate the less able students, the usual effect has been to lower the demands made on all students. This particularly affects the most able. The result was described by one educator: "What usually happens is that the teacher assigns a task, accepts a mediocre performance from the average and superior pupils, and accepts a less than mediocre response from the less able."

Evaluating such a situation in terms of preparation for work — certainly an important part of preparation for life — would indicate that under this system students often do not learn what it means to fulfill a given task according to objective standards. They may never understand the meaning of responsibility and thorough-

ness in terms of an actual work assignment. Nor will they be motivated to utilize their full capacities.

Thoughtful educators have conceded that the bright students
have often been the most neglected. The less able often have specially tailored programs and remedial classes; the gifted are usually
expected to find their own way. Yet it is known that if bright
students are allowed to coast through their earlier schooling, they
may develop poor study habits, the inability to concentrate on
demanding material, and an unwillingness to meet rigorous standards. These failings lead to poor preparation for work and to the
waste of valuable talents.

BASIC SKILLS AND DIFFERENTIATED NEEDS

When it comes to basic skills and work habits the needs of all
students are similar. One difference is the extent to which students
can develop their basic skills by taking more advanced work.
Another difference is the varied types of advanced work their skills
and interests lead them to study. In a sense the different yet similar
needs of the most able and the least able students illuminate the
major qualitative problems of secondary education and a possible
solution of at least some of them.

As educators have pointed out, the secondary school is now
a "common school" whose goal is to educate virtually the entire
school-age population. Yet faced with widely differentiated abilities and needs, the secondary school cannot provide equal educational opportunity by offering the same education to all. While it
must have common goals for all students and, therefore, some common methods and curricula, it must also differentiate its offerings
to meet the particular needs of different segments of the student
population.

Since certain basic skills and knowledge, previously outlined,
increase a youngster's eligibility for, and adaptability to, advanced
education in school and learning on the job, one of the goals of the
high school should be to provide as much education in these
subjects as possible for those able to absorb it. While the high

school makes education of this kind more broadly available, it must not debase the quality of the education offered to the more able students. Nor should it underestimate the average student's potential ability to absorb learning.

Regarding those who will enter employment immediately upon graduation from high school, the testimony of businessmen and industrialists emphasizes the value of educating for versatility. Technological changes and the consequent changes in skill requirements; the nature of many production jobs, which require only a short amount of time to learn the requisite machine operations; the training facilities and opportunities available in business and industry; the high degree of job mobility in our economy — all these point to the importance in most cases of providing an education in the general high school that enables students to adapt to changes in industrial technology and business methods.

Since most skills are usually gained through work experience and in training programs in industry and the armed services, often the best preparation for work the student can have is to acquire the skills that will make him eligible for such training and facilitate his learning. This adaptability is best developed by acquiring competence in the basic skills and subject matter that can be used in the widest variety of occupations.

Specific training beyond the basic skills can take various forms, depending upon the student's ability and interests. For example, spelling is a basic skill for which all students have a common need. One student might advance to courses in stenography, another to courses in creative writing. Similarly, arithmetic may help lead one student to courses in bookkeeping, another to courses in mechanical drawing, a third to trigonometry.

LIFE ADJUSTMENT AND PREPARATION FOR WORK

The schools consider that one of their functions is to help students adjust to life. Although preparation for life encompasses more than preparation for work, it is clear that the area of work is one in which the schools can most feasibly contribute to life adjustment.

When they leave high school and enter either the academic world or the working world, all students will encounter a series of training situations. Satisfactory adjustment to these situations requires certain work habits, attitudes, and motivations and is necessary for the student's advancement — academically or vocationally. The training situation in school offers one of the best means of preparing for these later adjustments.

Acquisition of the work habits and methods, attitudes, and motivations already discussed as preparation for work is, of course, a necessary part of effective preparation for life. So, too, is training in analytical habits of thought. The ability to come to grips effectively and creatively with a wide range of problems can also be part of the preparation for work given by the school.

The school can inculcate in the student an acceptance of present education by demonstrating its value in terms of later vocational advancement. By informing him of the nature of the work situation, it can teach him to anticipate and willingly prepare for subsequent training. Teaching him that change distinguishes the culture in which he lives will prepare him to accept technological changes and the retraining they will make necessary.

Such training in preparation for work is one of the most important ways the school can contribute to the student's life adjustment. This training can be given through a variety of courses and can be made an integral part of varied curricula. The specific ways of achieving this objective are for educators to determine.

EDUCATIONAL PRIORITIES

Preparation for work, although an essential aim of secondary education, cannot be its only goal. An inspection of curriculum offerings underlines the fact that the schools seek to serve many purposes. The question posed at the outset of this chapter, "What is *the* purpose of secondary education?" can, therefore, be said to misstate the issue. Nevertheless, many protagonists in the current debate about secondary education continue to postulate different single goals. Even if educational philosophers could reach agreement among themselves on a unified objective, the secondary school system as it now exists is too large, too diverse, and too much under local control to be effectively directed toward a single end.

Acceptance of the position that the school must serve many purposes can, however, obscure — if not completely obliterate — the points of reference required to give direction to this country's effort to provide mass education. Almost any course in the curriculum, from courtship to automobile driving, can be justified as contributing to a socially desirable purpose. Yet it is obviously impossible for the schools to seek to meet every student need. They should not attempt to do so. The family, the church, and community groups have important responsibilities they must continue to discharge.

This chapter has focused on the educational process from the point of view of education's role in preparing young people for work. This point of departure was dictated by the approach of the over-all study, which sought to illuminate the factors influencing the development of the nation's technical and skilled manpower. But it had the additional virtue of providing a fixed reference point from which to assess recent educational trends.

Educators have always recognized that their major responsibilities were to prepare young people for work and for life. Disagreements within and outside the profession have in the final analysis centered around the alternative ways of best accomplishing these purposes. Many educational leaders are convinced that the secondary schools could not possibly provide training for the tens of thousands of specific jobs which exist in our economy. They go further and argue that even if such specific training were practical it would be a mistake for the schools to undertake it. The young person would be prepared for his first job — but not for a working career.

These educators interpose a second objection to any effort to turn the secondary school into a training institution whose major objective is to assist its graduates to gain entry into a specific sector of the job market. They argue that if too much stress is placed on specialized occupational subjects, there will be no room left in the curriculum for providing the student with an understanding of his cultural past or for preparing him to play his role properly as a citizen in the future.

If preparation for work is defined broadly rather than narrowly, there need be no conflict between this aspect of the school's objectives and the other important goals of education connected with the transmission of a cultural heritage and an inculcation of the ideals of citizenship. Preparation for work involves a mastery over the fundamentals of communication and computation by a person who has acquired good work habits and who is strongly motivated to do his best. Clearly, these attributes are compatible with the other major goals of education.

This emphasis on a broad conception of preparation for work does lead to a reaffirmation of the importance of students mastering the Three R's, but it goes far beyond. There is need for a new departure in educational practice in order to develop the elements of a curriculum that can contribute not only to student acquisition of basic skills, but also to their development of good motivations and habits of work.

This approach has additional implications for the structure of the educational system and for students' choice of courses and their timing. Accepting the premise that preparation for work requires the mastery of fundamentals rather than a large amount of specialized training re-enforces the need for a common curriculum for all students through the tenth grade. Further, there is every reason to look askance at the practice of requiring young people to make fundamental educational or occupational choices prematurely, as so many must now do at the end of the eighth grade.

At the present time secondary education is buffeted by criticisms from within and without. In large part it has laid itself open to these criticisms by accepting a tremendously wide range of social objectives and by splintering its curriculum in an effort to meet these objectives. There is reason to believe that by establishing "preparation for work" as a fixed point of reference, secondary education will have a useful criterion for reassessing its present position and its future prospects. In this reassessment it will want to distinguish as sharply as possible between its primary responsibilities and the host of collateral objectives it has accumulated during recent decades. In a period of serious teacher shortages and vastly expanded enrollments, secondary education must utilize its limited resources to accomplish its primary missions and must beware of dissipating its facilities on peripheral undertakings.

CHAPTER VI

Issues in Vocational Education

IN MOST industrial countries there is only one route through which young men become skilled workers. The route is well marked, highly formal, and begins at an early age, usually fourteen or earlier, when the youth who is destined for a trade is separated from the small minority of his schoolfellows who enter a course of study which prepares them for higher education. The future craftsman may continue in school briefly, but by fifteen or sixteen he enters apprenticeship, which lasts for four or five years, sometimes supplemented by evening courses in school. Then, as he approaches his majority, he is formally accepted as a journeyman. If he misses one of the turning points, there are no detours likely to bring him to this destination.

By contrast, there are many ways of becoming a skilled worker in the United States. The potential skilled worker is likely to graduate from high school before he begins work, and in school the chances are that he followed a course of study not unlike that of his fellows who go on to college. In any case, he is likely to remain in the common educational stream at least until sixteen. The varied ways in which he may thereafter acquire his skills and knowledge are described in Chapter VIII.

In addition to the variety of its forms, the process of becoming a skilled workman in this country is distinguished by the unusual role played by formal education. There is no European country in which a substantial proportion of potential skilled workers remain full-time students until they are eighteen or older. And there is none in which the student may pursue a program designed to provide him simultaneously with a secondary education and the skills of a trade.

It would be a mistake, however, to assume that the exclusive, or even principal, reason for lengthening the school attendance of the potential worker has been to provide him with training for his work. Indeed, the extension of full secondary education to more and more young people has not even been conceived as a lengthening of school attendance for the future worker — although that is largely what it amounts to. It has been viewed, rather, as the extension of the values of education to all American youth, whatever their occupational destination. This is seen in the fact that vocational curricula for high school students are never devoted exclusively to teaching trade skills and knowledge, but always include a substantial number of general courses. It is seen even more obviously in the fact that the majority of young people who become wage earners do not pursue vocational courses in high school; they could not even if they would because the facilities are lacking. In short, in so far as the problem of schooling for future workers has been faced as a distinct problem by American educators, it has generally been posed in the following terms: How can young people who may (or may not) become wage earners be best educated? The question of how the schools can provide future workers with the skills they will need at work has been seen as only a part — though often a major part — of this larger problem.

FORMS OF VOCATIONAL EDUCATION

It has often been pointed out that all education is vocational education, since all the things taught in schools have some applicability to work. In contrast to the past, many employers now believe that the most important subjects the schools can teach as preparation for work are reading, writing, and arithmetic. The schools, of course, may also teach skills that are useful only in certain specific occupations. Although the extent to which they should do so is a lively issue, it has been widely accepted in the

United States for several decades that the schools, especially the high schools, should provide some specific occupational instruction.

The term vocational education is generally confined to instruction aimed at specific preparation for occupations not classified as professional. Most such instruction takes place in the secondary schools, though, as will be seen, an increasing amount is being provided in post-high school institutions. Whatever the level of the institution in which it takes place, formal school instruction in skills and knowledge applicable to nonprofessional occupations is the subject of this chapter and the next.

Vocational education occupies a unique place in the American educational structure, for much of it is financed in part by Federal funds, and when so aided, subject to Federal standards. Federal funds are channeled into the public schools for a variety of purposes, but the program of aid for vocational education is the only instance in which Federal money is available to all public school systems, contingent upon its use for teaching certain categories of subjects under certain conditions.

The aid program is based on the Smith-Hughes Act of 1917 and on subsequent supplementary legislation, primarily the George-Barden Act of 1946. Under the terms of this legislation, about $25 million has been made available to the states annually in recent years for financing instruction in four broad fields: trade and industrial occupations, agriculture, home economics, and distributive occupations. For the fiscal year 1955, Congress has appropriated about $30 million. Skilled worker and technician training is provided under the first of these categories. Education in distributive occupations — marketing and selling — is provided only on a part-time and evening basis for persons employed in the field, but in each of the other subject areas, instruction is also provided on an all-day basis for regular high school students. Home economics instruction is part of the same system, but since its aim is primarily the education of future housewives, and not training for gainful employment, it is not considered in this chapter. Courses designed to prepare for employment in dressmaking, cooking, and other skills that are also taught in home economics courses for home use are given as part of the trade and industrial program.

Although the term vocational education is frequently used to apply exclusively to the Federal-state program just outlined, a great deal of vocational education occurs outside of it. An unknown amount of training in the four fields subsidized by the Federal government takes place through courses for which Federal funds are not available because local school systems choose not to operate under Federal standards. Moreover, commercial and business education in the high schools — typing, shorthand, accounting, bookkeeping, office procedures, and similar courses — is not subsidized by the Federal government. Over half of all high school students take some commercial courses. Preparation for technician occupations in the public secondary schools takes place both within and without the Federal-state program. To be eligible for Federal aid, a technical high school program must meet the standards contained in the trade and industry section of Federal legislation.

One other aspect of secondary education that is closely related to vocational education, but is not part of the Federal-state program, is "industrial arts." In educational theory there is a clear distinction between industrial arts and vocational education. The latter is distinguished by the fact that its major aim is to provide effective preparation for employment in a specific occupation. It is intended only for students who expect to enter that occupation. Industrial arts, the outgrowth of what was once known as manual training, is intended to provide elementary knowledge of basic tools and processes for all students. In practice, however, the distinction between the two often seems to depend more on the goals of the student and on his over-all program of study than on the content of any given course. Over one million public high school students are enrolled in industrial arts subjects, compared to only about 225,000 full-time students in Federal-state trade and industrial occupations courses.

In addition to the public secondary schools, public institutions of higher education are also increasingly involved in vocational education. These institutions, variously designated as junior colleges, community colleges, city colleges, and technical institutes, also offer specific instruction for occupations below the professional level. Generally, they tend to emphasize preparation for technician occupations and for the more technical of the skilled fields, such as electricity or television. Many of them, however, also teach the traditional skilled trades. Federal vocational education funds are available only for instruction at less-than-college level. Nevertheless, some junior colleges accept Federal funds and thereby limit themselves in part to instruction at this level.

Finally, vocational courses are taught in a wide variety of private schools, both proprietary and endowed. These schools are especially well developed in the commercial and technical-industrial fields, and in such health fields as dental and medical assistant, physical therapy, etc. Usually, they concentrate on intensive, practical occupational training and ignore general and cultural subjects. Private correspondence schools perform similar functions for students who cannot or prefer not to attend a school in person. Some large enterprises, including manufacturing firms, retail stores, and hospitals, combine on-the-job training for skilled workers and technicians with formal, classroom instruction. Training for skilled and technical work in the armed forces is considered in Chapter IV.

TRADE AND INDUSTRIAL EDUCATION FOR HIGH SCHOOL STUDENTS

Although a few states and localities had begun to provide vocational courses before World War I, the widespread development of vocational education for high school students stems from the passage of the Smith-Hughes Act of 1917. Since 1948, aid to the states under the Smith-Hughes law and supplementary legislation has amounted to about $25 million annually. Allotted to the states on the basis of various population ratios, this money must be matched by at least an equal amount of state and local money spent according to the provisions of the law and the administrative regulations of the United States Office of Education. For many years most states have spent far more than the required minimum. In 1953 Federal expenditures were only about one sixth of the total of $146 million spent on vocational education under the terms of Federal legislation. This sum, moreover, does not represent the full cost of even the Federal-state program of vocational education, much less of all vocational education, since it includes only money spent for purposes specified in the law. These include instruction and counseling; teacher, supervisor, and counselor training; and some administrative activities. Only a small part of the costs of equipment and supplies and no expenditures for building construction or maintenance are represented in the figure.

In the last few years, the $25 million Federal contribution has been divided among the four fields of study roughly as follows: $10 million for agriculture, $8.5 million for trade and industrial courses, $6 million for home economics, and less than $500,000 for distributive occupations. To obtain Federal money a state must draw up a detailed vocational education plan which becomes a contract between the state and the Federal government. Federal money may be used only for instruction in public schools and for courses designed to fit persons over fourteen for useful employment in the field of study.

In 1953 about 190,000 boys and 35,000 girls were enrolled in all-day high school courses for trades and industrial occupations under the Federal-state program. This represents about 10 percent of the boys and less than 2 percent of the girls enrolled in grades ten through twelve of the public secondary schools, during which most vocational education is given. There are some 20,000 public high schools in the country (excluding junior high schools), of which about 5,500 are in urban localities. About 2,000 high schools offer trade and industrial programs. Of these, about 400 are schools operated primarily for vocational education. The remainder are general high schools with vocational departments. Since average enrollment in the vocational schools is much larger than in the vocational departments of general high schools, the majority of students are found in separate vocational schools.

Most trade and industrial courses are confined to the eleventh and twelfth grades, but there are still many three-year, and even a few four-year programs, especially in the older vocational schools of the Northeast. Because these schools are large, probably the majority of trade and industry students are in three and four-year programs. In the Western states vocational courses are rarely offered before the eleventh grade. In some California cities the great majority of students are in the thirteenth and fourteenth grades (junior college), and in North Dakota nearly all trade and industry students are high school graduates.

The term trade and industry has been very broadly interpreted by the Office of Education. It embraces any occupation directly involved in the design, manufacture, servicing, or repair of any manufactured product; any service occupation not classified as agricultural, business, or professional; and the technical occupations. Altogether, scores of different occupations are taught, some of them in only a single high school, ranging from janitor and waitress to industrial designer and tool and die maker. The trade and industrial program in at least one high school includes the performing arts: music, drama, and the dance.

Unfortunately, there is no current information on the numbers of students preparing for different occupations. A rough indication of the magnitude of training and the extent of facilities for each occupation is provided by a list of the states and cities in which various occupations are taught. There are now fourteen occupations or groups of occupations which may be studied in over 100 towns and cities. Two occupations are by far the most popular. Machine shop and automobile repair courses are given in the high schools of almost every state, and, respectively, of over 700 and over 600 cities. Three groups of occupations are taught in almost all states and in over 300 towns and cities: electrician and electrical repair; cabinet and furniture making and wood working; and carpentry. Other occupations taught in at least 20 states and 100 cities are: printing trades, drafting, radio and television, welding, sheet metal, practical nursing, building construction mechanic, bricklaying, and barbering and beauty culture.

In addition to the 225,000 full-time trade and industry students, there are other young people who have passed the age of compulsory full-time attendance and who have gone to work, but are continuing their secondary vocational schooling on a part-time basis. Many of these students are in cooperative programs, in which they spend half their total work-school time at paid work, receiving on-the-job training in a trade or industrial occupation. The other half is spent in school studying trade-related and general subjects. The size of this group cannot be determined from the data available. Almost 10 percent of the graduates of trade and industrial programs in the North Atlantic region in 1953 were cooperative students. Trade and industrial education for adults and for young people who have left school is considered in the following chapter.

THE BEGINNINGS OF VOCATIONAL EDUCATION

The permeation of the high school curriculum by vocational subjects, as has been seen, has not won unanimous approval from American educators. Indeed, the role of vocational education has been shaped by continuing conflict between vocational and general educators. The terms of the controversy began to take shape as early as the period following the Civil War, when proposals for adapting the schools to the requirements of an industrial economy and a changing school population received growing support. Manual training, advanced early in the nineteenth century as a means of broadening the cultural experiences of young people, received increasing support on the ground that it could provide students with general principles of craftsmanship which could then be applied to whatever specific vocations they entered. Vehement opposition, however, was expressed by those who believed that manual training represented a dangerous anti-intellectual trend in education.

Up to the close of the nineteenth century the idea that specific vocational preparation should be a part of "education" made little progress. The purpose of the schools, it was almost universally agreed, was to provide intellectual discipline, moral values, and a common body of culture. This was the task of the "common schools" at the elementary level, and it was therefore inconceivable that the elementary schools should undertake vocational training. Even if educators had wished to introduce vocational training into the high schools, the students who might have benefited were not there. In 1890, only 3.5 percent of the nation's young people were graduating from high school and most of the graduates entered college.

The real beginnings of the present programs of vocational education came in the first two decades of this century. The growth of professional schools in the universities and agricultural training in the land-grant colleges, and the founding of technical institutes helped to change the climate of educational opinion. The idea of free electives was beginning to modify the uniform classical curriculum in the high schools as well as the colleges. Most important was the spread of high school education, for this forced serious consideration of a secondary curriculum suitable for those who would become wage earners. By 1900, over 6 percent, and by 1920, 17 percent, of the nation's young people were graduating from high school. This expansion was in part the cause, and in part, no doubt, the result of the fact that the secondary curriculum, which had always been somewhat more "practical" than in Europe, became even more so. Courses were added in clerical skills, homemaking, civic intelligence, mechanical drawing, and sometimes handicrafts, while training in the classical languages declined.

There were two main lines of argument in favor of specific vocational education in the high schools, one economic, the other based on democratic values. Economists and businessmen emphasized the decline of apprenticeship, the expansion and increasingly technological character of industry, the superiority of European insti-

tutions for training workmen and technicians, and America's need
to improve its competitive position in world markets.

The second line of argument was advanced mainly by labor
leaders, social reformers, and a few dissident educators, who maintained that the schools in a democratic society are obliged to prepare all children for their life's work. Why, it was asked, should
the public pay for the preprofessional training of those who will
attend college, but contribute nothing toward the occupational
competence of the wage earner? Does not the emphasis of the
traditional secondary school on "academic" subjects reflect an undemocratic conviction that manual work is less worthy than brain
work? Should not familiarity with tools and with physical work
be a part of the background of all young people? It was argued
also that the competent, well-trained worker would somehow be a
better citizen with better attitudes toward work. Some advocates
of vocational education saw it as a panacea for the ills of a growing
industrial economy, from radicalism through unemployment.

In the early controversy over the role of vocational education,
three main positions, each of which has continued to receive strong
support, may be discerned. One viewed vocational education as a
final period of specialized training following the general education
received in the common elementary school. The regular high
schools, according to this view, should continue their traditional
function of preparation for college, but separate vocational high
schools should be added to the system to provide specific occupational training for future wage earners who would otherwise not be
in any school.

At the opposite extreme was the view that any form of vocational education would "contaminate" the schools. Its proponents
held that the primary purpose of schooling is the traditional goal
of training the intellect, and that the creation of separate courses
of study or separate schools for future manual workers is essentially undemocratic. To provide cultural and intellectual advantages and the qualifications for higher education to some students,

while denying them to others, they said, was clearly a way of introducing class distinctions into the schools. They agreed with the champions of vocational education, moreover, that there is not enough time in the high school course of study to provide both adequate occupational preparation and thorough intellectual and cultural training for the same students.

The third main position on vocational education held that it was wrong both to segregate vocational and academic students and to ignore the needs of the future worker and the educational values of manual work. Urging the extension of the "common school" approach into the high school, its advocates also wanted to modify somewhat the nature of the common educational experience. They believed that general education should be continued for all students throughout the high school years; that all students should also receive some manual training; and that those students who wanted and could profit from specific vocational training should be given enough to prepare them effectively for work. This position reflected an effort on the part of general educators to compromise with the growing pressure for specific and separate vocational education as well as changes in educational philosophy which emphasized practical knowledge and the education of "the whole man."

By 1910 the efforts of those who favored some form of specific vocational education were beginning to bear fruit. The National Society for the Promotion of Industrial Education had been founded four years earlier. This organization, the nucleus of the present American Vocational Association, played a significant role in the passage of the Smith-Hughes Act of 1917. Also by 1910 Massachusetts had passed the first act for state aid to local vocational education; high schools were teaching stenography, "typewriting," and other commercial skills; evening schools were offering specific trade training; and the first proposal for Federal aid had been presented to Congress.

Support for the Smith-Hughes bill came from business, farm, reform, and labor groups, with the active aid of a few educators who had espoused the cause of vocational training. The debates in Congress were not concerned with educational policy but with states' rights, Federal control, and the costs of the proposed program. One of the reasons for the bill's success was that World War I was then demonstrating the dependence of national security upon industrial supremacy and thus re-enforcing the arguments of those who urged the necessity of raising the skills of American workers.

The Smith-Hughes Act proved critical in the growth of vocational education. The states were eager to take advantage of Federal aid. Few educators had any knowledge of or experience or interest in vocational education. The Federal agency set up to administer the act was equipped with a paid staff of devoted vocational educators and had broad powers to assist the states in setting up their programs and to administer the expenditure of Federal money. The states, moreover, were required to draw up a fairly detailed vocational education plan which had to be approved by the Federal agency before the states were eligible for aid. The circumstances, in short, were highly favorable to the development of strong Federal influence. While the Federal government did not dictate the forms and content of vocational education, its influence gave this field more uniformity than any other aspect of public education.

The provisions of the act and the circumstances of the time encouraged the creation of a vocational education system largely separate from the regular high schools. Vocational specialists, convinced that most general educators were basically opposed to any vocational education, saw a separate system as the only possibility. Many general educators, on the other hand, were quite content to see this alien growth take place outside of their province. An important factor was the provision in the act for a completely independent Federal Board for Vocational Education responsible directly to Congress and consisting, not of educators, but of the Secretaries of Agriculture, Commerce, and Labor, the Commissioner of Education, and one representative each of business, farm, and labor groups. The functions of the Board were transferred to the Office of Education in 1933, but by then the Board had already left its imprint. Some states set up independent boards for vocational education, paralleling the Federal Board. Federal funds were made available only to help pay for instruction designed to fit young people for useful employment. The use of Federal funds to provide the supplementary general courses necessary for a well-rounded education was specifically forbidden. Day school trade and industrial programs were required to include three consecutive hours each day of "practical work on a useful and productive basis," which has usually meant shopwork.

CONFLICTING TRENDS

While these circumstances were pushing vocational education in one direction, a number of developments set up contrary pressures. By 1930, 30 percent, and by 1940, one half of the nation's young people were graduating from high school. As high school enrollment increased, the proportion of graduates who entered college declined. Although vocational enrollment increased rapidly, it still accounted for only a small fraction of the total. Those who had forecast a dual high school system, with one part preparing some students for college and the other preparing a much larger number for work, were proved wrong.

It was becoming clear that most students were using high school neither as preparation for college nor as specific preparation for work. Vocational educators urged, with considerable reason, that specific vocational training be made available for this growing group. At the same time, however, it was becoming difficult to retain the conception of vocational education as a period of primarily occupational preparation between general education and work. As attendance became more nearly universal, the high school was increasingly viewed, both by the general public and by educators, as a continuation of the common elementary school with an obligation to provide all students with certain minimum cultural and intellectual advantages.

The expansion of college attendance introduced further difficulties. If, at first, potential vocational school students were forced to choose between vocational school and no high school, it did not matter if the vocational graduate could not enter college. Once it became apparent that many students were being forced to choose at an early age between vocational school and a chance to attend college in later years, educators saw an additional reason for expanding the general education provided for vocational students. As one result, specific vocational training was delayed until the last three, and then the last two, years of high school, and even until junior college. Some schools gave vocational students the opportunity to qualify for college entrance by taking elective courses.

The gap between vocational and general high school education was also narrowed by increasing the occupational elements in general programs. Obviously, if the concept of public schooling as a common experience for all young people was to be honored and if some students were to receive vocational education, then all students had to receive some similar exposure. In addition, the trend toward practical "life-experience" education continued strong.

As a result of these developments, some communities have abandoned separate vocational and general high schools and are conducting all high school education in "comprehensive" schools which provide all students with both the traditional academic courses and more or less specific skill training, the precise mixture depending on the needs and abilities of the individual student. Industrial arts has become an important means of providing some exposure to skilled work for nonvocational students.

Elsewhere almost completely separate systems continue. As noted above, most trade and industry students are in separate vocational schools, especially in communities which are large enough to support several high schools. In three states the chief policy-making and administrative authorities for vocational education are completely independent of those who are responsible for the rest of the public school system. In fourteen other states, vocational education has some degree of independence at the highest state level. In some states, where vocational education is not independent at the state level, it is organized on a county or area basis, independently of the local school districts which run the other schools, in part simply because of the high cost of providing specialized vocational facilities in each district.

Each of the three major positions taken in the vocational education controversy a half century ago can claim some measure of success today. In some high schools the course of study is still primarily academic and college preparatory. On the other hand, a quarter of a million young people are officially designated as vocational trade and industry students, are enrolled in vocational schools or formally distinct vocational departments, and spend most of their time learning an occupation. Finally, in the majority of high schools there is a substantial measure of compromise between these extreme features of the educational scene. Even among the minority of schools which have no courses of study under the Federal-state program, there are very few in which some vocational elements have not entered the curriculum. In the vocational schools and vocational departments, increasing attention is being given to keeping the route to college open to all and to reducing the formal separation of vocational students from other students.

The extent to which the line between vocational and general education has been blurred, however, should not be exaggerated. Current educational theory emphasizes the common goals of secondary education for all youth, but in practice, whenever a school system offers a Federally subsidized trade and industrial program, the vocational student is distinguished from other students in several respects. He stays in school six hours a day, an hour longer than most other students, and he spends at least half this time in a shop learning a trade or industrial skill. Generally, he spends about four-and-a-half hours a day in vocational classes from which non-vocational students are excluded by law.

Together with the growth of high school attendance and the spread of vocational education, the separate status of vocational programs has led to a struggle over the assignment of students. As long as the vocational schools offered trade courses for a few students who would otherwise not be in school at all, the problem of selecting students for vocational courses was unimportant. The schools could offer training in the most common trades, and those young people who chose to, could enroll. But as enrollment in high school became nearly universal in most urban areas, selection and assignment became major problems.

Most vocational educators tend to regard their schools primarily as a means of producing potential skilled craftsmen. As vocational enrollment has increased, they have sometimes sought to protect this function by imposing high admission requirements and raising standards of school performance. Convinced that only those of average or above average intelligence are capable of becoming skilled craftsmen, they have sought to attract a larger proportion of the more able students.

Many general educators continue to feel, on the other hand, that the proper place for the able student is the academic program. In addition, faced with the necessity of doing something with many students who lack the ability or the desire to do well in high school, they have looked upon vocational courses as one means of providing course work commensurate with the ability of the less able students. Most vocational educators accept a responsibility for this group of students. At the same time, however, they protest when the vocational schools are used as the dumping ground of the general high schools and insist that they receive a reasonable share of students at all levels of academic ability. Frequently, in fact, there is a tug of war for the more able students and a battle of wits to avoid acceptance of the least able.

The Smith-Hughes and George-Barden Acts represent one answer to the still open question of how future workers can best be educated. For trade and industry students, the law declares, in effect, that the best education is that which is devoted primarily to training in the skills and knowledge of a specific occupation. The program which has been developed on this premise, it has been charged, inevitably involves some sacrifice of democratic values. The nonvocational courses taken by vocational students are rarely comparable in scope and quality to those available to other students. Usually, the trade and industry student has not been able to move from secondary school into college; frequently he has been segregated with other students who came from deprived economic backgrounds and lacked the ability or the motivation to succeed in academic work.

If the vocational program for trade and industrial education is vulnerable to the charge that it is "class education," it may also be questioned on other grounds. Even among vocational educators, few maintain that the full-time school is the ideal place for producing fully skilled workers. Vocational education is built on the premise that the student learns best by doing, by exercising the skills he needs under the same conditions he will encounter in a real job. At best, therefore, there are many things that cannot be taught as well in a school shop as in a well organized on-the-job training program.

The trade and industrial program has not enjoyed the continuous support of those interests which are most directly concerned with the training of skilled workers — industry and the unions. Business and labor groups supported the Smith-Hughes bill in 1917, but in later years there were few indications that major segments of industry or labor regarded the program as essential. At Congressional hearings on vocational education legislation and appropriations, farm groups backed the agricultural education program, retailers supported the part-time distributive program, and specialized educational groups endorsed the whole program, but industry and labor testimony was generally conspicuous by its absence. In the House and Senate, major support came from Southern legislators rather than from those from the more heavily industrialized areas of the nation. The National Association of Manufacturers and the U. S. Chamber of Commerce support vocational education but are opposed in principle to Federal grants-in-aid. Very recently both the CIO and AFL have given strong official support to the Federal-state program, and employer groups have shown renewed interest. Nevertheless, there are still signs that many employers and local union representatives view the program without great enthusiasm.

Why then, the vocational trade and industrial program? What is its justification? Defenders of vocational education present a number of cogent arguments for preserving and expanding specific occupational training in the high schools. Proceeding from the premise that, with few exceptions, everyone should have the advantage of high school, they argue that while the potential worker is in school, he should learn something that will be directly useful to him in his later work. There is no reason, they maintain, why manual skill should not have as honorable a place in the schools as intellectual skill — except for the prejudices of educators. Vocational education is represented as a healthy corrective to the ivory tower atmosphere of the schools. In earlier and simpler days when every child learned about work by watching and participating in the work of his parents and neighbors there was some justification for the schools' confining themselves to booklearning, then a rare and valuable asset. Now that work has been removed from the home and direct participation in work is often postponed until eighteen or later, the schools have an obligation not to turn young people loose in the world of work and adult economic responsibility without prior preparation.

Second, vocational educators argue that no one learns without interest. Many young people of high school age — particularly those who do not do well in the academic subjects — are primarily interested in going to work and earning money. Some have already developed an interest in a particular occupation, or in activities related to an occupation. When students come from a family and neighborhood background in which books and intellectual activities have a small role, it is often impossible for the schools to capture their interest through the traditional curriculum. For all of these reasons, it is argued, the school can best enlist the enthusiasm of many students by centering their studies about an occupational goal. Only in this way will it be possible for the high schools to hold the two-fifths of all students who now drop out before graduation. Moreover, once the student's interest in purely occupational training has been captured, it is then possible to extend his motivation into related courses such as mathematics and science, and sometimes into general education courses which had formerly seemed to have no connection with life.

Third, it is maintained, the high schools must provide systematic skill training because apprenticeship and other organized on-the-job training programs are not sufficiently developed to take care of the nation's needs. In view of the large number of skilled workers who pick up their abilities haphazardly and by chance, the contribution of the vocational schools to the nation's skilled labor force takes on added significance. For the high schools to neglect systematic preparation in the fundamentals of industrial work, it is asserted, would not be fair to the worker, wise for the economy, nor safe for the national interest.

Finally, according to vocational educators, the values of vocational education cannot be achieved through superficial shop courses. It is impossible either to generate sincere interest or to teach useful skills by having students make book ends or ash trays, and to pretend that it is possible is a fraud on both the student and the taxpayer. Learning by doing is the most effective method of learning. The vocational program, its champions insist, presents the schools with their best opportunity to teach through activity, but only if the activity is an honest, useful piece of work. If these requirements can be met only at the cost of setting the vocational

CHAPTER VII

Types of Vocational Schooling

THIS CHAPTER is concerned mainly with education for skilled trades and industrial occupations conducted under Federal law. It also deals with other vocational programs, including agricultural and distributive education in the high schools, commercial and business training, technician education, and correspondence schools.

Although Federal law has fixed the broad outlines of trade and industrial education in the high schools, state and local school systems have been free to fill in the details much as they choose. In describing trade and industrial education today, therefore, it is frequently impossible to do more than indicate the wide diversity of conditions and approaches in different communities.

Seeking current, specific information on the vocational programs in a representative group of communities, the National Manpower Council reviewed published materials and sent a questionnaire to thirty school officials in communities all over the country. In addition, the Council staff interviewed or corresponded with school authorities and other educators in states as widely separated as New York and California, Michigan and Georgia.

THE NUMBER OF FULL-TIME TRADE AND INDUSTRY STUDENTS

The great differences in trade and industrial programs are suggested by a comparison of the percentages of students enrolled. In most localities surveyed by the Council, the percentage of high school boys in trade and industrial programs is near the national average, about 10 percent. In such heavily industrialized areas as Gary and Providence, less than 5 percent are in such programs. In other communities over half the boys are enrolled.

These differences in enrollment are caused only in part by differences in the size, quality, and variety of shop facilities. Sometimes excellent, modern facilities are not fully used because not enough students apply. A recent survey showed that the vocational shops in Massachusetts were operating at only three fourths of capacity, with twelve vocational schools enrolling only two fifths as many students as they could handle. Surveys of high school students usually find that far more students plan to enter professional and managerial employment than can possibly get jobs in these fields. Many of them will later become industrial workers, but since they are aiming at white collar work they are not interested in the trade and industrial program in high school.

The vocational school has often been the "dumping ground" for students whom the regular high schools did not want. Even where this is no longer true, some teachers and parents urge young people to avoid the vocational school because they are not aware of the change. Where, for one reason or another, the schools and employers do not work closely together, there may be few channels through which potential vocational students can learn about and become interested in opportunities for employment as skilled workers.

The experience of communities like Allentown, Pa., where 60 percent of the public high school boys are in trade and industrial courses, indicates that this situation can be overcome. To do so, however, requires a combination of good shop facilities and teachers, school officials who are interested in vocational education, close cooperation with local employers and labor, and, above all, a guidance program which succeeds in attracting qualified young people to preparation for skilled work.

VOCATIONAL GUIDANCE AND VOCATIONAL EDUCATION

Vocational educators sometimes feel that the major role of guidance is to attract capable students into vocational programs.[1]

[1] Guidance problems are considered more fully in Chapter X.

It is not necessary to accept this view to admit that guidance activities in many school systems do not provide the student who is about to choose a high school program with adequate information about training and employment in skilled work. The teachers and counselors who are responsible for guidance are generally academically trained and often have little knowledge of industrial conditions. One common solution to this problem is to make sure that before the student has to make a final choice of high school program, he spends an exploratory year which gives him information about occupations and permits him to experience a variety of shop activities. This is one of the purposes of industrial arts courses.

The need for vocational guidance does not end when the student chooses a trade and industrial program. Changes in interests or mistaken estimates of ability and aptitudes may require a shift to another vocational course or to a nonvocational program. Some vocational educators, however, have little sympathy with guidance activities in high school. As one of them put it recently, "little real vocational guidance is needed after the boy has entered the vocational school. If the guidance is functioning properly in the junior high schools it is fair to assume that the boy was given all the necessary and available tests which pointed to the fact that he had mechanical aptitude and should go to a vocational school." This attitude is by no means universal. Many vocational schools do provide a continuous counseling program which includes a year of trial accompanied by various forms of guidance before requiring the final choice of a trade.

The methods, extent, and quality of guidance vary enormously. It is significant, however, that even in communities where guidance is highly developed, school officials are often dubious about its success. Federal funds are available for many vocational guidance activities under the terms of the George-Barden Act of 1946. Federal aid, however, does not strongly encourage the development of guidance. The states are not required to use any part of their Federal allotments for this purpose, and most of them

spend enough on other phases of vocational education to obtain
their full allotment without expanding guidance activities.

FITTING STUDENTS AND CURRICULA

One of the most difficult tasks in vocational education is the
guidance of students with varying degrees of ability into the
courses from which they can benefit most. The extent to which
vocational schools and departments face the special problems of
dealing with very good and very poor students varies considerably,
even within the same community. Among the twenty-six vocational
schools of New York City in 1949, the IQ distribution of new students was about normal in one school, while in another the average
was only 72. In the latter school, one fourth of the new students
were below 62, and only one fourth were above 80. The appalling
difficulty of operating a schoool with such a student body is indicated by the fact that persons with IQ's of 70 to 80 are generally
considered to be on the border line of mental deficiency, while a
score below 70 is usually a clear indication of feeble-mindedness.
In most of the communities surveyed by the Council, the average
IQ of vocational students was about the same as, or slightly lower
than, that of the whole population. Generally the most intelligent
students were attracted only to vocational programs that offered
preparation for technician occupations. But, unlike those in New
York City, most vocational programs had succeeded in excluding
the least intelligent students, occasionally through admission requirements, but generally through informal procedures.

Students of low ability have often been assigned to vocational
programs because they are incapable of mastering the academic
program and therefore, it is said, might as well spend their time
learning a few simple manual skills which will be useful when they
go to work. The protests of vocational officials against this policy
seem to have contributed considerably toward raising the average
ability of vocational students. Because of compulsory attendance
laws, the vocational schools still cannot avoid entirely the problem
of dealing with students of low ability. Generally the problem is

met by providing courses in jobs such as janitor or in the simple, repetitive skills of mass production industries. Sometimes a student is admitted to a course for automobile mechanics and taught only the simplest jobs — changing a tire, filling a gas tank, and lubricating a car.

Some schools do not provide special curricula for such students. In Chicago, the aim of the vocational schools is limited mainly to "the development of future skilled workers in the fields of design, tooling, maintenance, servicing, and sales engineering." The average IQ of the students, however, is quite low. As a result, one third to one half of them are incapable of completing their courses of study successfully. Some who should not be graduated manage to squeeze by, but the schools cannot recommend them to employers.

If average or above average intelligence is required to become a skilled worker, then it follows that a high proportion of those who can complete a rigorous vocational course of study could also succeed in the academic program and in college. A student who enrolls in a vocational course in the ninth grade may later demonstrate ability and interest in academic studies. Transfer to an academic program, however, is sometimes impeded by lack of academic credits in the early high school years, by inadequate guidance, and by the various barriers between vocational and general education already described.

Another way to prevent the vocational program from becoming a dead end with respect to higher education is to permit the vocational student to earn enough academic credits for college entrance, perhaps with the aid of a few courses taken after graduation. The importance of general education for all vocational students, quite apart from the question of college entrance, has been explored in Chapter VI.

Expanding the general and elective courses for vocational students, however, means taking time from skill training, and vocational educators feel that adequate skill training cannot be given unless most of the school day is devoted to it. Traditionally, vocational programs devote only about one fourth of the school day to "general" courses, usually English, physical education, and social studies. Some vocational educators resent any effort to merge vocational and academic preparation. They argue that by the time the student gets to the ninth, tenth, or eleventh grade, he should already have most of the general education he needs. Some maintain that vocational subjects are just as good, just as "cultural," just as challenging as academic subjects. Consequently, they say, there is no special need to worry about the general courses offered to vocational students.

On the other hand, expansion of academic studies is facilitated by the tendency to confine vocational programs to the last two years of high school, by the fact that the vocational school day is often an hour longer than the usual school day, and by the fact that it is frequently possible to combine "related" instruction with the required three hours of shop work so that the remaining three hours are free for academic courses. Many communities, including Chicago and Canton, Ohio, permit the able vocational student to pursue this combination of courses, and in Canton about 5 percent of the vocational graduates do enter college. In *The Double Purpose High School*, Franklin J. Keller describes twelve schools which seek to do this by eliminating wasted time and unessential courses from the curriculum.

The quality of general courses is just as important as the quantity, but in schools where most students are below average in intelligence the level of instruction is necessarily adjusted to the ability of the majority. Also, good academic teachers are reluctant to teach in vocational schools in which the enrollment includes a preponderance of problem students, the range of general courses is narrow, and the academic teachers are assigned second-class status. Until recently, New York City provided an extreme example of this problem. At the beginning of each school year, "substitute" academic teachers without tenure were hired for the vocational schools. Because many students dropped out before the beginning of the spring term, some of the substitutes were then released and some academic classes were turned over to shop teachers. This was done because it was known that at the beginning of the next year it would be much easier to hire new academic teachers than new shop teachers. Where the vocational courses are conducted on the same campus as academic courses, the problem of providing high quality academic instruction is often solved by combining vocational and nonvocational students in the same classes for academic subjects.

Another group of students who constitute a special problem for the vocational schools are those who have done poorly in school, not because of lack of ability, but because they are simply not interested. Studies have shown that this group is very large. Of the roughly 40 percent of young people who do not graduate from high school, many drop out not because of lack of ability or economic pressure, but because they do not like school or would rather work. Some vocational educators are convinced that vocational programs are uniquely suited to developing school motivation and therefore urge the extension to almost all students of occupationally-centered education. The data available, however, do not bear out these claims. Generally, the vocational schools lose at least as many students before graduation as do other schools.

VOCATIONAL EDUCATION AND THE EMPLOYER

Although the principal obligation of the vocational school is to the student, it is plain that unless he receives training useful to an employer the student's time is being wasted. Vocational programs employ a variety of means to keep their instruction in line with the current needs of employers, including advisory committees, "coordinators" who serve as liaison between industry and the school, surveys of local job opportunities, and informal contacts with industry.

The U. S. Office of Education strongly recommends the organization of advisory committees that include representatives of both employers and labor by all school units with trade and industrial programs. The extent to which this policy is followed in the country as a whole is not clear. Some large cities — San Diego is one example — maintain an elaborate network of active advisory committees, one for each of the trades taught. On the other hand, it has been charged that vocational educators frequently do not appreciate the importance of employer and labor cooperation and that, especially where vocational programs have been established for many years, officials sometimes view the vocational schools as their private preserve to be guarded jealously against outside influences.

However effectively the vocational school is geared to employers' needs, it cannot meet their requirements fully. The trade and industry graduate is seldom ready to step directly into a skilled job. At best he has a head start for apprenticeship or other on-the-job training. There is not enough time in high school to train a skilled worker. The shopwork per year of full-time school is the equivalent in hours of only about three-and-a-half months on a full-time job.

There are also many things a school cannot do because it is a school and not a factory. It cannot duplicate the specific requirements of each of the many jobs found in most localities, the pressures of production for profit, or the problems of getting along with other workers and the foreman in a real job situation. Vocational educators maintain that most schools do approximate real work situations closely enough to fit the graduate for a beginner's job in a skilled occupation. Some schools simulate work conditions by having the students produce goods or provide services on a commercial basis. This, however, is very expensive unless the products are sold, and some educators believe that, for both practical and ethical reasons, the schools should not become engaged in marketing operations. Also, labor unions and employers frequently object when goods made by unpaid students are placed on the market.

Vocational educators agree almost unanimously that the best answer to this problem is to be found in cooperative programs in which the advanced student spends half of his weekdays in school, studying trade-related and general courses, and the other half at paid work getting actual experience in the same occupation. Nevertheless, enrollment in cooperative trade and industrial programs has always been small, largely because it is difficult to interest employers in a program supervised by school officials and devoted to systematic training of the student. Newton, Mass., Allentown, Pa., Detroit, and other communities have demonstrated that when school officials make a concerted effort to enlist employer support, it is possible to run an extensive and successful cooperative program. Only the better students are usually admitted to such programs in order to encourage employer participation.

The fact that the vocational school does not duplicate factory conditions offers advantages as well as disadvantages. Because it is not concerned with production for profit in a changing market, the school is in a better position than the factory to concentrate on systematic, comprehensive training given in the proper sequence. While the vocational graduate may be no better prepared for the tasks of a specific job than the worker who is trained exclusively on the job, vocational educators assert that he is less likely to be totally ignorant about large areas of his trade, and, therefore, that he is in a better position to get another job or to win promotion.

The extent to which the vocational program meets the needs of the employer is a problem of policy as well as of method. The school must provide training which looks forward to placing most graduates in appropriate positions in local industry. Yet if the school is tied too closely to the needs of local employers, it may become a publicly supported adjunct of local business, neglecting the student in favor of the employer. Should the school base its curriculum on the expressed wishes of students or on the needs of employers? Should it concentrate on fitting students for the local labor market if this means reducing their opportunity to take jobs in other localities? In selecting occupations to be taught, should it give greatest weight to the cost of equipment, to the availability of good teachers, or to the local occupational pattern?

These considerations do not necessarily conflict — but they may. A school's specific problems depend largely on whether vocational education is separated from or closely integrated with the rest of the school system and on whether the school is located in a large city, a town dominated by one or two employers, or a diversified manufacturing community. These problems are rarely discussed but are reflected in the contrast between vocational programs that go their own way with little contact with employers, and others that are closely geared to the needs of a few major enterprises.

Relatively few school systems have undertaken surveys to find out how employers evaluate the graduates of vocational programs. Even fewer conduct systematic follow-up studies to see how well their graduates are doing after several years of employment. Consequently, most of the evidence on employer evaluations of vocational education is indirect, fragmentary, and inconclusive.

The National Manpower Council's survey found that in most communities there is a sizable group of employers who cooperate closely with the vocational schools. They help plan curricula, are eager to hire vocational graduates, support the program in the community, participate in cooperative work-study programs, and even contribute machinery and equipment. The Canton, Ohio, vocational school was built and equipped in 1940 with a $1,350,000 grant from the Timken Roller Bearing Company. Evidence that vocational education is valued by employers is also found in the fact that most vocational graduates today are placed in appropriate positions shortly after graduation. On the other hand, the excellent placement records of recent years are partly a reflection of continuing prosperity and abundance of jobs. There is considerable evidence that employers are frequently much less interested in specific vocational training than in good general background and in favorable attitudes toward work.

It is not surprising that employers differ on the merits of vocational education. Where vocational education is a neglected part of the school system or where school officials have not sought to enlist employer cooperation, employers are not likely to feel much concern. Large firms with well-developed training programs and a high degree of work specialization are likely to feel less need for specific training provided in school than are small firms. Because of financial considerations a vocational school system has to concentrate on training in a relatively narrow range of skills for which there is a steady and substantial demand. Since there are always many jobs for which vocational graduates are not prepared, many employers cannot have a vital interest in vocational education.

THE QUALITY OF VOCATIONAL EDUCATION

How well a vocational program accomplishes its goals depends in large part on the quality of its teachers, the suitability of its buildings, and the extent to which its equipment is kept up to date. Like public education as a whole, vocational education is often handicapped by the fact that its financial resources are inadequate to perform the tasks assigned to it by the community. The financial problems of the vocational schools are intensified by the relatively high cost of the required buildings and equipment. In addition, in seeking shop teachers the school must compete directly with industry which can pay more for workers with the broad skill and long experience desirable in a teacher.

Most of the communities surveyed by the Council reported increasing difficulty in securing good shop teachers. In one large city with a high salary scale, several courses had been discontinued because qualified teachers were not available. On the other hand, a substantial minority reported that getting qualified teachers is not a serious problem. The degree of difficulty encountered in finding teachers reflects great variation in both the standards of qualification for shop teachers and the salaries paid. Some communities require a few years of practical experience and very limited classroom training in teaching methods. Others require many years of experience plus college training in vocational education. All communities place primary emphasis on trade experience rather than on formal education.

About half of the communities reported that all their vocational school equipment is thoroughly up-to-date, in a few cases, more modern than in local industry. The other half have some obsolete equipment and varying degrees of difficulty in getting money to replace it. Providence reported that nearly all its vocational school machinery is obsolete.

Keeping facilities up to date seems to be less of a problem than providing training facilities for a variety of occupations. In the large metropolitan areas, trade and industrial enrollment is usually sufficient to justify the cost of training in a large number of occupations — frequently in specialized schools, each devoted to one group of occupations. New York City has thirty-one vocational schools offering training in over seventy occupations. In smaller communities, the schools usually provide instruction in only a few major occupations. Nassau County, Long Island, has a population of about a million, many of whom work in New York City industries or in the rapidly expanding industries of the county itself. Yet in the many independent school districts in the county, only four high schools offer trade and industrial courses in a total of only seven occupations. Sparsely settled rural school districts can rarely afford to offer trade and industry courses, even though many of their young people will eventually find industrial employment in the cities.

One result of the difficulty of expanding the number of occupations taught is that the traditional skilled trades receive strong emphasis while many newer, rapidly expanding occupations are neglected. It is possible to study cabinet or furniture making in the high schools of over three hundred communities, located in almost every state. On the other hand, courses for typewriter and office machine repairmen are given in only twelve communities, and for industrial laboratory technicians in only three.

To meet these problems, some states are beginning to develop centralized vocational schools to serve an entire county, an even larger area, or, as in Connecticut, a whole state. In addition to creating transportation or housing problems, however, this solution divorces the vocational schools from the normal administrative structure and intensifies the problem of coordinating vocational programs with other secondary education.

In the South, where segregated schools have been maintained, vocational education facilities, like all school facilities, are much less adequate for Negro than for white students. This remains true in spite of substantial progress in recent years. In 1952, in fourteen states for which data were available, Negroes constituted 20 percent of the population, but only 10 percent of the enrollment in trade and industrial programs. Even more important, opportunities for vocational education are limited mainly to those occupations in which Negroes have traditionally been employed and those in which Negroes can gain employment providing services for other Negroes. Almost 30 percent of the Negro trade and industry students were preparing for work in the building trades. Another 40 percent were in five other nonindustrial occupations: auto repair, barbering and beauty culture, domestic service, practical nursing, and sewing and tailoring. Machinist and draftsman, respectively, are the most commonly taught of the skilled and the technical occupations. Yet, in these fourteen states, there were only 263 Negro students in machine shop courses, and only 80 studying drafting.

Vocational educators in the South maintain that they cannot devote their limited resources to training Negroes for occupations in which they have little chance of gaining employment. Negro leaders respond that unless Negroes are trained for these occupations it will be impossible to break down the barriers which now keep them out. They add that Southern Negroes who cannot make use of their skills in the South can, and frequently do, migrate to the North.

These problems are not confined to the South. A recent survey by the Connecticut Commission on Civil Rights found that although Negroes constituted about the same proportion of vocational graduates as they did of the population of the state, the distribution of students among occupations showed the same pattern as in the South. "Negroes were represented proportionately less than whites in the electrical, machine, and drafting trades, and proportionately more than whites in auto repairing, dressmaking, and practical nursing. . . . No Negroes had ever attended private vocational schools specializing in tool and machine design."

AGRICULTURAL EDUCATION IN THE HIGH SCHOOLS

Most of the literature about, and most of the controversies over, vocational education have centered about the trade and industrial program. Meanwhile, agricultural training under the Federal-state structure has inconspicuously won a major place in the rural high schools of the country. Nearly half the high schools in the country offer vocational agriculture courses. About 430,000 high school students are enrolled in full-time agricultural programs in 10,000 high schools. The agricultural program involves about twice as many full-time students and about five times as many schools as the trade and industrial program. The number of all-day students in trade and industrial courses has remained relatively stable since the close of World War II at a level almost one third lower than the peak year of 1942. Even though the agricultural labor force has been declining, enrollment of full-time agricultural students is now nearly a third higher than in 1942. Most experts agree that the agricultural program has made an important contribution to the skills of the agricultural labor force and to the great increases in agricultural productivity.

Perhaps the outstanding contrast between the trade and industrial and the agricultural programs is the much closer integration of agricultural education with other parts of secondary education and with the outside experiences of students. Vocational agriculture courses are rarely conducted in separate schools. Enrollment in rural areas is generally not large enough to justify the creation of specialized schools. Since many of the practical aspects of agricultural schooling are conducted on the farm rather than in the school, it is not necessary to build and equip extensive shops.

In agricultural programs, moreover, Federal law and administrative regulations do not separate vocational students from other students to the extent they do in trade and industrial programs. While the trade and industry student must spend half of every school day — and generally spends three fourths — in classes from which other students are legally excluded, the student of farming is required to devote a minimum of only about seven hours a week to agricultural courses.

By its nature as well as by design agricultural instruction is also more closely linked with the student's outside learning opportunities and experiences. The problem of coordinating theoretical instruction with realistic practical experience — which is so difficult in trade and industrial programs — is relatively easy. Most students would be getting practical experience on family farms in any case. In addition, Federal regulations require the student to carry out actual farming projects under the year-round supervision of the teacher.

After he graduates, the young farmer finds well-developed public facilities for extending his training. If he enrolls in an evening vocational agriculture class, he can continue to take advantage of the individualized guidance of the teacher. The extension service, run by the Department of Agriculture and the state land-grant college, is equipped to help him in the continual development of the specific skills he needs on his farm. A relatively small proportion of vocational agriculture graduates, however, go into farming. Some critics have maintained, therefore, that rural high schools should place more emphasis on college preparation and on training for nonagricultural occupations.

Agricultural education in the high schools is likely to be part of a lifelong process of skill development consisting of formal instruction closely coordinated with practical needs and experience. Trade and industrial education is more likely to be the only contact of the individual with formal instruction and less likely to be as closely related to his job needs and experience.

Recognizing both the difficulty of and the need for closely coordinating trade and industrial education with the needs and experiences of the skilled worker on the job, many vocational educators feel that evening and part-time courses for employed workers are the most effective part of the trade and industrial program. The importance of such instruction is reflected in the provisions of Federal law requiring that at least one third of the funds supplied by the Federal government, and of the matching funds supplied by the states, must be used for part-time classes. Originally, one of the purposes of these provisions was to encourage the part-time continuation of the general secondary education of young people who had started to work. Part-time general continuation courses, however, are rapidly disappearing. Almost all evening and part-time courses are now devoted to extending the skills of employed workers.

Part-time and evening courses of the "trade extension" type in the Federal-state program now enroll over half a million students, more than twice as many as are enrolled in all-day trade and industrial courses for high school students. Several years ago a survey of adult education facilities found that more school districts offered evening courses in industrial subjects than in any field except recreation. In cities of over 50,000 population, 80 percent of the school districts offered evening industrial courses. Of the more than half a million "trade extension" students, about 120,000 are apprentices receiving related instruction in vocational schools as a regular part of their apprenticeship training. The U. S. Bureau of Apprenticeship recommends that apprentices receive at least 144 hours a year of related instruction in a vocational school. About two thirds of all apprentices in programs registered with the Bureau do so.

Most of the remaining "trade extension" students are young workers attending classes on their own time to help them to improve their skills in their present jobs or to qualify for promotion.

Evening classes generally meet for two hours an evening two evenings a week for a period determined by the needs of the students. They may meet during the day for workers employed at night. Recently, there has been a trend toward greater emphasis on theoretical and technical instruction and toward greater reliance on on-the-job experience and training for development of manual skills. About 20,000 workers are enrolled in courses for foremen and supervisors.

Because evening students attend on their own time and because many evening instructors are employed during the day as skilled industrial workers or foremen, most evening courses are closely related to job needs. Special classes are sometimes set up primarily for employees in a particular plant, and instruction may be provided by a foreman from the same company. It is even possible to hold Federally aided classes within the plant provided certain stringent Federal requirements are observed to insure that the primary purpose is the training of the students rather than the profit of the employer.

During World War II the Federal-state vocational system became the main instrument for government assistance in training of workers for war industries. The program's success in rapidly preparing large numbers of inexperienced men for semi-skilled production jobs led to the conviction that a similar program would be useful for reconverting war workers to peacetime pursuits. Consequently, when the George-Barden Act was passed in 1946, it provided for pre-employment trade and industrial training for unemployed workers.

Like the war-time program, these courses are designed to prepare men in the shortest possible time for a beginner's job in a new field of work. Frequently the sessions last eight hours a day, with the majority of the time spent in shopwork and with no time devoted to general education courses. In some states they have been used to retrain people on relief rolls. In New England these courses have been used to train unemployed textile workers for work in the electronics industry and other light manufacturing plants. How many workers are enrolled in such courses is not known.

DISTRIBUTIVE AND COMMERCIAL EDUCATION

All distributive education is conducted in evening and part-time classes for students employed in the field. The merchandising program began in 1938 and expanded steadily, except for the war years, until 1950. Since then, heavy cuts in Federal funds have led to a sharp reduction in enrollments. These cuts occurred for several reasons, including Congress' desire to reduce unessential expenditures during the Korean war and evidence that Federal money was poorly spent. The increased appropriation for Federal aid to vocational education for 1955 restored half of the previous cuts. Several considerations were involved — fear of recession, which served to emphasize the importance of salesmanship, improvement in the administration of vocational aid funds, and continuing protests from retailing organizations.

In the peak enrollment year of 1950 about two thirds of the distributive students were in evening classes on their own time. Less than 10 percent, about 30,000, were high school students in cooperative work-study programs. The remaining one fourth were employees given time off, usually with pay, to attend part-time courses closely coordinated with their work.

One of the goals of the distributive program is to reduce the rate of failure among small retailing establishments. A high proportion of enrollments have consisted of the owners and employees of such businesses. In 1950, slightly less than half of the students were enrolled in courses for store personnel — sales clerks, stock clerks, cashiers, etc. Less than a fifth were in managerial courses, including courses in finance, sales promotion, merchandising, etc. The remainder were in courses centering about the distribution of specific commodities or services, most of them in the restaurant and food fields. Recently more than half of the students have been women.

Although high school courses in business or commercial subjects are closely related to the distributive program, they are considered separately because general business courses are not aided by Federal funds. The main reason for this seems to be that Congress has felt that business courses are sufficiently developed not to require special encouragement. Bookkeeping and typing were among the earliest occupational subjects introduced into the high schools. At present, over half of all high school students take at least one business course.

This does not mean, however, that the majority of students are preparing for work in office occupations. First-year typing courses enroll the largest number of students, most of whom acquire some typing skill for personal use and do not take a second year of typing. Bookkeeping and shorthand courses rank next to typing in number of students. Most evening high schools also give business courses.

Like the trade and industrial program, business education in the high schools seeks to produce graduates with the skill needed to begin employment rather than fully skilled workers. Some of the graduates enter public or private post-high school institutions to develop their skills further, but the majority go right to work and learn whatever else they need on the job.

The precise number of students enrolled in post-high school courses in office occupations is not known, but is very large. These institutions range all the way from schools offering one or two years of instruction in typing and shorthand to four-year colleges which grant degrees in accounting and business administration. There are about 1,500 private business schools. Nearly 500 give courses of at least twenty-five hours a week for thirty-six weeks and otherwise meet the standards of the National Association and Council of Business Schools. Few of this group have less than 100 students and some have several thousand.

In the last few years enrollment in private business schools has decreased substantially. This is partly because few World War II veterans studying under the GI bill are still in school. In addition some employers have lowered their minimum hiring standards because of shortages of office help.

The Accrediting Commission of Business Schools has approved seventeen business schools which offer at least two-year programs at the collegiate level. These schools emphasize a broad understanding of business methods and problems rather than the stenographic and clerical skills, and devote at least one fourth of their programs to academic subjects. Many colleges and junior colleges that do not specialize in business courses also have large enrollments in these subjects.

TECHNICAL EDUCATION

The term "technical education" covers a variety of educational programs and institutions. Unlike vocational education for the skilled trades and collegiate training for the professional engineer, technical education has not yet evolved a substantial body of common theory and practice.

Perhaps the most important reason for this situation is the difficulty of separating the technical occupations from the skilled and professional occupations. In listing the occupations for which their graduates are trained, technical schools sometimes include jobs ranging all the way from semi-skilled equipment assembler to professional engineering consultant. Actually, a single graduate may pass through this range of jobs in the course of his career. Because many companies follow a policy of promoting from within to fill all positions below the professional level, the technical school must often prepare its students not only for their ultimate technical occupation, but for the semi-skilled and skilled jobs they may hold on the way up. Recently, however, a growing number of companies have been placing graduates directly in technician positions, in part because of shortages of engineers.

A second reason for the great variations in technical education is that the widespread development of educational programs designed specifically to prepare students for technician occupations is very recent. Most technical education takes place in institutions designated as "post-high school" but "noncollegiate." Their functions are not yet as clearly established as those of the elementary school, high school, college, and university, nor have they won the same degree of public understanding and support.

A substantial but unknown number of high school students are enrolled in technical high schools or departments. Some high school technical education is conducted within the framework of general or academic high schools. Such programs range all the way from traditional college preparatory courses with some extra work in shopwork and drawing to that of Brooklyn Technical High School, which offers such intensive technical training that many of its students are accepted into engineering colleges with advanced standing. Especially when they impose high admission standards, technical high school programs within the academic structure frequently tend to serve as prep schools for engineering colleges.

Since World War II, increased emphasis has been placed on technical courses of study within the Federal-state trade and industrial program in the high schools. Such courses are designated as "vocational-technical." This new emphasis is the result not only of the changing character of industrial operations, but also of an increase in the average age and intelligence of vocational students, which has enabled more of them to complete the necessary mathematics and science courses. Because of their close association with education for skilled work, vocational-technical programs often emphasize manual skills rather than theoretical knowledge. Some vocational educators feel that technicians cannot validly be distinguished from skilled workers, nor technician training from skill training. From their viewpoint, vocational programs should simply seek to match industry's increasing need for skilled workers who have broad theoretical backgrounds.

In the West and Midwest, junior colleges represent another important effort to provide technician training within institutions originally designed for other purposes. Many of the junior colleges were established to provide the first two years of the liberal arts college program. However, they have generally been closer to community needs than other colleges and less bound by traditional curricula. As the demand for technical workers increased, the junior college was the logical institution to fill the need in areas where there were few technical institutes. Technical training in the junior colleges also seemed the best way to meet the needs of the growing number of high school graduates who did not intend to go to college and had not prepared for any particular job.

More than half of all junior college students are in California. The philosophy that every young person should receive as much education as he can benefit from has been widely accepted there. Reinforced by the difficulties of coordinating vocational and general education in the high schools, this viewpoint has led to the conclusion that most vocational instruction should be moved from the high school into the junior college. The high school orientation of junior college vocational and technical education in California is increased by the fact that it is aided by Federal vocational funds. These funds are available only for instruction of less than college grade and many vocational and technical courses duplicate trade and industrial training in the high schools, except that they are adapted to take advantage of the greater maturity of junior college students. On the other hand, some of the junior colleges in California and elsewhere have made pioneering advances in the development of formal instruction for technical occupations.

Junior college enrollment is now about 570,000. Three fourths of the students are in the West and Midwest. More than 85 percent of the students are in publicly supported institutions, most of them locally controlled. About 35,000 of the students are preparing for jobs as engineering, science, or health technicians or as skilled workers. Another 56,000 are preparing for wholesale and retail distribution, and less than 20,000 each for agriculture and home economics. The junior colleges also offer part-time and evening courses. Most of them now admit non-high school graduates who can profit from the instruction, and about two thirds of all students are adults or special students.

Technical institutes, unlike junior colleges, concentrate exclusively on occupational training. The first technical institutes were founded in the United States over a century ago, but most of the early schools evolved into degree-granting engineering schools. The development of today's institutes stems mainly from the years after World War I. Almost all technical institute students are found in four types of schools, as shown in the following table:

Table 4. Students in Technical Institutes, January, 1954

	Day	Part-time and Evening	Total
State and municipal	10,200	7,900	18,100
Privately endowed	2,800	7,800	10,600
Extension divisions of colleges and universities	3,000	9,800	12,800
Proprietary	5,800	3,400	9,200
Total	21,800	28,900	50,700

Source: "Annual Survey of Technical Institutes for 1953-4," prepared by Leo F. Smith, Dean of Instruction, Rochester Institute of Technology, *Technical Education News*, August, 1954.

Of the twenty-two state and municipal technical institutes, thirteen are in New York State. The latter enroll about five sixths of the students. Six of the other nine are in the North Atlantic region, as are most of the twelve privately endowed institutes. The thirteen extension divisions and the twenty-four proprietary institutes are scattered across the nation. During the last four years, enrollment in publicly supported institutions has increased substantially. Enrollment in the endowed schools has remained stable. The proprietary schools, private schools run for profit, have lost substantial ground as World War II veterans have completed training under the GI bill. In business and technical education and in other fields, the GI bill led to rapid expansion of enrollments and to the hasty establishment of many new proprietary schools. Within a few years the sharp decline in veteran enrollments not only put many of the new schools out of business, but also endangered the financial positions of some old and reputable institutions.

The schools covered by the survey summarized in the preceding table graduated over 6,200 engineering and science technicians in 1953. The largest number, about 2,400, were electrical technology graduates. About 1,400 were in various mechanical fields, including drafting, machine and tool design, instrumentation, steam and diesel engines, and welding. Over 600 were graduates of aeronautical courses, and about the same number, of architectural, building, and civil technology courses.

These figures do not accurately represent the extent of technical institute education. They include only schools which concentrate primarily on industrial technology. They exclude not only junior colleges, but also medical technician and business schools. Perhaps one fourth of the listed enrollments, however, are in such non-industrial fields as agriculture, business, graphic arts, health services, and home economics. Some schools listed by the survey failed to supply enrollment data.

The figures for proprietary technical institutes are particularly incomplete. Some refuse to cooperate in the annual survey, and others are excluded because the survey is confined to schools of the type accredited by the Engineers Council for Professional Development and the National Council of Technical Schools. Scores of other private schools offering some technical training range from those which could almost qualify as approved technical institutes to trade schools with low standards. A directory issued in 1953 listed almost 4,000 private, non-degree granting schools, accredited or approved in one way or another, offering some form of occupational instruction.

Even among approved schools technical institute programs vary considerably, in part because they must be closely coordinated with the changing needs of industry. The students, many of whom are experienced workers paying substantial tuition fees in order to qualify for better jobs, know what they want. The private schools tend to concentrate on a single occupational field, such as electronics or aeronautical technology, while most of the public institutions offer courses in a number of fields. In any case, the student is likely to be prepared for a group of related jobs. Thus the graduate of a mechanical technician course might, with some experience, qualify as a laboratory assistant, a time-study man, a power plant operator, a tool designer, or a production supervisor.

Technical institute programs run from about one year to three and sometimes even four years, though the most usual length is two years. They are often arranged so that the student can drop out at the end of any semester with training which he can put to immediate use. By staying an additional term he can qualify for a more responsible position or a wider range of jobs. All accredited institutes require high school graduation or its equivalent for admission.

Curricula invariably include courses in mathematics and science, in the theory of the specific field, and in the practical application of general principles to specific problems in laboratory or shop. The relative emphasis on manual skills as opposed to theoretical knowledge varies considerably depending on the school and the field of study, but accredited schools place primary emphasis on mathematics and science. A few technical institutes offer cooperative work-study programs.

The role of general education is now a lively issue in the technical institute field, just as it is in the vocational high school and the engineering college. Originally, most institutes offered little or no general education. Many of the private schools still offer nothing in this area beyond a few courses in technical English. Students are generally not eager to devote their time and their money to courses which do not have an obvious relationship to their intended jobs. Some technical institute educators maintain that in such fields as electronics and aviation, qualified technicians cannot be trained in two years unless at least 80 or 90 percent of the curriculum is devoted to specialized courses. There is, however, a trend in the other direction. In the New York State institutes, one fifth of the curriculum is devoted to general courses.

The primary intent of all technical institutes is to provide practical, terminal training. Yet, since many of their students have the ability to complete engineering courses, the institutes have had to concern themselves with the needs of those who decide that they want to go on for a bachelor's degree. This has meant further changes in curricula, together with efforts to persuade the colleges to grant for institute work at least some credit toward a degree.

Because of these and other developments, technical institute programs have assumed many of the characteristics of junior colleges. At the same time, technical curricula in the junior colleges have assumed some of the features of technical institutes. The original differences between the two kinds of schools, reflecting the primarily academic orientation of the one and the industrial training orientation of the other, have been growing less pronounced. Admission requirements have become more formal in the institutes, less so in many junior colleges. The junior colleges have given increasing attention to specific occupational training, and less to general scientific background, academic education, and college preparation. The technical institutes have moved from training for single jobs to broad training for groups of related jobs. They have given growing attention to scientific background and general education. The five new institutes established in New York in 1946 are now legally designated as community colleges. Little distinguishes them from the junior colleges elsewhere except that they still concentrate mainly on occupational training.

Training for one group of technical occupations, health technicians, is concentrated in hospitals and in university schools of dentistry and medicine. Many of the hospitals combine in-school and on-the-job training programs. The number of students enrolled and the number graduated in 1951 from schools approved by the American Medical and Dental Associations is shown in the following Table:

Table 5. Enrollment and Graduation of Health Technicians, 1951

	Enrollment	Graduation
Occupational therapists	1,971	411
Physical therapists	723*	585
Medical record librarians	176*	58
Medical technicians	3,518	2,220
X-ray technicians	1,907*	1,080
Practical nurses	6,711	n.a.
Dental hygienists	1,454	632

n.a. — not available

* Capacity rather than actual enrollment

Source: *A Report to the President of the President's Commission on the Health Needs of the Nation*, 1952, Vol. 3, and *Journal of the American Medical Association*, Hospital Number, May 10, 1952.

Many schools not accredited by these associations, including some of the public technical institutes as well as private schools, also train health technicians. The term "technician," like the term "skilled worker," includes occupations with widely different minimum training requirements. Thus, occupational and physical therapists are usually college graduates with several years of postgraduate training. On the other hand, practical nurses are often trained through high school or correspondence courses. Practical nursing is taught as part of the vocational trade and industrial program in the high schools of 158 communities in 41 states.

CORRESPONDENCE SCHOOLS

For many years, a significant amount of technical instruction has been provided by correspondence schools. There are now some 300 private correspondence schools with estimated enrollment of about one million. Another 175,000 students are enrolled in correspondence courses given by university extension divisions. The forty-two schools accredited by the National Home Study Council account for about 80 percent of enrollment in private schools. Probably about 300,000 of these students are taking courses in the skilled and technician occupations.

Correspondence instruction, because of its nature, must concentrate on technical information even in courses for skilled workers. The vocational and technical correspondence courses serve the same types of people who enroll in parallel evening courses — young, ambitious workers seeking knowledge to qualify for promotion or to keep a new job. About 5,000 companies have contracts through which their employees may take at company expense either regular correspondence courses or specially developed courses. Because the larger schools have very large enrollments scattered all over the country, they are able to offer a great variety of courses, many not available in the residence schools of most localities.

A typical vocational-technical course, in radio or television repair, for instance, consists of 75 to 100 lessons, each based on a booklet of more than fifty pages and requiring about fifteen hours of work by the student. To pass the course the student must complete a written assignment on each lesson, which is sent to the school for grading and comment. The graduates of reputable schools seem to have considerable ambition and self-discipline, and the ability to read with understanding and to express themselves clearly in writing.

VOCATIONAL EDUCATION AND THE DEVELOPMENT OF SKILLED WORKERS

Vocational education for skilled workers and technicians embraces a great variety of public and private efforts. The total cost of the vocational training provided in the public high schools, junior colleges, and technical institutes has never been calculated but runs to many millions of dollars annually. The national importance of training for skilled and technical work is suggested by the extent to which the Federal government has become involved in it. Federally sponsored and supported training activities during World War II were directed mainly toward training workers, technicians, and foremen. Most of the enormous school structure of the armed forces today is devoted to training for skilled and technical positions. Federal law and Federal funds have made vocational education in the public high schools the closest approach to a uniform system of education that exists in the United States. Although the Federal government is deeply involved in vocational education, it does not have a comprehensive policy that relates its vocational education activities to its other educational programs, to its policies for skilled and technical manpower, or to the multiplicity of other institutions which contribute to the development of skilled workers.

Partly because it is, in some respects, a national system, the Federal-state program has dominated most discussions of vocational education problems. Each year, however, hundreds of thousands of people receive formal vocational instruction in other schools. High school education which is not specifically vocational also constitutes important preparation for work. The largest part of the skills and distinctive abilities of the country's skilled workers and technicians, moreover, is acquired on the job rather than in school.

Improving the means through which skilled workers are developed therefore requires careful consideration of all these institutions — and of how they can be better used together to increase the opportunities of individuals and the quality of the nation's labor force. ▸

CHAPTER VIII

How Workers Become Skilled

Skilled workers and technicians are developed in the United States in diverse ways. Some acquire their skills through apprenticeship or other formal training programs. Others become skilled workers through processes extending over considerable time in which formal training plays a small role. Thus a young man may become an apprentice when he completes high school, but this frequently occurs today only after he has tried out several jobs. More likely, he may simply pick up certain skills in several different jobs through observation and imitation, and he may also have the advantage of some measure of formal training organized by his employers. He may have gained some of his skills by pursuing a vocational course in high school or from his training and experience in the armed forces. His on-the-job learning may be supplemented by evening courses in public or private trade schools or by correspondence courses.

On the other hand, instead of going to work when he finishes high school the young man who later becomes a skilled worker may return to school full time to acquire certain skills. The school he attends may be a public vocational high school which admits high school graduates, a private trade school, or even a junior or community college. If he enters apprenticeship, it may be a formal training program, or it may consist only of an "understanding" that, as opportunities present themselves, he will be given the chance to learn parts of a given trade. Moreover, even if he leaves formal apprenticeship before completion, he may be able to secure employment as a skilled worker either immediately or after further work experience.

The technician may also acquire his specific abilities in many different ways. He is more likely than the skilled worker to be trained in a vocational high school, trade school, or junior college, but he, too, may acquire his skill through apprenticeship, informal on-the-job training or experience, part-time schooling, service in the armed forces, and through correspondence courses.

The existence of many ways for developing skilled and technical workers helps to explain why employers emphasize general qualities, rather than specific skills and abilities, in younger job applicants. At the time of hiring, it is often far from clear who among the new employees will become technicians or skilled workers or what particular occupations they will eventually enter. The conferences held by the National Manpower Council indicated that few employers regard the maintenance of an adequate supply of skilled and technical workers as a problem requiring exceptional attention. Many employers take it for granted that enough skilled workers are developed through a sort of "natural process" to meet normal needs.

Although it is well known to industrial managers, training specialists, and labor economists, the diversity of ways in which skills are acquired in the United States has not been adequately described. The literature on industrial training deals primarily with apprenticeship and the practical training problems faced by foremen. The experience of World War II, when a rapid expansion of war production was achieved by bringing large numbers of inexperienced workers into industry, intensified concern with supervisory and foreman training. The training of foremen during the war years provided them mainly with methods of instructing production workers, usually at the semi-skilled level. The interest in foreman training and methods of instruction has continued to the present. Increasing importance has been given to the "human relations" skills of foremen and to their functions as representatives of management who deal with workers on a day to day basis.

TRAINING IN INDUSTRY

Apprenticeship and the instruction of foremen in training techniques represent part of the total investment made by employers in training. Most industrial training is given informally on the job and is oriented to immediate production or service needs. It is largely in the hands of supervisory personnel in charge of operations. There has been a marked growth in the number of training departments within large firms in the past fifteen years, but these generally have staff responsibility for advising and assisting operating departments in meeting their training requirements.

Industrial training is seldom organized in a formal and continuing program. Training is used to meet spot needs, such as those arising when a new worker is added or an older worker changes jobs, when operations are expanded, or when new methods and techniques are introduced. Sometimes, when several workers are involved, special training groups or classes are set up. Such training at the semi-skilled level is generally part of the production process and of an *ad hoc* character, rather than part of a planned program in skill development. Yet it frequently contributes to the development of skilled workers.

The semi-skilled worker is often represented as an automaton who is quickly and easily trained to perform routine operations, but the title "semi-skilled" actually includes workers at many levels of skill. Many semi-skilled jobs can be mastered in a few days or weeks, but others require training over a period of several months, a year, or even more to insure average proficiency. During a more extended training period, the semi-skilled worker may be taught by his foreman or a skilled worker, but he is more than likely to learn as much by imitation and actual experience as from explicit instruction.

Some firms have established formal programs, which are not apprenticeships, for training technicians. For instance, several of the larger automobile and electrical equipment manufacturers, as well as companies in the communications fields, have their own technical institutes. Student-employees attend part time in the evenings, or on a combined work-study basis. Many firms, by covering all or part of the tuition costs, offer opportunities for employees to enroll in outside technical institutes or take correspondence courses.

Many companies also provide more general courses, usually in night-school classes, which contribute to an unmeasurable extent to the skills of their work force. Among these are courses in blueprint reading, mathematics, the scientific aspects of a particular industry (for example, electricity, electronics, metallurgy, physics, or chemistry), and the technology of the firm and industry. Participation in such courses depends on the initiative of the individual worker.

In addition to publicly supported vocational schools, technical institutes, and junior colleges, there are other public agencies upon which industrial firms may call for assistance with training programs. Some state university systems carry on foreman training in special institutes and night classes. The Federal and state apprenticeship agencies offer advice on methods of training apprentices. The Federal Bureau of Apprenticeship also provides advice through its Skill Improvement Program to help solve training problems of employers which involve semi-skilled workers as well as journeymen.

Trade unions have traditionally taken a great interest in the education and training of their members. Many unions play an important role in the development and administration of apprenticeship programs. In addition some in the printing, the electrical, the clothing, and other fields have established trade schools for training their members independently or in cooperation with employers.

SOURCES OF SKILLED WORKERS

Table 6 represents one attempt, following a method used by the Bureau of Apprenticeship, to indicate the relative importance of various sources of skilled workers. Of the approximately

8 million workers reported by the 1950 Census as "craftsmen, foremen, and kindred workers," about 5 million are in occupations which are registered in the Federal apprenticeship program. The Bureau estimates that approximately 250,000 workers leave apprenticeable occupations each year because of death, retirement, and shifts to other employment. Because of the stability of the total "craftsmen, foremen, and kindred workers" category, the replacement "need" indicated is a convenient reference point for showing the significance of the different sources from which skilled workers come.

Table 6. Estimated Annual Additions to the Skilled Labor Force to Meet Replacement Need

Estimated replacement need...................		250,000
Source		
Number completing apprenticeships registered with the Bureau of Apprenticeship............	30,000–40,000	
Number not completing registered apprenticeships, but subsequently qualifying as skilled workers	15,000–20,000	
Number fully or partially trained in nonregistered apprenticeships	35,000	
Number of skilled immigrants..	10,000	
Number graduating from vocational schools...............	1,000	
Additions from "identified" sources...............		91,000–106,000
Balance presumed to have acquired their skills through informal training and experience.........		144,000–159,000

Source: U. S. Bureau of Apprenticeship, Immigration and Naturalization Service, and Office of Education.

The Bureau of Apprenticeship reports that 30,000 to 40,000 apprentices who are registered with the Bureau complete their training each year and that about 15,000 to 20,000 workers who had left registered apprenticeships without completing training qualify as skilled workers. It is difficult to determine precisely how many skilled workers are developed by other formal training programs. Many apprenticeship programs are not registered with the Bureau of Apprenticeship. Moreover, there are other programs which produce workers with skills held to be comparable to the graduates of traditional apprenticeships. The Bureau of Apprenticeship estimates that nonregistered apprenticeships number from one fifth to one third of registered apprenticeships. But other estimates indicate that, each year, perhaps 35,000 workers who previously had partially or fully completed such programs enter the skilled labor force.

Since 1948, the highest reported annual figure for immigrants classified by the Immigration and Naturalization Service as "craftsmen, foremen, and kindred workers" was 21,832 in 1950. The lowest was 11,019 in 1948. In 1953 only 12,257 immigrants were reported as skilled and, under present immigration policies, there seems little reason to anticipate an increase. The shortcomings of classifying workers by job title have already been discussed. Some occupations classified as skilled in other countries are not so regarded in the United States. It seems safe to estimate the annual addition to the skilled groups through immigration now and in the near future at about 10,000.

Very few vocational school graduates spend enough time in shopwork to be able to enter the labor force as skilled workers, although it has been estimated that each year perhaps 30,000 graduates secure employment in the fields in which they were trained. The survey of vocational school graduates upon which this figure is based suggests that most of them were not skilled, since their reported average wage was far below prevailing wages in the skilled trades. Almost all vocational school graduates who later become skilled workers do so through apprenticeship, informal training, or on-the-job experience. A few may go directly into skilled positions, but probably no more than 1,000.

In summary, Table 6 suggests that less than two in five of the replacements required to maintain the present size of the skilled worker group in apprenticeable occupations have any contact with apprenticeship in the course of their training, although this ratio will vary widely in different occupations and industries. About 60 percent of the replacements acquire their skills informally through work experience and incidental training. Moreover, there are several skilled occupations which are not considered apprenticeable — for example, locomotive engineer and fireman, roller and mill hand, and log inspectors.

These estimates of replacements make no provision for growth in the skilled occupations. In recent years the skilled groups have been growing more rapidly than the labor force as a whole. It follows, therefore, that, of the number necessary for replacement and growth, well over 60 percent acquire their skills in some informal manner, and only one in four receive part or all of their training in apprenticeship or in similar programs. This conclusion is supported by a significant body of independent evidence. For example, the findings of a study made for the Social Science Research Council show that only one fifth of the workers who held skilled jobs between 1940 and 1950 had ever been in an apprenticeship program. Much remains to be learned about the ways skilled workers are developed. Enough is known, however, to make it clear that formal apprenticeship and similar programs, while important training institutions, do not account for the bulk of the skilled workers added to the labor force in recent years.

The available information also shows that much of the training of technicians is informal. Institutes and schools for technicians in the engineering, medical, and other fields are becoming increasingly important in providing formal training. Many graduates, however, have to be given additional training after they are employed, as do graduates of armed services programs for technicians. Many of the testing technicians and laboratory assistants currently employed in private industry have not had extensive formal training of any kind.

OCCUPATIONAL STRUCTURE AND INFORMAL ACQUISITION OF SKILL

Since very few new entrants to the labor force are employed as skilled workers, the growth of the skilled group is heavily dependent upon the development of skills in the course of experience in several jobs or work assignments. In the movement up the skill ladder, the combination of promotion and changing jobs plays a critical role.

Some understanding of the ways in which work is characteristically organized in industry is essential to an appreciation of how workers become skilled as a result of upgrading or changing jobs. The arbitrary division of labor into three grades — unskilled, semi-skilled, and skilled — obscures the existence of broad, overlapping categories of workers with varying degrees of skills. Within the total occupational structure, the range of jobs runs from the unskilled to the very highly skilled. Where there are related jobs at intermediate levels of skill, a worker may move from job to job with relative ease. Each successive job demands more in the way of distinctive abilities, but it also offers opportunities for learning additional skills. Where there are significant differences in the abilities required for successive jobs in the skill ladder, it may be difficult to move up without specific training.

The intensive specialization of function found in modern economies consists in part of the breakdown of skilled jobs. For instance, a number of metal machining operations may ordinarily be performed by one machinist, but, if the volume of production is large enough, individual workers may be assigned to component parts of the whole job. It may be more efficient to keep each worker at a particular machine on which he performs a few operations requiring a minimum of training. Many present-day production systems originally grew out of the breakdown of skills. With the passage of time, they underwent further change and became dependent on highly specialized machinery, with the result that the functions performed by the semi-skilled workers in these systems no longer resemble separate elements of a once skilled trade. There is also little continuity with earlier handicraft occupations in some production systems involving new products or based on new techniques. In modern production systems which consist of a series of single, specialized functions, most of the workers may be at the same limited skill level. The typical example is an assembly line operation, but even this requires some skilled workers in supporting roles.

In many other production systems it is more efficient to have a range of jobs extending from routine semi-skilled to highly skilled. In a modern machine shop, as well as elsewhere, it is common practice to distinguish three different grades of skill for each type of machine, such as Class A, B, and C drill press or milling machine operators. In addition, there will be "all-round," "set-up," and "lay-out" machinists who perform the more demanding tasks of organizing the specific operations to be performed by less skilled workers.

With large scale operations, many functions are moved out of the immediate production area, at least administratively if not physically. Thus departments are set up for research and design, engineering and drafting, model and pattern-building, and repair and maintenance, just as there are separate tool and die shops. In such departments or shops, operations are on a smaller scale than in the main production shops, and extreme specialization by function is less common. Normally, the proportion of professional, technical, and skilled workers found in these departments is large. Sometimes, however, a department or shop operates on a scale large enough to warrant the use of many workers at lower levels of skill.

In a small research department, for example, an engineer or scientist may be assisted by a few technicians, whose functions are general rather than specific. In a larger department, there are likely to be many technicians, each with specialized functions. Similarly, in a design department, drafting functions may be performed by workers of different grades of skill, beginning with tracers who merely copy the work of others. In a large maintenance department there may be anywhere from two to six labor grades in each trade group, such as pipefitters, electricians, machinists, and the like. On the other hand, if maintenance needs are small, handymen or general mechanics may be the only grades of workers found.

Where the system of production requires continuous or nearly continuous operations, as in oil, steel, and chemicals, extensive use is made of crews of workers. Here, the crew as a whole, as well as each of its individual members, has specialized functions. There are different grades of workers in a crew, with the more skilled workers performing a coordinating function in addition to being responsible for their own specific tasks. A graded crew or team system is also found sometimes in tool and die, design, and similar operations requiring considerable integration of duties.

The helper system found in the maintenance and building trades resembles the crew system. A skilled worker generally has one helper — sometimes two or more — who works under his immediate supervision. The helper gets supplies and tools, holds work in place, cleans up after a job, and assists the skilled worker in still other ways.

THE ROLE OF PROMOTION IN THE ACQUISITION OF SKILL

The practice of distinguishing grades of labor for the purpose of assigning functions and wage rates provides the basis for a system of promotion. Promotion is part of the process of skill development. When a worker is promoted from one job to another, he is exposed to a new range of experience, enabling him to acquire different and, presumably, more advanced skills. He may also have the benefit of special training, either before or after promotion, in order to fulfill the immediate requirements of the job. The promotion system thus operates as a means for developing skilled workers, as well as a means for advancing workers because they have acquired skills.

Broadly speaking, the process of progression from an unskilled to a skilled job consists of the following: training and experience in a given job; exposure to the work of more skilled workers; incidental experience in the next higher job; accumulation of seniority; and some specific training, usually in connection with promotion, if it is needed.

Promotion in large-scale industry frequently is strongly influenced by seniority. Workers who have been with a company longest have first claim to promotion when a position opens up. Even when such a claim is purely a matter of custom, it carries considerable weight, for the injury to morale and work performance which may result when it is ignored is well known.

The customary claim to promotion on the basis of seniority has been formalized in many collective bargaining contracts. Seniority provisions originally were used mainly to provide job security, by requiring that when workers are laid off, those with the longest service are laid off last and, when recalls to work are issued, are rehired first. However, seniority has been used increasingly as a basis for promotion. The provisions of most collective bargaining contracts state that management will consider some combination of abilities, aptitudes, and seniority in determining who is to be promoted. Practices vary with the union, the management, and the local situation. There has, however, been a growing tendency for unions to require that management prove that a worker, promoted ahead of other workers with seniority, has a greater measure of ability and aptitude for his new job. Management's mere assertion that a worker is more able does not always satisfy the unions, which frequently demand evidence based on "objective" criteria. To date, however, objective methods for determining what aptitudes are necessary for various jobs have been lacking.

Where a more or less rigid seniority structure exists, new employees are almost always assigned to relatively unskilled tasks. There may be several wage grades within the unskilled category. While a worker accumulates seniority, he normally works near or with employees in the next higher grade and can observe them. When a worker in the next higher grade is temporarily absent because of illness or vacation, some one in a grade below may replace him. This may set in motion a temporary upward movement among still lower grades of workers. When an employee has sufficient seniority to bid for an open position in the grade above his, he may already be able to perform some of the tasks attached to it and need very little additional training to handle his new job.

The structure of the seniority system and the way in which opportunities appear, as well as the particular industry, will largely determine which skilled or technical occupation an unskilled worker employed by a large firm will finally enter. Commonly, each major division or department of an enterprise — such as production, maintenance, and various specialized shops — has its own seniority system. There may also be separate seniority systems for each occupational group. Workers entering at the unskilled level in a particular department normally advance in grade within that department. Sometimes, however, different departments draw upon workers grouped in a pool of unskilled labor. In some cases workers can use their seniority in one department to bid for openings in another. Where workers bid out of production departments for openings in maintenance, their familiarity with the machines on which they will work has prepared them at least in part for their new tasks. In other instances the seniority structure may permit workers to bid for positions for which they have little preparation.

Under a strict seniority system promotion tends to be automatic, because even gross differences in skill or performance may be disregarded. Average performance at each assignment may be enough to warrant promotion where there is sufficient seniority, and, given enough time, most workers can progress at least part of the way up the skill ladder. Some workers, however, are unwilling to undertake the training required for more skilled jobs or to assume the greater responsibilities which they may involve. On the other hand, under a strict seniority system, management may have little opportunity to reward ambitious workers who have little seniority.

Where the seniority system is less rigid, the interests and initiative of individual workers are likely to have an immediate and important bearing on their development as skilled workers. Workers who are observant and make the most of their opportunities to learn are prepared, at less training cost to the employer, to move up when a higher position becomes open. Many workers strengthen their claim for promotion by taking advantage of such opportunities for skill acquisition as their employers may offer and by enrolling in night school and correspondence courses.

In research units many future technicians start as clerical or maintenance workers, messengers, bottle washers, and the like. As a result of their work experience, and depending on their interests, they acquire some familiarity with the techniques and language of the laboratory. They may then be assigned as assistants to professionally trained personnel. In their new assignments they will necessarily acquire a new set of skills. Many workers now classed as medical technicians were trained in this manner.

The extent to which an employee's experience prepares him for promotion also depends on the attitudes of his foreman and fellow workers. If foremen are insensitive to the organization's future needs for skilled workers and to an employee's desire to learn, the latter's opportunities to learn may be limited. The same situation will result where senior workers actively resist or are indifferent to the acquisition of skill by junior employees. On the other hand, indifference on the part of a skilled worker may enable an aggressive helper to take on more and more responsibilities. Where management realizes that the promotion system is also a training system, attitudes favorable to the acquisition of skill are encouraged. In a few cases, companies have encouraged skill development by rotating workers through several semi-skilled jobs at the same pay level.

CHANGING JOBS AND THE ACQUISITION OF SKILL

Many workers in moving from one semi-skilled job to another with different firms pick up abilities which eventually enable them to become skilled workers and technicians. This process of acquiring skill cannot be described with great precision. As in the process of skill development in which promotion plays a key role, the significant elements include experience; exposure to the work of more skilled workers; incidental instruction by foremen and other skilled workers; and supplementary training provided by technical, vocational, and correspondence schools.

For some occupations, fairly definite routes to the skilled level through changing jobs have been identified. For instance, many electronic technicians were employed in radio and television repair work before they found jobs in broadcasting, research, and various manufacturing operations. The Bureau of Labor Statistics of the U. S. Department of Labor reports that the training of construction machinery operators takes place in connection with changing jobs.

A man with aptitude for machinery and often some relevant experience, such as driving a truck, may get a job operating one of the simpler machines (a pump, an air compressor, a tractor without attachments, etc.). . . . As opportunity affords, he may get more exacting jobs (on a bulldozer, a tractor with other power attachments, a roller, various other machines) and then with more experience get a job on one of the top-grade machines.

Many helpers in the building trades acquire enough experience to undertake jobs as skilled workers on crude or rough work before undertaking work of higher quality with another employer. Some helpers obtain jobs as skilled maintenance workers in manufacturing plants where such positions are not filled by the training or upgrading of their own employees. Skilled factory maintenance workers acquire new skills by moving into the construction industry. Apparently it is a common practice for many who want to become tool and die makers and machinists to move from one small shop to another in order to acquire experience and skill. This kind of movement, for the purpose of gaining broader experience, frequently continues long after the status of journeyman machinist or tool and die maker is achieved. Some machinists become tool and die makers in the same way.

Small shops also afford training opportunities to many mechanics in the automobile, office machine, and appliance repair fields. Because there is less extreme specialization in small shops, a relatively unskilled worker who is interested has opportunities to learn a number of skills and prepare himself for a better job elsewhere. Many skilled repair mechanics begin in their occupations by doing work at home on a part-time basis. As they acquire experience and skill, they may devote more time to repair work.

As in the case of promotions which are not based solely on seniority, advancement by changing jobs depends very much on the initiative of the individual worker. In many cases the motivation to acquire additional skill may not appear until the worker has had related experiences in several jobs. These give him a basis upon which he can capitalize in seeking jobs which in turn provide opportunities for further enhancing his skills. Of course, many workers who move among semi-skilled jobs never acquire the experience that will enable them to seek skilled work.

In some cases workers change jobs primarily in order to use skills they already have. A helper's skill may never be recognized, for example, because he is not the product of a formal training program. If he secures employment as a skilled worker with an employer who does not know his job history, he may be able to perform satisfactorily enough to justify his skill classification. Where the helper is hired as a skilled worker, but still lacks some essential skills, he may be able to hide his shortcomings while acquiring additional skills on the job or in night school. In a tight labor market the employer may be satisfied to pay journeyman wages to a worker who is not fully qualified, but who will be willing to use his job to train himself.

Employment opportunities at all skill grades are likely to appear, of course, when new shops or plants are set up. Firms which ordinarily fill skilled positions through promotion may not be able to pursue that policy when expanding their skilled labor force rapidly. If there are not enough workers ready for upgrading, seniority systems may be overlooked and workers hired from the outside at intermediate or higher skill grades.

In the process of informal skill acquisition through changing jobs the worker's prior education and nonwork experience are significant. These may provide a solid foundation for subsequent training, both formal and informal. Experience with machine tools in vocational school will make it easier for a worker ultimately to become a machinist by picking up skills. Many people enter employment with some experience on automobile repair, carpentry, painting, and electricity, as a result of home and farm maintenance and repair. Radio construction as a childhood hobby contributed to the development of many electronic technicians.

Experience and training in the armed services, as has been seen in Chapter IV, also provide many workers with skills which help them obtain employment at an intermediate wage grade, as well as a foundation for the informal acquisition of further skills. Skill development by routes other than apprenticeship is thus likely to be more common in occupations found in both the armed forces and the civilian economy. Among these are motor vehicle and airplane repair mechanics and electronic technicians.

APPRENTICESHIP

Compared to the process of becoming a skilled worker through promotion and changing jobs, apprenticeship seems clear and simple. It involves a formal agreement covering a definite period of time which binds the employer to provide training in his shop in return for the work of the apprentice. The agreement stipulates the wages of the apprentice and the graduated increases he is to receive. Over the life of the agreement, most apprentices now average better than half the standard pay of the skilled workman or journeyman. Most apprenticeships run between two and four years, but some last as long as eight.

Most apprentices in the United States are in programs registered with the Bureau of Apprenticeship of the Department of Labor. The Bureau's statutory responsibility to promote apprenticeship is fulfilled by encouraging and assisting state apprenticeship authorities, employers, employers' associations, and labor unions to develop and establish apprenticeship programs. It also acts as a central research and statistical agency, maintaining a register of all apprentices in approved programs. The Bureau has no coercive powers, and apprenticeship programs exist on a voluntary basis.

The Bureau has established criteria for the occupations which fall within its program. An apprenticeable occupation, according to the Bureau's criteria, is one which (a) has customarily been learned in a practical way through training and work experience on the job; (b) is clearly identified and commonly recognized throughout an industry; (c) involves the development of skills sufficiently broad to be applicable in like occupations throughout an industry, rather than of skills the application of which is restricted to the products of one company; (d) requires at least two years of work experience to learn; (e) calls for related instruction supplementary to the work experience (144 hours of such instruction during each year of the apprenticeship is the minimum); (f) is not merely a part of an apprenticeable trade; and (g) is not a selling, retailing, or similar occupation in the distributive field, or a managerial, clerical, professional, semiprofessional, or agricultural occupation. These criteria are not always rigidly maintained, however.

Apprenticeship programs which do not meet one or another of these criteria lie outside the scope of the Bureau's activities. These criteria are traditional in nature and therefore tend to exclude new and developing occupations. As the technology evolves, new occupations may appear which combine old and new techniques and cut across established trade lines. For instance, welding techniques were originally introduced into the jobs of boilermakers, structural steel workers, machinists, and automobile mechanics. There are now many skilled welders, but the Federal program does not recognize welding as an apprenticeable occupation, even though many state apprenticeship programs do. On the other hand, the programs of state agencies are sometimes more conservative than the Federal program.

The Bureau of Apprenticeship recognizes some 300 apprenticeable skilled and technical occupations. Examples of these and of standard lengths of apprenticeship are given in Table 7. The standard period may be reduced because of prior related training or experience or rapid learning by the apprentice.

Table 7. Selected Apprenticeable Occupations Classified by Standard Length of Apprenticeship

Two Years
Alteration tailor
Construction ironworker
Cosmetician
Female bookbindery worker

Two or Three Years
Barber
Butter or cheese maker
Shoe repairman

Three or Four Years
Aircraft fabricator
Automotive mechanic
Draftsman
Dry cleaner
Farm equipment mechanic
Orthopedic-prosthetic technician
Stationary engineer

Four Years
Carpenter
Coremaker
Optical technician

Three to Five Years
Electrician (including electronic
   technician)
Wood carver

Four or Five Years
Die maker
Engraver
Plumber-pipe fitter
Printing pressman
Tool and die repairman

Five Years
Bank note designer
Patternmaker

Five or Six Years
Electrotyper
Photoengraver

Four to Eight Years
Die sinker

Before the Federal program started in 1934, apprenticeship as an institution was kept alive through the efforts of both trade unions and employers. Many collective bargaining contracts, consequently, contain provisions dealing with apprenticeship. The Federal program encourages the formation of employer-employee joint apprenticeship committees at the plant or, in the case of the building trades, at the community level. These committees deal with such questions as the age for entering apprenticeship; aptitudes, education, and physical fitness required; hours of work; wages; the number of apprentices to be employed; training standards; the scheduling of work and training; and classroom instruction in trade related subjects.

The question of how many apprentices are to be trained in a given shop or firm is of primary importance. The usual practice is to set a fixed ratio between the number of journeymen and apprentices. This ratio now runs from one apprentice for every three, to one for every twenty, journeymen. The most common ratios are one to five and one to ten.

The employment outlook in a particular trade is a major determinant of the actual ratio set. Many unions try to adjust the number of apprentices so as to maintain a supply of skilled workers which corresponds to fluctuations in demand. Most unions tend to be conservative in this matter, however, and prefer shortages to over-supplies in the trade. Sometimes the actual ratio set seems to bear no discernable relationship to demand. In *Union Policies and Industrial Management,* published in 1941, Sumner H. Slichter concluded that, with some exceptions, unions do not unduly restrict the supply of apprentices. "As a rule," he wrote, "the union members wish to place more boys as apprentices than the employers are willing to take." More recent studies confirm these findings. Unions in printing and the building trades, however, have been charged with maintaining restrictive practices. By and large, unions have actively promoted apprenticeship and have sought to induce employers to expand their training activities, although sometimes there are differences between national policy and local practice.

The content of apprenticeship training is ordinarily set forth in a schedule worked out by the local apprenticeship committee which specifies so many hours of experience for each type of work or machine. Because apprenticeship is institutionalized, training content may not be easily adjusted to changes in technology. Such adjustments, however, are constantly being made, as in the railway repair trades, following the change from steam to Diesel locomotives. Modification of training content usually comes in response to major, practical difficulties. Some changes are made on the initiative of the local union, firm, or both. Several national unions, including the brickmasons, the electricians, and the plumbers, in cooperation with national employers' associations, have recently completed an extensive analysis of the training content and methods of their apprenticeship programs. Training content is annually reviewed in the CIO United Automobile Workers' apprenticeship programs.

It is frequently asserted that unions arbitrarily set longer terms for apprenticeship than are necessary. The evidence, however, shows that the length of apprenticeship for a given occupation is much the same in union and nonunion shops. It may be noted that the terms of apprenticeship for bricklayers in the Bricklayers, Masons and Plasterers Union and for tool and die makers in the UAW-CIO have recently been reduced. As Table 7 indicates, the standard training time for a single occupation can vary considerably, sometimes as much as four years. There are several reasons for this. An occupational title is frequently only a broad classification. One industry may require better trained toolmakers than another. The skills of a maintenance electrician in a factory are different from those needed by a construction electrician. The existence of different training periods within a single industry suggests that skill requirements alone do not determine the length of the apprenticeship term. It is also influenced by such factors as tradition; the strength of a national or local union or an employers' association; and union rivalry in the same industry.

Most apprenticeship programs include a certain amount of classroom instruction in applied mathematics and sciences and in the production methods of the particular trade and industry. Usually these classes are held at the local vocational school, and a practicing journeyman is the instructor. In some cases, employers and unions permit apprentices to attend classes during working hours, for which time they are paid regular wages. In rural areas or where the number of apprentices does not justify setting up a class, correspondence courses are used. Many programs require more than the minimum of 144 class hours each year recommended in the Federal program. When the labor market is tight, employers show some reluctance to enforce class attendance.

TRENDS IN REGISTERED APPRENTICESHIP

The records of the Bureau of Apprenticeship show a rapid postwar growth in apprenticeship and a decline since the peak year of 1949, when there were some 235,000 registered apprentices, primarily because of the training of veterans receiving government benefits. The Bureau estimates 155,697 for 1954. The exact number of apprentices not registered with the Federal program is not known. The Bureau reports that they probably come to about one fifth the number of registered apprentices. In addition to non-registered apprenticeship programs there are other formal training programs designed to produce skilled workers. The total number of trainees in both these types of programs has been estimated as high as 300,000. Nonregistered apprenticeship is particularly important in the metal trades.

The construction trades currently have 54 percent of all registered apprentices. The metal trades — metal smithing, metal founding, and metal machining — now account for about 16 percent; the automotive and other repair trades for about 10 percent; the printing trades for some 8 percent. The remaining 12 percent are distributed in a number of other fields.

Apprenticeship has traditionally been a youth training program, but in recent years this has not been true. The minimum entering age still remains sixteen, but in 1952 only 2.5 percent of the registered apprentices were eighteen or less. At that time over half of the registered apprentices were twenty-six years or older; 22 percent were thirty or older; 7 percent were thirty-five or older; and more than 2 percent were forty or older.

In 1952 over 60 percent of the apprentices were veterans. Military service raises the average age of apprentices by interrupting or delaying training. Local Selective Service boards, employers, and apprentices fail to make full use of the current regulations which provide for the deferment of apprentices who have completed a year of their training, or six months if in a critical occupation.

A more important reason for the high average age of apprentices is that a great many enter registered programs with advanced standing on the basis of prior training and experience. One study indicates that 40 percent of those who either completed or withdrew from Federal apprenticeship programs in 1949 and 1950 had received some credit for previous training and experience. Half of them had received more than one year, and one fifth over two years, of credit. It has been charged that immediately after World War II, veterans received credit more generously than was warranted on the basis of their actual experience. Nearly 50 percent of the veterans who either completed or withdrew from apprenticeship in 1949 and 1950 had received advanced standing, but so did over 30 percent of the nonveterans. The practice of extending credit automatically to apprentices because of prior military service, work experience, schooling, or the like, is open to criticism. The Bureau of Apprenticeship, consequently, has encouraged local committees to grant credit on an individual basis for skills actually possessed. Many programs are protected from the consequence of gross errors made in granting advanced standing by the examinations which they set for their apprentices. A number of programs, however, have refused to extend advanced standing, although they have been under pressure to do so.

Apprenticeship does not stand apart from the development of skills by upgrading and changing jobs. This is shown by the large number of apprentices who receive advanced standing and by the extent to which apprentices who did not complete their training later became skilled workers. About as many apprentices leave before completion as complete their registered apprenticeship. According to a recent study, about three out of every ten of those who terminated their training in 1951 and 1952, without completing apprenticeship, were by 1954 working as journeymen in the trade for which they had trained. Another 12 percent were working in a closely related trade, and 7 percent were in some other trade.

Of the more than half who terminated apprenticeship some time after the second year, 42 percent were working as journeymen and 8 percent as foremen in trades for which they had trained. Another 9 percent were working in closely related trades. Some apprentices left training because they were able to obtain jobs as skilled workers, but others required more experience.

ASSESSMENTS OF INFORMAL AND FORMAL SYSTEMS

By the time a worker has had several years of experience in a skilled trade, it is likely to make little difference how he came to acquire his distinctive abilities and competence, particularly if learning on the job has been supplemented by background courses in vocational or correspondence schools. Yet a number of reasons may be cited to show that apprenticeship is a more desirable source for skilled workers than informal training. As a planned program, apprenticeship develops workers trained for an occupation, rather than for a job, who have been systematically exposed to the whole range of situations which they are likely to encounter in their trade. The formal system deters supervisors and foremen from diverting the apprentice from training to fulfill production needs. The worker broadly trained through apprenticeship can usually adjust more easily to changing conditions. He is likely to be more versatile and able to work on a wide range of jobs. As a result, management's task is made easier, because foremen are not compelled to match jobs to the skills of narrowly specialized workers.

Apprenticeship gives the skilled worker a recognized status and apparently an advantage in seeking new jobs, as well as greater job security. Moreover, just as the professions develop certain ethical standards of conduct, the traditions of apprenticeship tend to create a sense of job pride and responsibility and to maintain standards of work. Many firms select their foremen from among their apprentice-trained workers on the ground that they are thoroughly familiar with all phases of the work in a shop.

There is general agreement that apprenticeship training results in the benefits just outlined. However, it should also be noted that the establishment of some apprenticeship programs appears to be related only slightly to the question of the quality of training. There is evidence that some employers maintain apprenticeship programs rather than informal training programs chiefly because apprenticeship provides a better basis for requesting deferments from military service. Also, it is easier to obtain veterans' benefits for trainees in apprenticeship programs. There are also instances where apprenticeship programs are set up as a result of internal plant problems. Foremen under pressure to reduce wage costs may respond by using trainees in an informal program as fully as possible as production workers, with a consequent reduction in the time devoted to training. To reduce this pressure and to protect essential training, the informal program may be converted to an apprenticeship program with the wages of apprentices carried as a training, rather than a production, cost.

The advantages of informal training lie in the greater freedom, flexibility, and opportunity it affords. When training is formally organized, it may take three or four years to secure a large increase in the supply of skilled workers. Where there are many workers at an intermediate level of skill, it is possible to advance them to the skilled level in a relatively short time. Because formal programs respond less quickly to changes in demand, major dependence on them necessitates greater accuracy in forecasting future requirements for skilled workers. Where apprenticeship is the primary source of skilled workers, however, the program may be actively promoted by employers in order to insure an adequate future supply.

Changes in occupational content are usually more easily introduced in an informal training program. Such changes may be resisted by a union until it is certain that they do not threaten its members' security. Informal methods are also necessary in new occupations, where the nature of skill requirements is still emerging.

Many employers prefer the upgrading system as a device for providing incentives and improving morale for a greater number of employees. Informal methods enable older workers, who did not enter formal training while they were young, to advance by changing jobs as well as by promotion. While it is a more extended process, learning skills through upgrading and changing jobs entails less immediate sacrifice of income, and many workers are unwilling to accept the low wages apprentices receive.

Some employers, who prefer to deal with only one union for all employees, avoid apprenticeship because it may lead to the establishment of separate craft bargaining units within the plant, although some industrial unions are active in apprenticeship. On the other hand, some employers prefer separate units for bargaining purposes. Some employers avoid the Federal apprenticeship program, if not apprenticeship itself, because they do not want a governmental agency to play any part in the determination of their training programs. Others are said to object to registering with the Federal program on the grounds that this requires filling out many special forms and records. On the other hand, many employers indicate that advice from the state and Federal apprenticeship officials has been quite helpful.

What can be said in summary about the ways in which skilled workers and technicians are developed in the United States? In relatively few occupations, and in the case of some workers in all occupations, the primary path to becoming a skilled worker or technician is found in apprenticeship or training schools. The largest group of workers become classified as skilled workers or technicians in the course of their employment history. Labor mobility, both within the firm and among firms, is a crucial factor in the development of the skilled labor force in the United States. In the case of many workers, essential skills are not acquired early in life, but over a long period of time.

The development of skilled workers, consequently, must to a great extent be viewed as a "flow" process. At any one moment in time, there are a number of workers who, as opportunities open up, are moving into the skilled group of the labor force. This is what makes much of the development of skilled workers appear to be a "natural" part of living, working, and producing.

CHAPTER IX

Opportunities, Incentives, and the Acquisition of Skill

For PURPOSES OF ANALYSIS, it is helpful to consider separately the opportunities and the incentives which encourage workers to become skilled. For the most part, the acquisition of essential skills takes place in the course of working. Access to work and, therefore, to training is one aspect of the way in which the market for labor in a free economy operates. The use of the nation's human and other resources, even in periods of emergency, is largely determined by the decisions of individuals, of business enterprises, and of voluntary groups. Both freedom of opportunity and of choice are considered essential to the working of a free economy and for the maximum well-being of the individual and the society as a whole. In a system which depends upon freedom of choice, the role of individual motivation and response to incentives is of central importance.

Opportunities for the development of skills are determined basically by the kinds of jobs available and the level of employment in the worker's locality. But an opportunity is real only if it is known, and most workers know little about the range of job openings and the future prospects of different jobs even in their own locality. Moreover, there are many formal and informal barriers which make access to certain opportunities difficult or even impossible for some workers. Workers are frequently excluded from skilled and technical training on the basis of race, sex, or ethnic characteristics. Any hiring or promotion practices which are selective obviously favor some workers to the disadvantage of others.

LOCAL INDUSTRY AND OPPORTUNITIES

The range of occupations in which an individual worker has the opportunity to acquire skills is influenced by the jobs open to him in his local labor market. The level of employment in the nation as a whole and the total number of skilled and technical occupations in the economy may have little bearing on the job opportunities open to any individual worker. Most young workers look for their first jobs in their home communities. Unless jobs are very scarce, moreover, they give serious consideration to relatively few of the total number of jobs open locally. Even the minority who are willing to move elsewhere merely substitute one local labor market for another. Although the opportunity to get a job that can lead to skilled work may be greater in the new community, few workers move primarily in order to find an opening that will enable them to become skilled.

Almost every community offers opportunities for skilled and technical work in construction, printing, public utilities, and in custom production, repair, and service occupations. Nearly 40 percent of the country's "craftsmen, foremen, and kindred workers," however, are employed in manufacturing which is heavily concentrated in the region north of the Ohio and east of the Mississippi rivers and in California. Moreover, each locality has its own distinctive industrial complex. Detroit is dominated by the auto industry; Gary, by steel; and Hartford, by the manufacture of machinery and transportation equipment. Small towns built around a single industry, such as shoe or textile manufacturing, provide opportunities for obtaining jobs which may lead to skilled work in fewer occupations than large urban centers.

The concentration of particular industries in certain areas — and, therefore, of opportunities for becoming skilled — is reflected in the geographical distribution of skilled workers. One fifth of all the tool and die makers in the nation work in Michigan, primarily in the automobile industry and its suppliers. Two fifths of the loom fixers are residents of North and South Carolina, and another fifth are in the neighboring states of Virginia, Georgia, and Alabama. For the country as a whole, the opportunities to acquire skills are quite abundant, but the horizons of young workers are usually confined to their local labor market and each local market has a distinctive and limited range of job and training opportunities.

THE JOB MARKET AND OPPORTUNITIES FOR SKILL

At any given time, it may be more or less difficult to find jobs in a specific locality which provide opportunities for training for skilled and technical work. When a firm is expanding, more workers than usual are promoted. Others are likely to be taken on at intermediate and higher skill levels, and training programs are likely to be established or enlarged. Rapidly growing industries attract young people seeking their first jobs. They also draw experienced workers from declining or stable industries. Some of the latter move to a higher skill grade in their new employment. When new plants or departments are being opened, workers may climb from the bottom to the top of the skill ladder in three to five years. In a stable situation, it may take a worker twenty years to move the same distance. In declining firms, most workers may never be promoted, and they may have few, if any, opportunities to secure additional training. This means, of course, that in boom times, either in peace or war, workers have greatly expanded opportunities for training and on-the-job experience which will increase their skills.

In an expanding labor market, workers are more inclined to change jobs voluntarily and in the course of the process broaden their experience and acquire additional skills. A striking case was recorded in a recent study of tool and die makers by the U. S. Bureau of Labor Statistics. For five years after graduating from high school, one worker held only unskilled jobs. In 1940 he got his first job in a tool and die shop, where he worked for one year. During the next two and a half years, he reported, he held jobs in eight different tool and die shops, changing each time to broaden his experience. He obtained his first job as a full-fledged tool maker in 1943, and has remained with the same firm since then.

The increased opportunities to acquire skills when jobs are plentiful is illustrated by the fact that nearly 40 percent of all tool and die makers employed in 1951 had acquired their skills after the beginning of World War II. The Bureau of Labor Statistics' study of tool and die makers also suggests that informal methods of gaining skill through changing jobs and promotion become more important in boom times. About half of the tool and die makers who qualified during World War II developed their skills informally.

The recent history of technician training indicates that when the demand for trained workers is high, formal as well as informal training opportunities are very likely to expand. Since 1940, the growing military and civilian demand for technicians has been met, in part, through the wartime training programs conducted in colleges and universities with government sponsorship and funds; in part through armed forces technical schools; through the expansion of technical programs in high schools, junior colleges, and university extension departments; and also through the establishment of many new technical institutes. Where large firms have organized their draftsmen, testing technicians, and laboratory assistants into formal skill categories, they have an opportunity for promotion and further on-the-job training when the firm expands.

In addition to those that are created because firms, industries, and the economy at large are growing, many job opportunities become available each year because workers retire, die, or enter other lines of work. These opportunities fluctuate widely in particular industries or occupations. Rapidly expanding industries usually attract a high proportion of young workers, for older workers are less willing to change jobs. Some twenty-five to forty years later, the young workers hired during the period of expansion will be retiring. As a result, there are likely to be many new openings for skilled work and training.

Because the automobile industry expanded rapidly around World War I, many of its skilled workers will retire during the next few years, and many new opportunities for training will develop. The railroad industry stopped expanding after World War I, and by 1940 most engineers and many firemen were over fifty. During the 1940's many retired, creating new openings in both occupations and bringing promotions to many firemen who were no longer young. The firemen who were promoted, consequently, are due for retirement after a decade or so of additional service. The result will be that those who became firemen recently will probably become engineers much faster than those who became firemen in past years.

On the other hand, industries and occupations in which employment has expanded recently but is now comparatively stable will present relatively few training opportunities. The oil refining industry is not now adding substantially to the size of its work force, and upgrading opportunities in the traditional skilled trades will be limited for some time. The rapid increase in the use of electricity and telephones since 1930 has led to the hiring of a large number of young workers. In 1950, the average age of telephone, telegraph, and power linemen was only thirty-one years. Unless employment in the electrical, power, and telephone industries increases sharply, opportunities for new workers to acquire skills as linemen will be relatively limited for several decades.

BARRIERS TO SKILL DEVELOPMENT

The opportunities for employment and training in skilled occupations are not equally accessible to all workers. Many obstacles prevent or make it difficult for some workers to take advantage of existing opportunities. It has already been pointed out that the worker is for the most part limited to the opportunities in a particular locality, and that most workers are poorly informed about job openings even in their own community.

Even in times of severe labor shortages management always has some options in deciding who should be hired, trained, or promoted. Management, of course, seeks to select the "best" workers in terms of the needs of the company and the demands of the job. Because it is impossible to devise completely objective and accurate methods of picking the best workers, however, the selection of some workers — and the rejection of others — is always somewhat arbitrary. Workers, of course, are also concerned with the criteria for employment, training, and promotion. Unions and associations of technicians seek to expand or to limit access to certain opportunities in the interest of their members.

Finally, management, workers, and community pressures, acting separately or together, frequently erect specific barriers against workers of a particular race, religion, ethnic background, age, or sex. These barriers may reflect the efforts of workers to protect their own advantages as well as deep community prejudices.

LACK OF INFORMATION

Surveys of local labor markets have shown repeatedly that most workers have an extremely limited knowledge of the different jobs that are open and of the future prospects for training and promotion in different firms. Frequently, workers are unaware of the substantial differences in the wages paid for similar work in their own community. The worker who is looking for a job is not likely to know about more than two or three openings. Few new entrants in the labor market have specific occupational goals. Many accept the first job offered to them. Those who have attended vocational schools are likely to be somewhat better informed. More workers rely on relatives and acquaintances for information on jobs, working conditions, and training prospects than on any other source.

A worker usually obtains his first job by applying to a firm that is conveniently reached from his home. Although he probably has little accurate information about the jobs that are open at this or near-by plants, he is not likely to shop around. Management commonly insists that the worker accept or reject a job on the spot. Except when confronted with serious labor shortages, management does not bid for workers, and hesitates to publicize definite information on wage rates, promotion prospects, and working conditions. Neither management nor workers rely to any large extent on public or private employment services, except for white collar workers, or when unusual problems arise in securing workers or in finding a job. Only after he is on a job can a worker really find out about his future prospects, supervisors, working conditions, and fellow workers.

This system of finding jobs explains why many young workers shift from one job to another, when the state of the labor market permits it, until they find satisfactory employment. A worker seldom obtains a new job before he leaves his old one. It is difficult to learn of new openings while one is still employed. Moreover, many firms refuse, except in tight labor markets, to hire a person who is currently employed or who is temporarily unemployed but expects to be called back. Although he may have a general idea of how plentiful jobs are, and may even know of a few firms that have been hiring, the worker must do most of his investigating and decide on his new job in the relatively short interval after he quits his old job and before he feels pressed by the lack of current income. Only after he has tried several jobs, and thus has some experience in the job market and some skills, is the worker who wants to become more skilled likely to find a job that affords the opportunities he desires.

HIRING STANDARDS

The criteria used for hiring or admission to training programs, it has been noted, automatically exclude certain workers from opportunities to acquire skill. Aptitude test scores, age, formal schooling, character references, and other standards are used for selection purposes. They are intended to assess the individual's suitability for a particular position. Selection methods, however, are frequently based on hunch or prejudice. When hiring standards are based on careful research, they can increase the probability that the workers selected will be suitable for the job or the training program, thereby reducing turnover and training costs, but no criterion can surely predict the future performance of a particular individual.

Many companies require that all new employees hired for jobs likely to lead to skilled or technical work be high school graduates. Satisfactory completion of high school is considered a good sign of strong motivation to learn and to complete a task as well as of the possession of useful knowledge. This requirement, however, excludes many young people with the intelligence and other qualities required for becoming skilled. Some employers refuse to hire individuals who have changed jobs "too often." When the individual is an older worker with a long history of changing jobs, this practice may be justified. On the other hand, as has been seen, many young workers hold a series of jobs in order to broaden their skills and competence and not because they are unstable.

Hiring standards are inevitably somewhat flexible. They are usually adjusted to the qualities of applicants and to the urgency with which firms need workers. In a tight labor market, qualifying test scores may be reduced and other standards altered. Where high school graduation is not usual, as in much of the South, it is not generally required for employment.

BARRIERS TO INFORMAL TRAINING

Many unions exercise considerable control over entry to work and training in the skilled occupations. Unions frequently participate in the selection of apprentices, and it is an old complaint that in some fields the sons and relatives of union members have first claim on apprenticeship openings. Unions seek not only to limit entrance to apprenticeship, but also to secure for their members first claim on all job openings within their jurisdiction. In addition, of course, unions seek to extend their jurisdiction to unorganized workers.

Most unions in fields where apprenticeship is established actively promote its further development. At the same time, however, they frequently seek to prevent workers from acquiring skills through informal methods. Some craft unions, such as the electricians, usually forbid the employment of helpers, who might learn the trade while assisting journeymen. Other unions restrict the kinds of work that helpers are permitted to perform. The bricklayers, for instance, have a rule against helpers using the standard tools of the trade. Some joint apprenticeship committees refuse to reduce the length of apprentice training for those who have acquired some skills in the armed forces, through experience, or in schools.

The worker who has become partially or fully skilled through informal processes may, particularly under conditions of less than full employment, have difficulty in getting a skilled job. When there are many more jobs available than there are members, unions usually allow informally trained workers to take jobs within their jurisdiction. Sometimes a "permit" allowing the nonmember to work on a union job is issued for a fee. Since the permit can be withdrawn, the worker's future is not very secure. In most unions that follow this practice, however, a man who has worked for several years on a permit can obtain full membership.

Very few occupations are so fully organized that the union can exercise complete control over entrance to training or employment. In most fields, the union cannot insist too rigidly on apprenticeship as a prerequisite for membership and employment. Many workers acquire skills informally in nonunion shops, and unions hoping to organize them cannot bar such workers from membership. The degree to which unions restrict informal training varies widely in different occupations and fields. The building and printing trades place strong emphasis on apprenticeship. But even in the building trades, apprenticeship is not the usual method of becoming a construction machinery operator or an elevator constructor. Even in strong craft unions that place great emphasis on apprenticeship, many members have acquired their skills in other ways. Only 30 percent of the new members admitted to the building trades branch of the United Association of Plumbers and Pipefitters in 1953 came in as apprentices.

Not all of the barriers against informal skill acquisition are erected by unions. Frequently employers as well as unions are reluctant to reduce the length of apprenticeship for a worker who has already gained substantial skills through schooling or experience. Since the pay of apprentices rises as they approach completion of their training, prolonging the period of formal training helps to reduce labor costs. In selecting skilled workers for promotion to higher skill grades or to supervisory positions, some employers give strong preference to workers who have passed through their own apprenticeship programs. In these plants, informally trained workers have little chance of obtaining the best jobs.

Because some employers narrowly restrict the scope of training given to semi-skilled workers, it is difficult for their employees to acquire significant skills. Many semi-skilled jobs have such narrowly defined functions that work experience contributes very little to a worker's ability to seek a more skilled job with either his present or another employer. Moreover, where there are wide gaps between the skill levels in a production system, it is almost impossible for workers in the lower grades to acquire gradually on the job the skills necessary to hold a higher grade position. Without extensive formal training, such workers cannot be promoted. Training and production along these lines is often justified in terms of greater efficiency. It has been charged, however, that in many cases such practices are the result of overemphasis on short-run efficiency and failure to consider long-run disadvantages.

LICENSING AND REGISTRATION

In some occupations, the efforts of organized groups of workers to restrict entrance to training and employment are re-enforced by legal licensing requirements. The Federal government requires licensing of certain skilled workers and technicians in the radio, television, maritime, and aviation industries. In many states and localities a person cannot work in certain occupations unless he has obtained a license. In its 1952 study of *Occupational Licensing Legislation in the States,* the Council of State Governments pointed out that while "such laws provide minimal safeguards for the protection of the public health, safety and welfare . . . . they may impose barriers to the free choice of occupations and help to create monopolistic conditions for established practitioners." The skilled and technical occupations most commonly licensed by the states are shown in the following table.

Table 8. Skilled and Technical Occupations Licensed by States

Occupation	Number of States Requiring License
Barber	46
Beautician	45
Surveyor	33
Dental hygienist	29
Plumber	17
Physical therapist	15
Miners and inspectors	13
Electricians	9
Opticians	7
Watchmakers	7

Source: Council of State Governments

Other occupations licensed by a few states are boiler and elevator inspectors, dry cleaners, hoisting and stationary engineers, horseshoers, medical technicians, motion-picture machine operators, and practical nurses. Data are not available on licensing by local governments, which generally cover the same occupations.

The Council of State Governments declared that in many cases the legal qualifications have been drawn up by interested private groups which have most to gain from limiting the supply of workers. "Requirements vary greatly for applicants seeking licenses as barbers, beauticians . . . electricians, plumbers, and practical nurses . . . in accordance with the beliefs and powers of state and local associations." Trade school training or apprenticeship is frequently required, but the length and value of this training are often questioned. Residence requirements for licensing place a barrier in the path of workers who move from one locality to another.

Licensing of medical technicians has not been common, but the organized societies of technicians in the health field have pressed for formal requirements for employment in their respective fields. Some societies maintain a register of members limited to those who have received formal training in a school affiliated with a hospital or medical school. Technicians trained informally or in public and private technical institutes find it difficult to obtain registration. Some hospitals prefer to employ registered technicians, but the need for technicians has been so great that most hospitals accept those who are not registered. In 1952, less than one half of medical technologists and X-ray technicians employed in hospitals were registered.

SENIORITY

Seniority systems constitute still another means by which access to employment and training opportunities is restricted. Employers as well as unions sometimes prefer to rely on seniority in order to regularize their procedures and forestall charges of favoritism. Under a rigid seniority system a worker may not compete for a skilled opening — no matter how able or ambitious he may be — unless he is at the top of the seniority list. Consequently, seniority systems may impede the efforts of a worker to add to his skills by changing jobs and employers. If his new employer has a strict seniority system he must start in a low-skill job at the bottom of the seniority ladder no matter what his prior experience. However, if the employer wishes to promote him and can convince the union that none of the workers with greater seniority are qualified, he may be moved up the ladder. In the actual operations under many collective bargaining contracts, workers who have demonstrated greater ability than others with more seniority have a definite advantage when opportunities for promotion appear.

Seniority systems may also discourage a worker from changing to a related job in the same company or plant. Ordinarily, large plants do not have a single seniority list for all workers. Jobs are grouped on the basis of the usual promotion sequence, and the seniority rights of an individual worker generally apply only to one group of jobs. The established promotion sequence, however, may fail to reflect technological developments which make different promotion sequences more desirable. It may also fail to recognize unusual but perfectly reasonable shifts from one job to another. Production workers frequently become familiar with the construction of their machines and learn a great deal about their maintenance. When there are separate seniority systems for production and maintenance workers, the production worker with some knowledge of repair will not have an opportunity to be promoted to a maintenance position. Seniority rules are often relaxed when the demand for skilled workers is high. To meet emergency production needs during the Korean war, the United Automobile Workers (CIO) permitted new workers to be brought into certain shops at intermediate skill grades. Under the union's "change over rule," the new men could not acquire permanent seniority. When the demand for skilled workers fell off, they were released.

DISCRIMINATION AGAINST MINORITIES

Large segments of the American population are denied access to work and training in many skilled occupations because of widespread prejudices against racial and ethnic groups. Discrimination is strongest and most widespread in the case of Negroes, but there are similar barriers for Spanish-speaking persons, Orientals, Jews, and other groups. Chapter VII noted the extent to which high school vocational training for Negroes is limited. While discrimination against Negroes is most rigid in the South, it exists in every section of the country. Throughout the South, Negroes are employed for skilled work in only a few service occupations or in trades in which they have long been established, such as carpentry, bricklaying, and some other construction trades. Negroes are not accepted in even these trades in many communities.

Negroes have usually gained a foothold in occupations which white workers consider undesirable because they involve arduous labor or hot, dirty, or otherwise unpleasant working conditions. Thus, Negroes work as bakers, blacksmiths, auto mechanics, locomotive firemen, and cement finishers. Negroes have sometimes been excluded from trades which were formerly open to them when working conditions in these occupations became more agreeable. After cement finishing was mechanized, many white workers entered the trade. The switch from steam to diesel locomotives made the job of railroad fireman more attractive, and Negroes are now being excluded. On the other hand, continuing unpleasant working conditions in foundries, together with the continuance of a tight labor market, has led many white workers to avoid foundry work. Opportunities for skilled work in this field have opened up for Negroes, as well as for workers of Mexican extraction and white workers with limited education.

In some cases the exclusion of Negroes is a stated policy. Where the ban is not overt, there are nevertheless many ways in which Negroes are denied access to skilled work and training. Elaborate rules that are overlooked for white employees are applied to Negroes. Since jobs are frequently located through information supplied by relatives and acquaintances, and since so few Negroes are in skilled work, they are not likely even to learn about job openings. A smaller proportion of Negroes than whites attend high school. Many Negroes who have the basic ability to become skilled workers find the opportunity closed because they fail to meet educational requirements. The difficulties encountered by all informally trained workers in gaining full status as skilled workers are multiplied many times over for Negroes. Most seniority systems, particularly in the South, maintain separate lists for service and production workers. Negroes hired for janitorial and other unskilled service work have no opportunity to acquire seniority rights to skilled production jobs.

During the last few years, many companies and national unions have adopted an official policy of nondiscrimination. Local managers and union officials, however, respond to the pressures and practices of the community. Some of the more venturesome are willing to take the lead in breaking through local discriminatory practices; others are ready to use local pressures as a reason for doing nothing.

Outside of the South, the last few years have brought considerable progress in broadening the employment opportunities of Negroes. In many states, the basic principle that every man has an equal right to employment opportunities, regardless of race, religion, or ethnic background, has been written into law. Practice is still lagging behind precept, but significant gains have been made.

The picture in the South is less clear. Major advances have been made under the aegis of the Federal government and particularly the armed forces. In military establishments, qualified Negroes are admitted to apprenticeship and integrated into the skilled work force. In some Southern companies, Negroes are hired for production jobs which afford opportunities to advance in the skill-seniority system. Usually, however, they work in segregated departments. Where they do not, they are frequently restricted to particular lines of work. Although some white workers will leave or avoid lines of work where Negro workers gain admittance, and special problems often arise when Negroes gain positions above white workers, there has been increasing proof that Negro and white skilled workers will work together in integrated units without great difficulty. The status of the Negro as a skilled worker in the South has improved little in the last decade, but there are sufficient signs of change to suggest that in another ten years conditions will be noticeably different.

While Negroes and other minority groups encounter greater or lesser difficulties in gaining entrance to many skilled occupations, it is also true that some skilled occupations are dominated by particular ethnic or religious minority groups. This situation reflects the heavy immigration of workers during the period of America's most rapid industrial expansion. Immigrants came in large numbers from different parts of Europe at different times and entered the industries which were expanding rapidly when they arrived. Those who arrived later tended to settle in the same localities and enter the same occupations as their countrymen who had preceded them. In addition, employers frequently recruited skilled workers from European countries in which the same industry was well developed. These concentrations have been preserved in part because workers seeking their first jobs generally rely on the help and information of relatives and friends. Thus, even today, many of the tinsmiths in Eastern Pennsylvania are of Welsh extraction. Most skilled garment workers in New York are Jews of Eastern European origin or Italians. Many tool and die makers are of British and German extraction. While these concentrations are gradually disappearing, workers with particular ethnic backgrounds still have an advantage in gaining entrance to some occupations.

Although women account for a high percentage of medical technicians and many work in the skilled service trades, the barriers to the training and employment of women found in many sectors of the American economy are particularly significant in the case of skilled work. In part, this may be justified where women leave without a significant period of productive work after their employers have made a training investment in them. However, discrimination against women seems to be primarily a reflection of widespread social prejudices.

The preceding catalogue of barriers to the acquisition of skill might well leave the impression that, for all but a favored few, it is exceedingly difficult to become a skilled worker. In spite of all the barriers — and they are more complex than described here — the fact remains that the extent of opportunity is governed primarily by the rate of expansion of the skilled labor force. With the exception of occasional periods of depression, the skilled labor force has been expanding rapidly for many decades. Consequently, opportunities to acquire skill have generally been abundant. It should be added that when the skilled groups are growing most rapidly — that is, when the demand for skilled workers is very high — the barriers that have been erected against various groups are generally reduced or can be overcome by workers who make special efforts.

Skilled workers generally enjoy higher incomes and higher status than other workers. Their jobs are usually more secure and afford greater opportunity for independent judgment and action than those of semi-skilled workers. Technicians also enjoy higher income and status, and greater job security. In spite of these advantages, workers respond differently to the alternative opportunities to acquire skill. The sons of skilled union members may have first claim to apprenticeship openings, but some pass them by to enter college, while others are satisfied to become semi-skilled workers. Some work hard to acquire skills, while others expend a minimum of effort. Still others complete a training program only because their parents insist on it and some may dislike their work all their lives.

Some workers who do not have ready access to apprenticeship seek out training openings while others have to be pushed into training by their employers. Some make great sacrifices to attend a technical institute, but others continue with their schooling because it is the easiest thing to do, and still others leave school as soon as they can. A worker caught up in a strict seniority system may advance up the skill ladder step by step without special effort. Some workers refuse to accept the added responsibilities which come with promotion.

When promotion is not forthcoming, some workers change jobs to improve themselves. Others accept their current status, while still others remain on the same job and work hard to merit promotion when an opportunity does arise. Some study in night school or pursue correspondence courses, while others will not put forth such effort even when they know they could be promoted if they did. Some workers qualify for promotion through long service with one employer. Others quickly become bored with one type of work and move from job to job. In this process, however, they may acquire additional abilities that enable them to seek and obtain skilled work.

Some workers seek skilled status because of its prestige. Similarly, one of the appeals of the technician occupations is that the technician frequently works in close association with professional personnel. On the other hand, some are not interested in most skilled or technical work because, for them, office work carries greater prestige than factory work.

The range of possible responses to technical and skilled occupations underlines the complexity of the values that can be sought and found in work. Different individuals respond differently to money income, prestige, working conditions, and to the specific character of the job, and the way in which they respond largely determines their behavior in seeking or utilizing opportunities in the world of work.

Until recently the study of the motives that lead men to seek training and employment in specific occupations has been dominated by a belief in the power of economic incentives. Consequently, attention has been focused on wage differentials, and concern has been expressed because in the last fifty years the average differential between the wages of the skilled and the unskilled has declined by about one half. Some observers have argued that this development may result in a shortage of workers willing to invest in training for skilled work.

Relatively little is known about the complex processes through which individuals make choices between alternative opportunities for training and work in different occupations. It is clear, however, that the size of the wage differential is only one important factor among many. A particular job may pay lower wages than another, but still have higher prestige. Students are only beginning to understand how workers respond to such characteristics of a job as the variety of tasks involved, the degree of independent judgment possible, the pattern of supervision, and the organization of work groups.

Knowledge of the personality characteristics that lead individuals to respond to these various incentives in different ways is also rudimentary. Some individuals are much more concerned than others with choosing and preparing for a career. They plan more carefully and are more willing to make sacrifices of income and leisure to reach their goals. The process through which an individual finally reaches a particular occupation begins in childhood, and is influenced by his family background, the kind of community in which he lives, his school experiences, the attitudes of family and friends, and many other circumstances.

Adequate understanding of how and why some workers decide to enter skilled occupations awaits further study. The discussion of incentives in the following pages centers upon money income, both because it is the influence about which most is known and because there is no question that it is an important incentive in leading individuals to become skilled or technical workers.

Social values in the United States place great stress on the amount of money a man earns and spends. Because of social and family pressures which may not even be consciously perceived, most young people hope at least to reach, and preferably to surpass somewhat, the occupational and income levels of their fathers. Even if a young man quits school and takes the first job that comes along, he is likely to start looking for opportunities to advance by the time he has had several years experience and begins to acquire family responsibilities.

In addition to its direct importance, money income is also closely related to other incentives for choosing skilled work. There is generally at least a rough correspondence between the wages, the prestige, the desirability of working conditions, and the degree of variety and independence on the job in different occupations.

An individual's choice of occupation may be influenced not only by current rates of pay but also by his estimate, however rough, of earning prospects during his working lifetime. Steadiness of employment and income varies considerably among occupations. For example, hospital technicians enjoy relatively stable employment, while construction workers do not. The employment of tool and die makers has been irregular, especially in the machine tool industry.

Occupations also present varying opportunities for advancement. The prospect of becoming a contractor is an important incentive for some people who enter the building trades. Many repair trades are carried on in small shops. This affords the ambitious person an opportunity to open his own business. With additional training, tool and die makers can become designers and a few even become engineers. In the medical field rigid requirements foreclose advancement from technician to professional status, but some dental technicians own their own laboratories. Such opportunities are frequently perceived, not when a person enters an occupation, but only after he has had considerable experience.

The long-term employment outlook in an occupation may influence a person's decision to enter it. One of the primary attractions of technician occupations is their rapid growth in recent years and their prospect for continued growth. Some repair trades, especially in aviation, have been attractive for similar reasons. Shoe making and repairing, tailoring, and blacksmithing have been less attractive because employment opportunities have been declining.

In assessing the influence of the long-term outlook on the decisions of individuals, it would be helpful to know expected lifetime earnings in various occupations. Such data are not available, however. Statistics on average annual earnings provide the best available indication of money rewards in various occupations.

ANNUAL EARNINGS

The 1950 Census collected information directly from individuals on their earnings during 1949. Table 9 presents the average earnings for male workers in nonfarm occupational groups. The average income of "craftsmen, foremen, and kindred workers" is higher than that of all groups except professional workers and business owners and managers.

Table 9. Annual Earnings of Male Workers, by Occupational Group, 1949

Occupational Group	Median Income
Professional, technical, and kindred workers	$3,958
Managers, officials, and proprietors, except farm	3,944
Craftsmen, foremen, and kindred workers	3,125
Sales workers	3,028
Clerical and kindred workers	3,010
Operatives and kindred workers	2,607
Service workers, except private household	2,195
Laborers, except farm and mine	1,961

Source: U. S. Bureau of the Census

Actually, the average income of skilled workers in 1949 was greater than Table 9 indicates. The distribution of annual earnings in a number of technical, skilled, and other occupations is shown in Table 10, which indicates that a substantial number of workers classified as skilled earned less than $2,000. Wage-rate surveys, however, indicate that regularly employed workers in even the lowest paid skilled occupations averaged considerably more than $2,000 in 1949. Undoubtedly, some of those shown in Table 10 as earning less than $2,000 were not regularly employed. Nevertheless, the high proportions in the less-than-$2,000 groups suggest that the Census counted as skilled many semi-skilled workers. Their inclusion substantially lowers the average earnings shown for craftsmen, foremen, and kindred workers.

Most skilled and technical workers undoubtedly received an income of about $3,000 or more in 1949. Table 10 indicates that in many occupations many workers earned more than $5,000.

Some earned as much as $7,000 and even $10,000. Women in skilled and technical occupations received less than men, partly because many women worked only part time, but mainly because of the lower wages in occupations usually open to women.

Table 10. Annual Earnings of Workers in Technical, Skilled, and Other Occupations, 1949

			PERCENT EARNING		
		MEDIAN ANNUAL	LESS THAN	LESS THAN	$5,000
RANK	OCCUPATION	INCOME	$2,000	$3,000	OR MORE
	Male Workers				
1	Locomotive engineers	$4,590	3	9	37
2	Printing craftsmen, except compositors and typesetters	4,211	9	23	34
3	Foremen not elsewhere classified.....	3,949	5	20	23
4	Compositors and typesetters.........	3,742	12	31	22
5	Toolmakers and diemakers and setters.	3,741	6	21	14
6	Locomotive firemen	3,688	10	27	12
7	Power station operators[a]...........	3,655	5	22	8
8	Stationary engineers	3,604	9	28	15
9	Designers and draftsmen...........	3,600	11	31	18
10	Brakemen and switchmen, railroad[a]...	3,592	9	28	7
11	Electricians	3,449	13	34	13
12	Mechanics and repairmen, airplane...	3,437	8	28	6
13	Structural metal workers...........	3,428	14	34	13
14	Millwrights	3,413	8	30	7
15	Boilermakers	3,385	11	33	8
16	Linemen and servicemen, telegraph, telephone, and power.............	3,363	10	36	9
17	Plumbers and pipe fitters...........	3,344	17	39	13
18	Firemen, fire protection[b]..........	3,298	5	31	4
19	Motormen, street, subway, and elevated railway[a]	3,278	3	20	3
20	Machinists and job setters..........	3,242	11	37	4
21	Policemen, sheriffs, and marshals[b]...	3,228	10	38	5
22	Tinsmiths, coppersmiths, and sheet metal workers	3,203	15	41	6
23	Welders and flame cutters[a].........	3,146	16	43	5
24	*Craftsmen, foremen, and kindred workers*	3,125	20	46	9
25	Bus drivers[a]	3,116	20	44	2
26	Cranemen, hoistmen, and construction machinery operators	3,115	15	45	8
27	Filers, grinders, and polishers, metal[a]..	3,019	19	49	3
28	Bakers	2,917	21	53	5
29	Technician, medical and dental......	2,915	23	53	11
30	Masons, tile setters, and stone cutters..	2,895	28	52	10

RANK	OCCUPATION	MEDIAN ANNUAL INCOME	PERCENT EARNING		
			LESS THAN $2,000	LESS THAN $3,000	$5,000 OR MORE
31	Cabinet makers and pattern makers...	2,881	25	53	6
32	Plasterers and cement finishers.......	2,842	30	53	11
33	Tailors and furriers	2,841	26	55	9
34	Molders, metal	2,826	20	57	2
35	Surveyors	2,805	28	55	8
36	Blacksmiths, forgers, and hammersmiths	2,701	32	58	4
37	Mechanics and repairmen, automobile.	2,689	27	60	3
38	Carpenters	2,456	37	64	4
39	Painters (construction), paperhangers, and glaziers	2,295	41	69	3
40	Shoemakers and repairers, except factory	2,079	47	76	4
41	Mechanics and repairmen, radio and television	2,059	34	63	4
	Female Workers				
1	Designers and draftsmen............	2,504	32	64	10
2	Foremen not elsewhere classified.....	2,268	37	78	2
3	Technicians, medical and dental......	2,122	44	84	1
4	*Craftsmen, foremen, and kindred workers*	1,999	50	83	2
5	Dietitians and nutritionists..........	1,951	52	80	3

a Classified as "Operatives and kindred workers."
b Classified as "Service workers, except private household."
Source: U. S. Bureau of the Census

These figures understate the full economic returns received by employees. Fringe benefits have been estimated to equal 10 to 20 percent of total earnings. These fringe benefits take the form of paid holidays, vacations, and sick leave; Christmas, year-end and other bonuses; profit-sharing plans; health, hospitalization, and life insurance benefits; and pensions and other welfare arrangements. Some fringe benefits are included in the annual earnings statistics, but others are not.

Table 10 also includes a number of occupations not classified as technical or skilled in the 1950 Census in which average income is comparable to that of skilled workers. Among these are firemen and policemen; railroad brakemen and switchmen; street, subway, and elevated railway motormen; bus drivers; welders and flame cutters; and metal filers, grinders, and polishers. These groups share with craftsmen and foremen a significant income differential.

DECLINE IN THE WAGE ADVANTAGES OF SKILLED WORKERS

Although skilled workers are paid considerably more than unskilled and semi-skilled workers, the relative difference has been declining for many years. Because of changes in the skills required in particular jobs, in systems of skill classification, and in the regularity of employment in different occupations, it is impossible to make precise comparisons of relative earnings at widely separated times. While the available data do not indicate exact differentials, they do show that the earnings of skilled workers have fallen substantially compared to those of unskilled workers.

According to one estimate, the average wages of skilled workers in manufacturing were more than double those of unskilled workers in 1907. The differential declined to 75 percent by 1919, increased slightly to 80 percent by 1932, and then declined steadily to 65 percent in 1940, 55 percent in 1947, and less than 40 percent in early 1953.

The difference between the wages of skilled and unskilled workers has always been greater in the South than in other regions. In 1947 the average differential was 70 percent in the South but only from 45 to 55 percent in other regions. In some Southern industries it is not unusual to find highly skilled occupations with rates three times as high as for unskilled occupations. Since rates for skilled workers, who are relatively scarce in the South, are about the same as or slightly lower than in the North, the major reason for the large differential is that unskilled workers in the South receive very low wages. In recent years, however, the differential between the wages of skilled and unskilled workers has been declining more rapidly in the South than elsewhere.

The narrowing difference between the pay rates of skilled and unskilled workers in manufacturing is paralleled in other sectors of the economy. Journeymen in the building trades averaged 85 percent more than laborers and helpers in 1909 and about 100 percent more between 1912 and 1916. The differential dropped sharply during and after World War I, remained stable through

1935, and since then has declined steadily. By 1952 it had fallen to less than 40 percent. The same general pattern holds for the wage rates of the principal skilled occupations in book and job printing relative to wage rates of press assistants and feeders. Similarly, machinists and other skilled shopworkers for the railroads received 50 percent higher wages than helpers in 1922, but only 17 percent higher in 1952. Yard conductors and firemen received 44 percent more than switchtenders in 1922, but only 17 percent more in 1952.

Although still earlier evidence is fragmentary, it appears that the difference between the wages of skilled and unskilled workers has been falling for about a century. According to one estimate, skilled wage rates were approximately three times unskilled rates before the Civil War. In Great Britain and other Western European countries, the skill differential has also declined and is even lower than in the United States. In some industries, the top skilled wage rates are less than 20 percent above unskilled ones.

The relative wages in skilled occupations decline fastest during periods of increasing demand for labor. During sharp declines in employment, the relative difference between skilled and unskilled rates has tended to widen again, but not to the previous level.

DOLLAR DIFFERENCES

Expressed as a percentage of unskilled wage rates, skilled rates have been declining. On the other hand, the actual cents-per-hour differences have been rising. In other words, the wages of both skilled and unskilled have risen, but skilled wages have increased less rapidly than unskilled wages. For example, average union wages in the building trades in 1936 were $1.24 per hour for journeymen and $0.71 for laborers and helpers. The difference was $0.53 or 75 percent of the unskilled rate. By 1947 rates of journeymen had increased to $2.13 and for laborers and helpers to $1.49. The difference was $0.64, but only 43 percent. These growing dollar differences are probably more important to the worker than the decline in percentage differentials.

The extent of such dollar differences is indicated by estimates of annual earnings based on a number of surveys made in 1950 and 1951. In steel foundries, interstate telephone service, and radio and television manufacturing, the differences between the annual earnings of unskilled workers and the highest paid skilled occupations ranged from $1,700 to $2,000. In steel foundries and radio and television manufacturing, the typical skilled worker received, respectively, $640 and $680 more than the typical semi-skilled worker. The range within the skilled worker category was even greater than the difference between the wages of the typical skilled and the typical semi-skilled worker. In steel foundries some skilled workers received $860 more than other skilled workers. In radio and television manufacturing, men in the highest paid skilled occupation averaged $780 more than men in the lowest paid skilled jobs.

The effect of income taxes must be considered in appraising these differentials. A worker with three dependents paid no taxes in 1951 if his income was less than $2,675, but a worker with the same sized family paid taxes of slightly less than one fifth on all income between $2,675 and $5,000. On the other hand, these figures on average income conceal the fact that there were still larger differences among the earnings of individual workers. Wage rates for nearly identical jobs frequently vary widely among firms in the same locality for a number of reasons, including differences in unionization, the profit position of individual firms, company policy, and varying respect for historical wage relationships.

REASONS FOR THE DECLINE IN DIFFERENTIALS

The long-run decline in relative wage differentials for skill has been attributed to a number of factors. Modern technology has made it possible to employ persons with little or no specialized training effectively. This has been reflected in the rising wages of unskilled and semi-skilled workers. The benefit of small productivity gains which take place continually in manufacturing is more likely to accrue to production workers, who are often paid piece rates, than to skilled workers, who are usually paid by the hour. The unusual demand during war and postwar booms for additional labor has been responsible for much of the decline in skilled wage differentials. Changes in the character of the labor supply because of better education, a later school-leaving age, a declining birth rate, and limitations on immigration have apparently affected wage differentials. The rise of industrial unions, with strong concern for the welfare of the main body of their members, has also been cited as a contributing cause. The trend toward smaller wage differentials for skilled workers is part of a much larger movement to reduce the upper and raise the lower extremes in income distribution, which has been reflected in the policies of management, unions, and government.

WAGE INCENTIVES AND THE SUPPLY OF SKILLED WORKERS

The concern here is with wage differentials only in their role as incentives for training and work in the skilled occupations. It must be asked, therefore, whether the decline in the relative income advantage of skilled workers has resulted in an inadequate supply of workers willing to undertake the necessary training.

There is evidence that in at least some skilled occupations and communities, there is a shortage of well-qualified young men willing to enter and to complete apprenticeship. An unpublished survey of local and national representatives of the International Association of Machinists undertaken for the National Manpower Council indicates that many of the union's representatives believe the declining wage differential has seriously reduced the incentives for becoming an all-round machinist, although a minority, about 30 percent, held a contrary opinion. Many of the respondents emphasized that the starting wages of apprentice machinists are only about half the journeymen's wage and less than the wages of unskilled workers. For many able young workers, the wage advantage they would enjoy ultimately as skilled machinists apparently does not seem large enough to warrant the temporary sacrifice of income entailed by entering apprenticeship. This view is supported by a recent study by the U. S. Bureau of Labor Statistics, which found that over one third of all those who enter apprenticeship leave voluntarily before completing training. Of these, about one third drop out largely for financial reasons.

Recent apprenticeship conferences held in various parts of the country, however, do not indicate any general shortage of candidates. There are shortages in some localities and occupations, particularly in declining fields such as blacksmithing. There are also occasional complaints about the quality of applicants. On the other hand, some apprenticeship programs have from ten to fifty times as many applicants as they accept.

During the last few years many union contracts have increased the differential in favor of skilled workers. Some observers have seen in this development strong evidence of concern over inadequate incentives for entrance to skilled work. A number of contracts have raised the starting wage for apprentices relative to the journeyman's rate. Skilled workers in the automobile industry recently received an extra increase of ten to twenty cents an hour. Similar increases for skilled workers have been given in the electrical machinery and equipment and radio industries. Between 1947 and 1952, wage increases in the steel industry were on a percentage basis which maintained existing differentials. According to the U. S. Bureau of Labor Statistics, at least one third of all contracts negotiated since the end of the wage stabilization program during the Korean war maintained or increased existing relative differentials. There is reason to believe that these developments reflect a desire to deal more equitably with the older workers in certain skilled trades more than they reflect a concern with incentives for entering skilled occupations. In any event, they point up the fact that when and if these incentives become inadequate, they can be increased.

While it may well be that some apprenticeship programs are encountering a shortage of well-qualified workers willing to complete training, there is no sign of an over-all shortage of skilled workers and little indication that employers are having difficulty in finding workers willing to be upgraded through informal training. The employers who attended conferences held by the National Manpower Council in 1953 and 1954 were not finding it difficult to get young people to enter training. Some employers had encountered shortages when they were organizing new plants, especially in the South, or when their needs were suddenly increased as a result of contracts with the armed forces. But even these employers did not indicate that the shortages were acute or prolonged. Although many employers declared that a significant number of their workers had little desire to advance, they all seemed to find enough ambitious, capable workers to keep their training systems and their openings for promotions filled. Two economists, Lloyd Reynolds and Richard Lester, have studied the effect of wage differentials in widely different industries and locations. Neither of them found reason to conclude that declining differentials for skilled work have reduced the supply of workers willing to accept promotion and training.

Indeed, if the need for skilled workers is defined in terms of the requirements of employers, it is difficult to see how declining wage differentials could possibly result in a prolonged and general shortage of skilled workers. In a profit economy, without wage controls or heavy, progressive taxes on the incomes of skilled workers, there is nothing to prevent employers from raising wages to the point where they attract as many workers to skilled occupations as are needed for profitable operations. Because of rigidities in the wage structure introduced by contracts with unions and by traditional differentials in an industry or area, the monetary incentive may be inadequate temporarily in particular industries or firms. But it is difficult to conceive that all employers in the economy would consistently pursue wage policies resulting in shortages of skilled workers that would impede their operations and jeopardize their profits.

The persistence of monetary incentives inadequate to attract new skilled workers is likely only when the demand for workers with a particular skill is declining, or when a high proportion of the workers in an occupation are employed by government agencies, hospitals, or other nonprofit organizations where special conditions affect wage rates. Since it takes time to train skilled workers, adjustments in wages or other incentives for training cannot bring about an immediate increase in the supply. As has been noted, however, even sudden increases in the need for skilled workers can usually be met in various ways. A company can reduce its total needs for skilled workers through changes in job assignments, products, or technology.

Still another set of considerations also suggests that it is unlikely that declining wage differentials have seriously impaired the supply of skilled workers. Most skilled workers become skilled, not through prolonged formal training, but through a gradual process of picking up skills on the job. This means that, in order to become skilled, it is not necessary for the worker to make a major sacrifice in terms of extra effort or postponed earnings. He must be prepared to work satisfactorily, to learn from fellow workers and supervisors, to accept the added responsibilities of promotion, and perhaps to attend night school for a while or to change jobs in order to broaden his experience. There is every indication, however, that there is no shortage of able workers willing to meet these demands in response to present wage differentials, which, in terms of dollars, are greater than ever. It is noteworthy that a substantial proportion of the apprentices who drop out before completing their training later become skilled workers through less demanding informal processes. That many workers are willing to make special efforts to acquire skills is indicated by the fact that enrollment in evening trade and industry classes under the Federal-state vocational education program has been consistently much higher in recent years than formerly. It should also be pointed out that because of the spread of high school education there has been an increased supply of young people who enter employment with an adequate background for further training.

In short, the evidence now available points to the conclusion that the long-term decline in the relative wage advantage of skilled workers has not produced and is not likely to produce a general shortage of skilled workers. It may be that workers as a whole are somewhat less willing than formerly to make sacrifices of time, effort, or money to develop their skills and merit advancement. Even to the extent that this is true, however, it is not possible to attribute it entirely to the decline in wage differentials. The complicated processes of occupational choice are still poorly understood, but it is clear that financial considerations alone do not determine the decisions of most individuals.

Along with wage differentials, many other parts of the opportunity-incentive structure have also changed. A half century ago, skilled work offered the major opportunity for young people from poor backgrounds to raise their standard of living. Today, this is no longer true. Increased opportunities for employment in professional, service, clerical, and well-paying semi-skilled industrial jobs, as well as wider access to secondary and higher education, have greatly broadened the range of attractive alternatives. At the same time, shorter hours and higher pay have given workers the leisure and the means to seek important satisfactions outside of their work. Because of the rising school-leaving age, compulsory military service, and the declining marriage age, many young men today have family responsibilities shortly after they begin work. They are therefore unwilling to undertake prolonged training which requires a temporary financial sacrifice regardless of the wages for which such training would eventually qualify them.

Existing training opportunities and incentives seem adequate to maintain a supply of skilled workers which meets the demands of employers. This analysis, however, deals with wage rates only in relation to their influence on the supply of skilled workers. It should not be taken to express a judgment on what the general level of wages should be or on the proper distribution of income among various classes of workers. Moreover, the demands of employers are not the only relevant criteria for judging the adequacy of opportunities and incentives for training for skilled work. Barriers to employment and training based on ignorance, prejudice, or the private interests of small groups not only reduce the nation's resources of skill, but contradict democratic values. Finally, the needs of employers for particular kinds of skilled workers are not necessarily identical with the long-term manpower needs of the country as a whole. Employers are necessarily preoccupied with the profitable operation of their own concerns. The responsibility for building a labor force which facilitates long-run economic development and is readily adaptable to the requirements of full mobilization must be shared by the many individuals, groups, enterprises, and public institutions which play a part in the development of skilled manpower resources.

CHAPTER X

Vocational Guidance and Counseling

IN THIS COUNTRY freedom of opportunity is an article of national faith. The vast majority of Americans believe that every American youngster should be free to enter any occupation for which he can qualify. When discriminatory practices restrict freedom of opportunity, they arouse nation-wide controversy.

Yet freedom of opportunity is restricted by a condition far more widespread and far less obvious than discrimination — the general ignorance among youngsters, and almost equally among their elders, of the myriad types of trained personnel required by our complex society. Ignorance of available vocational opportunities can as effectively prevent access to them as restrictions rooted in racial, ethnic, or religious discrimination.

Although a youngster often reads about different kinds of work with which he can have no firsthand experience, when he thinks about choosing a field of work he is likely to be most influenced by the occupations he has actually encountered. Generally, these occupations are limited to the principal professions and the services and trades he becomes acquainted with in the course of his daily life. Consequently, the average youngster becomes familiar with only a tiny fraction of the many different types of work which exist.

As our economy has grown, so has the number of occupations that support it. As our technology has become more specialized, so have the kinds of jobs that maintain it. The *Occupational Outlook Handbook* of the U. S. Department of Labor describes 433 occupations. The U. S. Employment Service's *Dictionary of Occu-*

pational Titles describes 22,028 different jobs — that is, the specific duties performed by individuals in their work.

Casual familiarity with an occupation may leave one ignorant of its actual diversity and requirements. For example, the *Dictionary of Occupational Titles* lists about 60 different job categories under the main title of carpenter. To name only a few, there are acoustical carpenters, foundry carpenters, stage carpenters, ship carpenters, and refrigerator carpenters. The much newer occupation of draftsman is similarly subdivided. The latter is an example of an occupation in which even the specializations have become subspecialized. Not only does the *Dictionary* list approximately 30 different kinds of draftsmen, it also, for example, details 7 different kinds of marine draftsmen.

GUIDANCE IN THE SCHOOLS

With such an enormous diversity of job opportunities open to the qualified, it is obviously desirable that some systematic procedure exist through which a youngster is informed about the occupations for which he might qualify and told how he can prepare for them properly. Such assistance becomes critically important at the time the young person is ready to enter secondary school. No longer can he simply accept an assigned curriculum as he did in elementary school. He has reached the point where he must begin to make choices. Shall he take a general, college preparatory, or vocational course? Does he expect to graduate from high school or does he anticipate leaving early? Does he show signs of any special aptitudes or interests, and, if so, how can they best be developed? What vocational goals is he beginning to set for himself?

While in secondary school, the individual is going through a period during which he should be making a tentative occupational choice. Occupational choice is a gradual process in which a compromise is eventually reached between a person's abilities, interests, and values, and the realistic necessities presented by his actual opportunities for preparation and employment. Although knowledge of the world of work is clearly not the only element needed to make sound decisions about one's high school education, it is highly valuable. Unless deliberate steps are taken to supply such knowledge, most young people will be handicapped in attempting to make sound educational plans.

Learning about the relationship between education and occupational opportunity is important to youngsters for a second reason. As they move into their teens, they often become less willing to attend school and take it seriously unless they understand the advantages of doing so. The realization of how their education helps determine the work they can later do will help motivate youngsters to take full advantage of their educational opportunities.

If youngsters understand that their early selection of courses of study may restrict their freedom to make subsequent educational and occupational choices, if they can perceive the importance of their schooling in preparing them for the work they might want to do — in short, if they are shown the relationship between education and their future vocational opportunities, most of them would probably be far more interested in their education. The inability to understand the function of education as preparation for work often causes youngsters to leave high school early or to become recalcitrant students who merely go through the motions of attending school until they reach the legal age at which they can withdraw.

As an institution, the secondary school has come to occupy the most effective position for giving a youngster the guidance he will need to prepare himself for work. The schools have access to most teenagers in this country, since the great majority enter high school. The school must acquaint incoming students with its curriculum and in the process can indicate the value of education as a whole and the specific usefulness of different parts of the curriculum in terms of the individual's aptitudes and interests. The school is able to draw on government and industry for vocational data and information so that students can have a better idea of how their preparation will affect their chances when they look for a job. For all these reasons, vocational guidance and counseling have a critical role to play in secondary education.

A survey covering the school year 1952-53 revealed that there are slightly over 18,000 persons in the junior and senior high schools of the nation who are doing counseling. The study does not differentiate those who are primarily concerned with vocational guidance. Although the results are not strictly comparable to those of a survey made in 1946, it is apparent that the number of counselors has risen sharply from the older figure of a little over 8,000. There is now approximately one counselor for every 453 school pupils. But less than half of these 18,000 counselors devote as much as half their time to counseling.

At the present time, thirty-nine states employ state supervisors of guidance. There is still, however, a wide variation in the scope of guidance programs. California has over 1,200 counselors who devote at least half their time to counseling, while New York and Massachusetts have 700 and 530 respectively. At the other extreme North Dakota has 4, and Alabama has 9.

In the fiscal year 1952 about $400,000 in Federal funds were expended under the George-Barden Act to help states with their guidance programs. The states reported the expenditure of a little over $1 million in order to qualify for the Federal contribution. Much more money was expended by states and localities other than that reported under the Act. Massachusetts, for example, reported that local school committees spent just under $2 million for guidance in the fiscal year 1952. Responding to the same 1952-1953 survey noted above, Washington reported over $1 million; Texas, about $850,000; and Georgia, $450,000.

OTHER VOCATIONAL GUIDANCE FACILITIES

Although this chapter is primarily concerned with vocational guidance in the public schools, it should be noted that other institutions also provide vocational guidance. Among these are various social agencies. Of outstanding importance has been the work of the Young Men's Christian Association. B'nai B'rith has pioneered in group guidance methods, and facilities are provided in a number of cities by Jewish Vocational Service agencies. The Catholic Youth Organization and various service clubs, such as the Rotary and Kiwanis, have long been interested and active in the field of vocational guidance.

In many communities throughout the United States, vocational guidance services are provided either by an independent agency, such as the Vocational Advisory Service in New York City, or in connection with the placement work which is undertaken by various social and religious groups. Since these placement efforts are usually directed towards helping special groups, a careful investigation of vocational aspirations, abilities, and interests is required.

A directory compiled by the American Personnel and Guidance Association, which was formed in 1951 by the amalgamation of the National Vocational Guidance Association and several other societies, lists the vocational counseling services approved by the Association. In 1953 there were slightly over 150 such services. More than 40 percent of these operate as part of a college or university, but are also open to the public. Another large proportion consists of services provided by such organizations as the Y.M.C.A. or Jewish Vocational Service agencies. A small number are private agencies or individual guidance counselors in private practice. These approved counseling services are concentrated in the larger cities and more industrialized states. About one fifth of them are located in two cities, New York and Chicago, and many important cities do not have a single approved service. Twenty-two states lack approved services of any kind.

The Federal government also contributes to vocational guidance services. Through its support of vocational education under the George-Barden Act, it contributes to the training of counselors and to the payment of guidance supervisors' salaries at the state level. During recent years, in connection with its large-scale educational and training program, the Veterans Administration has become deeply involved in advisory programs that are primarily focused on vocational guidance. About 600,000 disabled veterans who sought benefits under Public Law 16 were required to secure guidance. Millions of other veterans who pursued training or education under Public Law 346 were entitled, and in some cases required, to use these guidance services. The Veterans Administration estimated that it spent $26 million on counseling services during the first six years after World War II.

Guidance functions have also been part of the work of Federal and state employment services. The state agencies affiliated with the U. S. Employment Service placed considerable emphasis on counseling during the 1930's. Guidance was particularly important during the depression because the many people seeking employment possessed a wide variety of qualifications. Counseling was sharply de-emphasized under the federalized U.S.E.S. during World War II, when there was a shortage of workers and the need was to fill job openings as quickly as possible. Since the war, efforts have been made to rebuild the guidance and counseling aspects of the employment services. These efforts have been handicapped by the lack of trained personnel.

The Bureau of Vocational Rehabilitation, located in the U. S. Department of Health, Education, and Welfare, seeks through its affiliated state agencies to appraise and counsel clients, as well as support them through the period of necessary training and initial employment. This service is intended for any handicapped person, but insufficient funds have limited the Division's aid to a relatively small number. Very recently, Congress has enacted legislation which will progressively increase the funds available over the next five years to nearly triple the 1953 appropriation. The use of some of these funds for the training of additional counselors and for research is also authorized.

Every young man who enters the armed services takes a comprehensive battery of tests. Their purpose is to discover his present skills and his potential for acquiring new ones. The kind of training he will receive largely depends on his test scores and his civilian background. This has the effect of introducing many young men to new fields they might otherwise never have considered. During the demobilization after World War II, the services operated extensive counseling programs designed to assist men in their return to civilian life.

The Federal government also contributes to vocational guidance through its various information services. The U. S. Department of Labor, in cooperation with the Veterans Administration, has developed an *Occupational Outlook Handbook,* which carries the subtitle "Employment Information on Major Occupations for Use in Guidance." Within the compass of two brief pages for each occupation it seeks to provide the following information: a summary of the prospects for employment throughout the next five or ten years; a short description of the nature of the work; training and other qualifications required for employment; a more detailed analysis of the factors affecting the demand for and supply of workers which have been noted in the outlook summary; some statistical information about earnings and the range of earnings in different parts of the country; finally, where to go for more information.

Several divisions of the Department of Labor, particularly the Bureau of Employment Security, have also been engaged in the compilation of occupational information. Basic to the collection and effective utilization of such information was the development of the *Dictionary of Occupational Titles,* first published in 1939, which introduced a system of job classification and shows the relationships that exist within job groupings. The Bureau of Employment Security has also contributed to guidance by developing tests and job analyses, and by doing some counselor training.

A good deal of the existing literature on occupations and vocational opportunities is sponsored by trade associations and professional societies. Much of it is designed, however, to attract entrants into particular fields. A number of private publishers have also tried to meet the sizable market that exists for up-to-date and usable information about the world of work.

Tests, which play so important a role in current guidance, received great impetus from their extensive use and development in the armed services. Even more extensive use of tests is made by the public schools. Tests are now available that are intended to reveal an individual's general intelligence, special aptitudes, present achievements, interests, values, and personality — nearly all the psychological factors considered important for vocational guidance. One current textbook for students of guidance devotes eleven pages of small type just to list available achievement tests.

THE DEVELOPMENT OF VOCATIONAL GUIDANCE

Professor John M. Brewer of Harvard University, the historian of vocational guidance in the United States, offered six reasons for the rise of the movement. First, the removal of work from the home, which meant that most children were no longer in intimate contact with the world of work. Second, the increasing complexity of technology, which multiplied the types of work available. Third, the failure of many who had undertaken vocational training for which they were not suited. Fourth, the difficulty of finding appropriate employment in a world of increasing technical specialization. Fifth, the transformation of secondary schools from specialized institutions serving the minority of youngsters preparing for college to common schools serving most adolescents. Finally, Brewer stressed the importance in a democratic society of insuring that vocational choice is not only free but based on sound knowledge.

The vocational guidance movement was started in the United States by Frank W. Parsons. In 1908 he established a vocational bureau in Boston which he called the "Breadwinner's Institute." During the same period E. M. Weaver, a teacher in the public schools of New York City, was pioneering in attempts to find the right vocations for young people when they graduated from high school. Parsons was convinced that, "Society is very shortsighted as yet in its attitude toward the development of its human resources. It trains its horses better as a rule than its men. It spends unlimited money to perfect the inanimate machinery of production, but pays very little attention to the business of perfecting human machinery, though it is by far the most important in production."

In his book, *Choosing a Vocation*, Parsons presented three conditions necessary for wise vocational choice:

1. A clear understanding of yourself, your aptitudes, abilities, interests, ambitions, resources, limitations, and their causes; 2. A knowledge of the requirements and conditions of success, advantages and disadvantages, compensation, opportunities, and prospects of different lines of work; 3. True reasoning on the relationship of these two groups of facts.

Every young person needs help on all three of these points. He needs all the information and assistance he can get. He needs a vocational counselor. He needs careful and systematic help by experienced minds in making this greatest decision of his life.

Parsons further stressed the evil of unbalanced specialization and argued that children require broad culture and experience if they are to develop properly.

Parsons' methods included all the elements of present vocational guidance, from aptitude tests to occupational forecasts. Subsequent developments in psychology and psychiatry have caused the guidance movement to concentrate at different times on specialized aspects of guidance and to broaden enormously the original goals of counseling.

Psychological testing on a large scale was introduced by the Army during World War I. In the next decade business and industry began to use tests on a large scale. Educators were introducing them into the public schools during this period, and testing has since been adopted by almost every school system in the country. Psychological measurement is now an important tool of guidance.

In the 1940's and the 1950's, the whole guidance movement became increasingly concerned with personality problems. This concern had always been felt by some within vocational guidance. It had already been expressed in the 1920's when the National

Vocational Guidance Association drew up a statement of principles and practice. In it, the point is made that, "Problems of adjustment to health, religion, recreation, to family and friends, to school and work, may be included under the general term 'guidance.'" Counselors have always been aware that some individuals who repeatedly seek occupational counseling often do this as a substitute for counseling on their deep-seated psychological problems.

Recently, furthermore, many preparing to become counselors have been doing graduate work in psychology. Such preparation makes them interested in over-all problems of adjustment in addition to the narrower problems of occupational guidance. This broadened emphasis has resulted in the emergence of a new psychological specialty, "counseling psychology." Another indication of how the field has expanded far beyond Parsons' original goals is the four areas into which guidance problems are divided in a recent textbook for students of guidance. These areas are: vocational pursuits; vocational activities; activities concerned with maintaining mental and physical health; and social and civic interests. The term "guidance" clearly encompasses much more than vocational guidance. Vocational guidance has become one facet of a larger movement. The importance of vocational guidance within the whole guidance movement appears to be constantly declining.

APPRAISALS OF VOCATIONAL GUIDANCE

Many who are enthusiastic about the potentialities of vocational guidance admit that its achievements have so far been modest. Improvement, it is often felt, will come about through the training of a large number of competent guidance counselors, in securing improved occupational information, and in improved methods of individual appraisal and counseling.

Vocational guidance has been handicapped by the fact that the educational and training program recommended for guidance personnel has not been adopted by all states and school systems. School superintendents have been free to appoint almost anyone in the school system to be a guidance counselor. Recently, however, many states have adopted certification requirements. The most recent survey shows that twenty-one states and the District of Columbia now have mandatory certification. Eighteen states either have optional standards or are working on certification plans. All these states require a certificate to teach and several years teaching experience. Most require also a period of work experience and courses of particular relevance to guidance and counseling. Nine states still have no plans for certification nor are they preparing any.

Another handicap has been the lack of occupational outlook materials that local guidance counselors can apply to their particular problems. At present, good occupational outlook data usually deal with national situations. But individuals involved in preparing themselves for work need, if not local, at least regional information. Some communities are now making special and successful efforts to provide the essential local information.

Although some guidance workers believe that more emphasis on psychological testing would improve the effectiveness of vocational guidance, many leaders in the field do not believe that such efforts will result in much improvement unless guidance is first strengthened in other ways. After making a special review of the guidance movement, Dr. Nicholas Hobbs of George Peabody College for Teachers declared in his paper entitled *The Social Scientist and the Field of Guidance* that the movement, which "started in the interest of the fullest human development" seems

to have become a vast technology, almost completely absorbed in its own operations, rather vaguely concerned about the nature of the individual it proposes to serve, and seemingly oblivious to the demands of the society in which the individual must work out his destiny. I came away from this experience feeling that we in guidance have been captured by our methodologies and that we have lost sight of the meaning of what we are doing. In our preoccupation with how to do things, we seem to have lost interest in why we do them.

After a careful review of ten of the leading textbooks in the field, Dr. Hobbs concluded that, "The texts are skimpy on discussion of the nature of the child and young person, and almost completely barren of any discussion of the society in which the effectiveness of guidance efforts will be validated."

Elaborate special aptitude tests, to which so much effort has been devoted, do not enable one to predict with high accuracy performance on most jobs. The important determinants of success in many occupations are: higher general intelligence than that of others in the same job; competence in the basic skills — reading, writing, and computation — and willingness to learn and to work hard. Although guidance people tend to exaggerate the importance of psychological testing, it does have many valuable applications. One, for example, is in discovering exceptional aptitude which would otherwise not be revealed.

The effectiveness of vocational guidance would no doubt be increased by improving the training of those becoming counselors, by providing better forecasting materials, and by the wiser use of psychological tests. But one other factor continues to hamper vocational guidance. This is the ever-growing emphasis in the guidance movement on counseling for over-all adjustment.

Even if vocational guidance were to restrict itself to helping individuals prepare for work, it would still have to provide an imposing array of services. Most experts have agreed that a well-organized public school vocational guidance program should provide the following: (1) a vocational information service, which collects occupational information; (2) a personal data collecting service, which obtains information about the individual; (3) a counseling service, in which the individual is helped to study himself, his occupational opportunities, and his occupational goals and plans; (4) a placement service, which helps the individual get into contact with job opportunities and work out a job-getting program; (5) a follow-up and research service, designed both to evaluate the program and to help the individual make job adjustments.

How far guidance has attempted to go beyond even these ambitious goals is illustrated by "The Illinois Secondary School Curriculum Program," specifically the part dealing with guidance services. The study is oriented toward a set of guidance objectives that go far beyond the vocational area. Questions are raised, for example, asking how those responsible for guidance can help the student overcome difficulties in personal relations, choose companions wisely, and develop attitudes that will lead to a happy marriage and satisfying family life.

In theory there is no reason why young people cannot be provided with broad counseling for life adjustment in addition to more restricted vocational guidance. In practical terms, however, school systems have a limited amount of money, personnel, and time to devote to guidance and counseling activities. The newer emphasis on dealing with the pupil's adjustment problems may compete with vocational guidance for the available resources. Or, counselors now concerning themselves primarily with vocational guidance may turn their attention to other areas of counseling. It seems likely that the increasingly broad goals of guidance may work against more effective vocational guidance.

THE NEED FOR EFFECTIVE GUIDANCE

Unless the vocational guidance services provided for young people during the period they are in school are performed effectively, the most important contribution guidance and counseling could make to individual satisfaction and to economic and social efficiency will be lost. Effective vocational guidance could encourage many young people to derive more value from their education.

Perhaps the most important reason many adolescents derive little value from their schooling is that they cannot see the relevance of their current education to their future lives. They drift along within the school system more or less doing the required work and choosing courses they consider easy or that their friends are taking. It is not only students with limited intellectual ability who act this way. Even some gifted children show a marked drop of interest in school work after they enter high school.

The second reason many young people fail to get as much from their secondary schooling as they might is that their occupational objective is too modest. Many who have the ability to go through college never consider doing so because they are unaware of the possibilities for financial assistance. Most American families, even those in the lowest income level, are able to maintain their children in high school. But a considerable number do not have the financial resources to support their children's education after high school, especially if they have to study away from home. Yet there are many opportunities for young persons with limited financial resources to secure either a college education or some type of specialized training. Many young persons needing financial aid fail to learn about scholarship opportunities for which they might qualify.

Many young people do not foresee the jobs that would be open to them if they received a solid education. They are not made aware of the enlarged opportunities for training or employment that may be open to them in communities in other parts of the country or in the armed services. It has already been pointed out that the armed services offer the young man with a good high school background opportunities for technical training. Moreover, he can also take advantage of educational benefits after his discharge. The restricted employment opportunities of rural areas or one-industry towns may give young people a very limited picture of the world of work. They fail to consider that they are likely to migrate to other parts of the country. Such ignorance of possible future opportunities is undoubtedly an important reason why approximately 40 percent of young Americans terminate their education before they graduate from high school.

Making sound vocational plans is not easy for a young person under even the most favorable circumstances. He must take into account his abilities and interests, the advanced education and training he can hope to secure, occupational prospects, and such other goals as marriage and raising a family. Ideally, sound vocational planning requires a youngster to make tentative vocational commitments that help to give him a sense of direction and purpose as he goes through school. But he must also maintain sufficient flexibility to shift his plans as he matures, his interests stabilize, and his knowledge expands. This requires that he does not make the type of premature choice of courses or schooling that can prevent him from later changing his plans.

Occupational choice goes on during adolescence, the period when a youngster is being transformed from a child into an adult. A process involving such a radical transformation is never smooth and easy. Further, the most insistent pressures of the period relate, not to occupational choice, but rather to emancipation from parents and adjustments to the opposite sex. In a period of such turmoil, even able and well-balanced individuals will make errors. Many will inevitably fail to make maximum use of their opportunities. They will delay making choices, or they will, for a long time, pursue the wrong choice.

OBJECTIVES OF IMPROVED VOCATIONAL GUIDANCE

In trying to reduce this waste, vocational guidance faces many difficulties. Yet even after acknowledging the scale of these difficulties, it is not unfair to assert that vocational guidance is far from effective. Because of the dangers to vocational guidance implicit in the ambitious goals of the total guidance movement, it becomes necessary to ask what are reasonable goals for vocational guidance.

The previous discussion has already implied what these objectives should be. A fundamental objective of vocational guidance must be to make young people aware of the need to give more deliberate thought to the problem of their occupational choice. A second objective should be to help young people avoid early acceptance of overly modest occupational goals. This is closely related to the third objective, keeping young people from committing themselves to curricula or courses that will prevent them from changing or raising their occupational sights later in their educational careers.

Next, vocational guidance needs to help a young person discover the range of occupational goals he can reasonably expect to attain and the opportunities available to him for education and training. Lastly, the success of all of these objectives depends upon the vocational counselor's helping youngsters to learn the value of getting as much as they can out of their high school education.

Guidance counselors are already trying to meet three of these objectives — inducing awareness of the problem of occupational choice, providing information about jobs and educational and training opportunities, and emphasizing the value of high school education. The activities of some counselors, however, hinder the fulfillment of the other two objectives. Seeking to make sure the youngster will be certain to prepare himself for a specific occupation, the counselor may guide him into curricula or courses based upon too modest a goal. By following such a course, the youngster is often unable later to raise or revise his occupational objective.

A youngster's occupational choice and preparation for work are molded by several powerful influences apart from the direct vocational guidance he may receive — for example, his family, friends, school experiences, and the prevailing economic situation. Formal vocational guidance may not be encountered until relatively late in the occupational choice process, when the youngster's direction may be firmly set.

Vocational guidance cannot be expected to act as the overriding factor in the occupational choice process. The occupational adjustment of the population does not depend upon vocational counselors any more than the mental health of the population depends upon psychiatrists. Yet just as psychiatrists have a contribution to make to raising the emotional health of the population, so there is much that guidance experts can contribute to vocational adjustment. The responsibility for contributing to sound occupational choices must be borne not only by the vocational expert, but by all the sectors of the community capable of making effective contributions — the family, teachers, industry, mass communications media, the armed services, and government at local, state, and Federal levels. A key task for the guidance movement is to stimulate these contributions and, by integrating them, encourage their effective use.

Even within the narrower confines of the school system, individual counseling by the guidance specialist is not the only, and probably not the major, factor in vocational guidance. Much of it must be accomplished by the teacher in the course of teaching. A good teacher knows how to show the implications of what he is teaching for the future lives and working careers of his pupils. He knows how to stimulate and encourage those of ability to set high goals for themselves. He also knows how to persuade a young person who has set his goals too high or in the wrong direction to alter his choice and to make it more realistic, without discouraging him. A competent guidance specialist assists the teaching staff to bring out the occupational implications of the subject matter presented to the students.

By the eighth grade, youngsters already need to be made aware of the considerations that must influence their early occupational decisions. The school system forces the youngster to make critical educational choices before he enters high school. For example, he must make a choice between courses that are either narrowly vocational or broadly academic. Postponing vocational guidance until the eleventh grade, as frequently happens, often limits its usefulness. By then, numerous students have already cut themselves off from many possible lines of development. Fortunately, a trend is developing to start vocational guidance activities as early as the elementary school.

The effectiveness of vocational guidance may be endangered by the increasingly ambitious goals of the guidance movement. These goals lead to programs which seek to counsel the youngster regarding all his adjustment problems. They may thus divert attention and effort from the specific objectives of vocational guidance. If attention were concentrated on the basic objectives of vocational guidance more youngsters would derive greater benefit from their secondary education and a greater number would seek advanced education and training. This would be a significant contribution to the more effective utilization of the nation's human resources.

CHAPTER XI

Public Policies and Skilled Manpower

Force of circumstance has been altering the traditional attitudes of Americans toward the nation's human resources. As they have come to understand the direct connection between the size and skills of the population and their economic strength and security, they have increasingly recognized the need for a comprehensive and long-range approach to manpower problems and policies. This has been reflected in a host of statements by governmental bodies, special study groups, and individual experts. Thus, the Report of the Committee on Manpower Resources for National Security to the Director of the Office of Defense Mobilization observed that the United States "must be certain that" it is "doing what is necessary to conserve and increase all our resources. This is particularly true of manpower — of men, women, and youth — the most vital of our resources to support and defend our national security."

THE NATIONAL GOVERNMENT AND MANPOWER POLICIES

Since the Federal government is responsible for the nation's security, it must give high priority to ways of strengthening and making effective use of the country's manpower resources. It faces difficult and continuing problems in determining, in the light of changing world conditions, how to maintain the armed services and to train and utilize young men of military age. An effective military reserve system, for example, still remains to be created, and the establishment of a system of universal military training is still being vigorously debated. The international situation compels agencies of the Federal government to plan how to meet the extraordinary civilian and military manpower requirements of full mobilization. In developing a program for dealing with the problems of full mobilization on a voluntary basis, the National Labor Management Manpower Policy Committee of the Office of Defense Mobilization has pointed out that "Manpower will be the ultimate limiting resource in the Nation's capacity for full mobilization." Even in this period of partial mobilization the Federal government must be sensitive to the ways highly trained scientific, professional, and technical manpower are developed and utilized, if for no other reason than because it is responsible for two thirds of all current expenditures for research and development.

In concentrating on manpower problems arising out of considerations of national security, the government must remain fully responsive to manpower requirements for civil defense, as well as for the economic, educational, health, and other essential needs of the civilian population.

The size and character of existing manpower resources shape many key policies of the Federal government. Less immediately apparent is the extent to which policies and actions of the Federal government affect the nation's resources of skilled workers and technicians.

IMMIGRATION POLICY

The supply of skilled manpower depends in part upon the size of the total population. The latter is directly influenced by policies governing immigration. Since the 1920's, immigration policy has severely restricted the number of people entering the United States from every part of the world except the Western hemisphere. In recent years relatively few skilled immigrants have entered the country. Out of a total of 170,000 immigrant aliens admitted during the year ending June 30, 1953, only about 12,000 were classified as "craftsmen, foremen, and kindred workers," and an uncertain proportion of even this small number probably has been improperly classified.

Under present law, immigration from outside the Western hemisphere is limited by a system of national quotas. However, preference is given to immigrants with special abilities or skills up to one half of the quota for each country. This preference provision of the McCarran-Walter Act has made little practical difference because nine out of ten quota immigrants have been coming from countries in western Europe that have been using up only a part of their quotas. The Act also permits the temporary entrance of skilled and certain other workers to alleviate labor shortages.

The present immigration act has been criticized on many counts, including the charge that it deprives the economy of skilled and technical workers who could contribute to its growth. It has been maintained that there are a number of trades, formerly dominated by immigrant workers, in which there have been shortages in recent years because native-born Americans are reluctant to enter them. The occupations that have been specified include custom tailoring, shoemaking, mining, and stonecutting. The point has also been made that an expanding economy can absorb many more immigrants than can enter under present quotas.

TRAINING ACTIVITIES

Other Federal policies affect the nation's resources of skilled and technical manpower less directly than immigration policy. The specialist training provided in the armed services makes an indirect as well as an immediate contribution to the skills of the working population. The consequences of this training for the skills of the nation's civilian working population have not yet been adequately evaluated. It is clear, however, that the training which many young men receive while in service helps them to acquire further skills when they return to civilian life.

Other agencies of the Federal government operate training programs for their civilian employees, but existing information does not permit an evaluation of their contribution to the nation's manpower resources. The Tennessee Valley Authority and the Atomic Energy Commission offer examples of agencies which have found it desirable, and in some cases necessary, to develop special training programs. Since 1936, the Tennessee Valley Authority has been conducting apprenticeship programs in cooperation with the unions in several skilled trades. The TVA points out that this training program contributes to the manpower resources of the whole region, and not merely to its own operations. The TVA has also established special programs to train steam and hydroelectric power and chemical plant operators because it was unable to meet its requirements through regular hiring procedures. As a matter of personnel policy, the Atomic Energy Commission has declared that "Employees will be provided with an opportunity to fill in any gaps in their knowledge, skill, or ability in order to enable them to perform the tasks assigned to them in the best known ways." This policy has been applied in the case of skilled workers and technicians as well as scientists.

It has already been seen that the Bureau of Apprenticeship in the U. S. Department of Labor plays a positive role in encouraging apprenticeship training. The Bureau of Apprenticeship is also responsible for a broader Skill Improvement Program which is designed to assist employers who request help in solving problems they encounter in training workers.

In the summer of 1954, the Federal government sought to conserve the skills of a highly trained group of workers not by providing additional training facilities but by protecting their jobs. By Presidential order the tariff on some watches imported from Switzerland was increased for the declared purpose of protecting the employment of some 4,000 watchmakers whose skills are acquired only through long years of training and experience. It was argued that if these men left the watchmaking industry, the core of highly skilled workers essential to produce the large volume of precision devices required in wartime would be lost. The validity of this argument need not be argued in this context. It is sufficient to note that the Federal government was able to use tariff laws to achieve a particular goal with respect to skilled manpower.

Earlier chapters have shown that the level of employment, occupational information and guidance services, and secondary education significantly influence the development of the nation's resources of skilled and technical manpower. The policies and actions of the Federal government have important consequences for each.

Since most workers become skilled in the course of their work experience, the level and pattern of employment affect the size and characteristics of the skilled worker component of the labor force. It is significant, therefore, that the Employment Act of 1946 declares

that it is the continuing policy and responsibility of the Federal Government to use all practicable means consistent with its needs and obligations and other essential considerations of national policy . . . to coordinate and utilize all its plans, functions, and resources for the purpose of creating and maintaining, in a manner calculated to foster and promote free competitive enterprise and the general welfare, conditions under which there will be afforded useful employment, for those able, willing, and seeking to work, and to promote maximum employment, production, and purchasing power.

It is not necessary to detail all public policies which have affected or could be utilized to influence "employment, production and purchasing power." In seeking to achieve particular employment objectives, the Federal government's taxation, credit, foreign trade, and farm policies could all have a decisive impact upon the nation's resources of skilled and technical manpower. Today, expenditures for national security, which still account for roughly two thirds of total Federal expenditures, have a direct effect upon the demand for skilled workers and technicians and in this way upon the future supply. Legislation on housing, public works, and health has similar results.

EMPLOYMENT PRACTICES AND INFORMATION FUNCTIONS

Members of minority groups are frequently deprived not only of opportunities for education and training but also of access to the type of employment that enables a man to move up the skill ladder. To the extent that the Federal government has used its authority to reduce or eliminate discrimination against minority groups in the armed services, in Federal employment, and in work performed for government agencies by contractors, it has contributed to expanding the sources from which skilled manpower is drawn. Within the area of direct Federal employment, significant strides have been taken toward the total elimination of discriminatory practices. The Federal government has sought ever since 1941 to eliminate such practices on the part of contractors who work for it. Progress has been substantial, but much remains to be accomplished. The complete elimination of discriminatory practices where the Federal government has authority will substantially increase the opportunities for employment in skilled and technical work for sizable groups in the population.

Earlier chapters have emphasized that freedom of the individual to choose his occupation or career can be thwarted not only by artificial barriers erected by prejudice, but also by lack of sound information. An effective vocational guidance program and sound occupational decisions cannot be realized without adequate information. Because it is the key source for data about the trends in the labor force, the Federal government influences in still another way the nation's resources of skilled workers and technicians. The materials bearing on vocational guidance developed by the Bureau of Labor Statistics and by the Bureau of Employment Security of the U. S. Department of Labor, even though they could be refined and expanded, contribute significantly to providing a basis for occupational decision-making.

FEDERAL EDUCATIONAL ACTIVITIES

The part which Federal legislation and funds play in vocational education has already been reviewed in detail. This effort, however, represents only part of the government's contribution to the educational resources of the country, which play a central role in preparing young people for work. The Supreme Court decision of

May 17, 1954, which found a segregated school system to be unconstitutional, is highly important in enlarging opportunities for Negroes to acquire basic preparation for becoming skilled. The scale of Federal educational activities is impressive. A study by the Library of Congress in 1950 listed almost 300 separate Federal educational activities carried on in the Executive Office, Executive Departments, independent offices and agencies, the Legislative Establishment, and the District of Columbia. Total expenditures in 1950 exceeded $3.6 billion. Four fifths of this sum was accounted for by the Veterans Administration. The policy of granting educational and training benefits to veterans continues to help raise the skill level of the working population.

About $160 million went to public elementary and secondary schools. This Federal money was used for school lunches; aid for vocational education; assistance to local school districts to help cover the cost of educating the dependents of servicemen, government employees living on Federal installations, personnel working on large government projects, and Indians on government reservations; and still other purposes.

Until a critical study of the various Federal programs aiding education is undertaken, it will be impossible to evaluate their relationship to the educational and training facilities or to the skilled manpower resources of the country. Some critics have contended that such a study would point to a consolidated program of assistance to public education rather than a continuance of the multitude of special purpose Federal assistance programs. Others hold that the current role that the Federal government plays in vocational education is not effectively correlated with other educational efforts of the Federal government.

Yet, the support given to vocational education by the Federal government continues to meet approval. The present program of vocational education makes a genuine contribution to the preparation of boys and girls for skilled work and to the skills of adult workers. It should be pointed out, however, that the legislative foundation of this system of Federal grants-in-aid was adopted in

1917 and has been modified in the intervening period only in detail. During those three and a half decades, the character of public education, the technology, and the composition of the labor force — to mention only three significant factors — have changed greatly. Whether the objectives of the law, the sums voted by Congress, and the ways the funds are used are consonant with these and other changes warrants an objective inquiry.

Existing legislation, for example, does not directly recognize the development of the technician occupations or of technical training in post-high school institutions, particularly in junior colleges and technical institutes. Only a small part of Federal funds for the land-grant colleges and for vocational secondary education is used for the training of technicians. An unsuccessful effort was made at the end of World War II to revise substantially the Federal grant-in-aid program for vocational education. More recently, a bill was introduced in the Second Session of the Eighty-third Congress to repeal present legislation and place Federal aid to vocational education on a new basis. However, this bill never emerged from committee.

THE LIMITS TO GOVERNMENTAL RESPONSIBILITY

To say that the nation is being challenged today to find the best possible ways of developing and using its manpower resources must not be taken to mean that only the Federal government has a responsibility to act. Nor should one conclude from this brief recapitulation of the impact of Federal policies on skilled manpower that the Federal government is the sole or major determinant of the nation's resources of skilled workers and technicians.

State and local governments play the dominant role in education, and consequently they are primarily responsible for the basic preparation for life and work that the individual acquires as a result of his elementary and secondary schooling. The structure of the school system, the school leaving age, the pay schedules for teachers, the guidance programs in the schools, the availability of post-high school public education in the form of junior or community colleges and technical institutes — the responsibility for these and a host of other educational matters belongs to the states and local government.

State and local actions likewise help to determine employment opportunities. Southern states have used governmental and non-governmental means to attract industries and to help provide the trained manpower they will require. Again, state and local action can contribute to solving employment problems created by a declining industry, as in the case of anthracite coal mining in Eastern Pennsylvania. Eleven states and twenty-five municipalities have some form of fair employment practice laws aimed at opening up job opportunities for members of minority groups. It has been estimated that enforceable fair employment practice laws now cover areas containing one third of the total population and one eighth of the nonwhite population. State laws provide the legal framework for apprenticeship agreements, and state agencies promote this form of training. The licensing provisions for skilled occupations are largely determined by state and local law. State governments and communities provide employment services, including some occupational guidance counseling.

Federal, state, and local governments all make important policies affecting the nation's manpower resources. But government is only one center of policy-making. In a democracy, responsibility for manpower policies is not only widely diffused throughout the society, but it resides to an overwhelming degree in the individual, either as an individual or as a member of voluntary groups.

Every employer contributes to manpower policy through the practices he follows in hiring and promoting employees and through the training opportunities he provides. Every labor organization is, in greater or lesser degree, a center of manpower policy determination. They may affect the conditions of entry into a trade, the training requirements of an occupation, the wage incentives for skill training, and, through seniority provisions, the process of promotion. Other voluntary organizations also influence manpower policies. An association of technicians may be instrumental in securing registration requirements for the occupation, and an employer organization can be the source of important occupational information.

Every individual plays a part in the determination of manpower policy. As a citizen he participates in the political process and thereby helps to determine the public policies that affect the nation's manpower resources. It is the individual who is for or against universal military training or increased expenditures for education. The attitude of every individual towards the development and utilization of skilled manpower is strongly influenced by the consensus in his community, but he helps to make that consensus. It is the individual who will decide in the long run whether his community assigns as much importance to investing in the well-being of its citizens as in its roads and public buildings.

Finally, it is the individual who decides to pursue a particular course of education and training, to enter a specific occupation, to seek employment with one firm rather than another. This freedom of choice is frequently restricted by conditions over which the individual has no immediate control. Yet, it is the decisions of the individual which play the key role in the development and use of the nation's manpower. In a democracy the freedom to choose one's occupation is as crucial as the right to think and speak freely.

Bibliography

Accrediting Commission of Business Schools. Directory of Accredited Institutions, 1953–1954. Washington, 1953.

American Council on Education. What the High Schools Ought to Teach. Washington, 1940.

American Vocational Journal. Various issues.

Bakke, E. Wight, and others. Labor Mobility and Economic Opportunity. Cambridge, Mass., 1954.

Bell, Bernard Iddings. Crowd Culture. New York, 1952.

Berthoff, Rowland Tappan. British Immigrants in Industrial America, 1790–1950. Cambridge, Mass., 1953.

Bestor, Arthur E. Educational Wastelands. Urbana, Ill., 1953.

Bezanson, Anna. "Promotion from Without," *Quarterly Journal of Economics,* Vol. 36, November, 1921.

——— "Skill," *Quarterly Journal of Economics,* Vol. 36, August, 1922.

Brammell, P. Roy. Your Schools and Mine. New York, 1952.

Brewer, John M. "Vocational Guidance," in Encyclopaedia of the Social Sciences.

Bureau of Apprenticeship. Apprentice Completion? or Cancellation? Technical Bulletin No. T-130. Washington, 1951.

——— Apprenticeship Statistics, 1953. Technical Bulletin No. T-137. Washington, 1953.

——— Minutes of Seventy-seventh Meeting of Federal Committee on Apprenticeship. Washington, June 22, 1954.

——— The National Apprenticeship Program. Washington, 1953.

——— The Skilled Labor Force. Technical Bulletin No. T-140. Washington, April, 1954.

Bureau of Labor Statistics. The Mobility of Electronic Technicians, 1940-52. Bulletin No. 1150. Washington, 1954.

——— The Mobility of Molders and Coremakers, 1940-1952. Bulletin No. 1162. Washington, 1954.

——— The Mobility of Tool and Diemakers, 1940-51. Bulletin No. 1120, Washington, 1952.

——— Occupational Outlook Handbook. Bulletin No. 998. Washington, 1951.

Bureau of the Census. Current Population Reports, Labor Force. Monthly Reports on the Labor Force. Series P-57. Various issues. Washington.

——— 1950 Census of Population. Bulletin P-C1. U. S. Summary, Detailed Characteristics. Washington, 1953.

—— Occupation by Industry. 1950 Census of Population, Special Report P-E No. 1C. Washington, 1954.

—— A Projected Growth of the Labor Force in the United States under Conditions of High Employment: 1950 to 1975. Series P-50, No. 42. Washington, December 10, 1952.

California State Department of Education. Vocational Education in the Junior College. Sacramento, 1949.

Caswell, Hollis L. (ed.). The American High School: Its Responsibility and Opportunity. Eighth Yearbook, John Dewey Society. New York, 1946.

Chamberlain, Neil W. The Union Challenge to Management Control. New York, 1948.

Clark, Victor A. History of Manufactures in the United States. 3 vols. New York, 1929.

Cohen, Nathan M. Vocational Training Directory of the United States. Washington, 1953.

Commissioner of Labor. Seventeenth Annual Report. Trade and Technical Education. Washington, 1902.

Committee on Manpower Resources for National Security. Manpower Resources for National Security. Washington, 1953.

Conant, James B. Education and Liberty. Cambridge, Mass., 1953.

—— Education in a Divided World. Cambridge, Mass., 1949.

Connecticut Commission on Civil Rights. Training of Negroes in the Skilled Trades. Hartford, 1954.

Council of State Governments. Occupational Licensing Legislation in the States. Chicago, 1952.

Davis, Hiram S. The Industrial Study of Economic Progress. Philadelphia, 1947.

Department of Agriculture. Employment Distribution of Korean Veterans. Agricultural Information Bulletin No. 120. Washington, January, 1954.

Department of Defense. Catalog of the United States Armed Forces Institute. 7th edition. Washington, April, 1954.

—— Reenlistment Rates in the Armed Services, Washington, April, 1954.

—— Report of Working Group on Human Behavior under Conditions of Military Service. Washington, June, 1951.

—— A Review of Research on Military Instructor Problems. HR 202/3. Washington, April 1, 1953.

Department of Labor. Job Guides for Young Workers. Washington, 1954 edition.

Department of the Air Force. USAF Program, Technical Training. PTT 55-3. Washington, June 16, 1954.

—— USAF Training Prospectus. Washington, March, 1953, plus revisions.

—— Warrant Officer and Airman Classification Manual. Air Force Manual, 35-1, revised. Washington, 1954.

Department of the Army. The Army School Catalog. Army Pamphlet 20-21. Washington, June, 1953, plus revisions.

Department of the Navy. Naval Air Technical Training Command. 1954 Bulletin of Schools and Courses. Washington, 1954.

——— U. S. Navy Occupational Handbook for Men. Washington, 1953.

Dewhurst, J. Frederic, and Associates. America's Needs and Resources. New York, 1947.

Diebold, John. Automation: The Advent of the Automatic Factory. New York, 1952.

Douglas, Paul H. American Apprenticeship and Industrial Education, New York, 1921.

Durand, John D. The Labor Force in the United States, 1890–1960. New York, 1948.

Edwards, Alba M. Bureau of the Census. Comparative Occupation Statistics for the United States, 1870 to 1940. Washington, 1943.

Encyclopedia of Vocational Guidance, New York, 1948.

Evansville Manufacturers and Employers Association. Your Career Opportunities in Evansville Industry. Evansville, Ind., 1953(?).

Filene Foundation. Skilled Labor in Massachusetts. Industrial Development Reports. Boston, 1952.

Fisher, Allan G. B. Economic Progress and Social Security. London, 1945.

Folger, John K. Southern Regional Education Board. Future School and College Enrollments in the Southern Region. Atlanta, 1954.

Froelich, Clifford T. Office of Education. Guidance Workers' Qualifications. Washington, March, 1951.

Ginzberg, Eli, and Associates. Occupational Choice: An Approach to a General Theory. New York, 1951.

Grace, Alonzo G. and Staff. Educational Lessons from Wartime Training. The General Report of the Commission on Implications of Armed Services Educational Programs. Washington, 1948.

Greenleaf, Walter J. Occupations. Office of Education, Vocational Division Bulletin No. 247. Washington, 1951.

Haber, William, Frederick H. Harbison, Lawrence R. Klein, and Gladys L. Palmer. Manpower in the United States: Problems and Policies. New York, 1954.

Hart, L. Lane. "Modern Farming Needs Occupational Skill," Employment Security Review, Vol. 21, No. 3, March, 1954.

Harvard Committee on the Objectives of a General Education in a Free Society. General Education in a Free Society. Cambridge, Mass., 1945.

Hecht, Reuben W. and Glen T. Barton. "Skilled Regular Workers Essential to Modern Farming," Employment Security Review, Vol. 21, No. 3, March, 1954.

Hope, John, II. "Industrial Integration of Negroes: The Upgrading Process," Human Organization, Vol. 11, No. 4, Winter, 1952.

Horchow, Reuben. Careers for Young Americans in the Army and After. Washington, 1950.

Human Factors Operations Research Laboratories, Air Research and Development Command. A Survey of On-the-Job Training Procedures in the Air Defense Command. Washington, January, 1954.

Illinois Secondary School Curriculum Program. Consensus Study No. 3. Inventory A., Inventory B. What Do You Think About Our School's Program of Guidance Services? Springfield, 1951.

Immigration and Naturalization Service, Annual Reports. Washington.

Industrial Relations Center, University of Minnesota. The Relation of Vocational and Technical Training to Work Experience and Mobility of St. Paul Workers, 1940–1949. Minneapolis, 1952. (Mimeographed)

Industrial Relations Research Association. Behavior of Wages. Annual Proceedings, Part III, 1953.

International Labour Office. Vocational Training of Adults in the United States. Vocational Training Monograph No. 3. Geneva, 1948.

International Social Science Bulletin. Social Implications of Technical Change. Vol. 4, No. 2, Summer, 1952.

Jaffe, A. J., and Charles B. Stewart. Manpower Resources and Utilization: Principles of Working Force Analysis. New York, 1951.

Jerome, Harry. Mechanization and Industry. National Bureau of Economic Research, New York, 1934.

Jones, Arthur J., and Leonard M. Miller. "The National Picture of Pupil Personnel and Guidance Services in 1953," The Bulletin of the National Association of Secondary School Principals, Vol. 38, No. 200, February, 1954.

Journal of the American Medical Association. Hospital Number. May 10, 1952.

Kahler, Alfred, and Ernest Hamburger. Education for an Industrial Age. Ithaca, N. Y., 1948.

Kanninen, Toivo P. "Occupational Wage Relationships in Manufacturing, 1952-1953," Monthly Labor Review, November, 1953.

Keller, Franklin J. The Double Purpose High School. New York, 1953.

Lefever, D. Welty, Archie M. Turrell, and Henry I. Weitzel. Principles and Techniques of Guidance. Revised edition. New York, 1950.

Lester, Richard A. "A Range Theory of Wage Differentials," Industrial Relations Review, Vol. 5, No. 4, July, 1952.

Library of Congress. Legislative Reference Service. Federal Educational Activities and Educational Issues before Congress. Washington, 1951.

McCarthy, John A. Vocational Education: America's Greatest Resource. Chicago, 1950.

McCauley, John S. "Employment Status of Former Apprentices in Early 1954," Monthly Labor Review, July, 1954.

McLaughlin, Glenn E., and Stefan Robock. Why Industry Moves South. Washington, July, 1949.

Mays, Arthur B. The Concept of Vocational Education in the Thinking of the General Educator, 1845 to 1945. University of Illinois, Bureau of Educational Research Bulletin No. 62. Urbana, Ill., 1946.

Moore, Wilbert E. Industrialization and Labor. Social Aspects of Economic Development. Ithaca and New York, 1951.

Mumford, Lewis. Technics and Civilization. New York, 1934.

Myers, Charles A., and George P. Schultz. Patterns of Mobility of Skilled Workers and Factors Affecting Their Occupational Choice, Six Cities, 1940–1951. Massachusetts Institute of Technology, 1952. (Mimeographed)

National Association and Council of Business Schools. Business Schools in the United States. Washington, 1954.

National Association of Secondary School Principals. Functions of Secondary Education. Bulletin of the National Association of Secondary School Principals, Vol. 21, No. 64, January, 1937.

—— Imperative Needs of Youth of Secondary School Age. Bulletin of the National Association of Secondary School Principals, Vol. 31, No. 145, March, 1947.

—— Issues of Secondary Education. Bulletin of the National Association of Secondary School Principals, Vol. 20, No. 59, January, 1936.

National Council of Technical Schools. Directory of Technical Institutes. Washington, 1954.

National Education Association. Educational Policies Commission. Education and Economic Well-Being in American Democracy. Washington, 1940.

—— Research Division. The Three R's Hold Their Own at the Midcentury. Washington, 1951.

National Home Study Council. Home Study Blue Book and Directory. Washington, 1953.

National Manpower Council. A Policy for Scientific and Professional Manpower. New York, 1953.

—— Proceedings of a Conference on the Utilization of Scientific and Professional Manpower. New York, 1954.

—— Student Deferment and National Manpower Policy. New York, 1952.

National Planning Association Committee of the South. Selected Studies of Negro Employment in the South. Washington, 1953.

National Security Training Commission. 20th Century Minutemen: A Report to the President on a Reserve Forces Training Program. Washington, 1954.

National Society for the Promotion of Industrial Education. Bulletins, various issues, 1907–1917.

National Vocational Guidance Association. The Principles and Practices of Vocational Guidance. Cambridge, Mass., 1930.

Nelson, Lieutenant Dennis D., USN. The Integration of the Negro into the U. S. Navy. New York, 1951.

New York State Apprenticeship Conference. First Report. Brooklyn, N. Y. October 28-30, 1953.

New York State Education Department and Board of Education of the City of New York. Vocational Education in the New York City Schools. New York, 1951.

North American Conference on Apprenticeship. Proceedings of the First Conference. San Diego, Calif., August 2-9, 1953.

Norton, T. L. Public Education and Economic Trends. Cambridge, Mass., 1939.

Office of Education. Administration of Vocational Education. Vocational Education Bulletin No. 1. Washington, 1948.

—— Adult Education Activities of the Public Schools. Report of a Survey, 1947-48. Pamphlet No. 107. Washington, 1949.

—— Biennial Survey of Education in the United States. Washington, various years.

—— Counselor Competencies in Occupational Information. Misc. 3314-3. Washington, 1949.

—— North Atlantic Regional Conference for Trade and Industrial Education. What Becomes of the Trade School Graduate — Class of 1952. Washington, D. C.

—— 100 Evening Schools. Bulletin No. 4. Washington, 1949.

—— The Structure of State Departments of Education. Miscellaneous Bulletin No. 10. Washington, 1949.

—— Vocational Division. Digest of Annual Reports of State Boards for Vocational Education. Washington, various years.

—— Vocational Division. Directory of All-Day Trade and Industrial Education Programs Qualified for Federal Aid. Washington, 1954.

—— Vocational Education in the Years Ahead. Vocational Division Bulletin No. 234. Washington, 1945.

—— Vocational Education of College Grade. Bulletin No. 18. Washington, 1946.

—— Vocational-Technical Training for Industrial Occupations. Vocational Division Bulletin No. 228. Washington, 1944.

Palmer, Gladys L. Labor Mobility in Six Cities. New York, 1954.

Pancoast, Omar, Jr. Occupational Mobility. New York, 1941.

Parsons, Frank. Choosing a Vocation. New York, 1909.

President's Commission on the Health Needs of the Nation. 5 vols. Vol. 3. America's Health Status, Needs, and Resources. Washington, 1952-53.

Reynolds, Lloyd D. The Structure of Labor Markets. New York, 1951.

Russell, William F. How to Judge a School. New York, 1954.

Slichter, Sumner H. Union Policies and Industrial Management. Washington, 1941.

Society for the Promotion of Engineering Education. A Study of Technical Institutes. Lancaster, Pa., 1931.

Southern Regional Vocational Association. Summary Proceedings, Seventh Regional Conference. Washington, 1952.

Southern States Apprenticeship Conference. Fifth Annual Proceedings. Fort Worth, Texas. September 10-12, 1953.

Spaulding, Francis T. High School and Life. New York, 1938.

Super, Donald E. The Dynamics of Vocational Adjustment. New York, 1942.

Tanneyhill, Ann. From School to Job: Guidance for Minority Youth. Public Affairs Pamphlet No. 200. New York, 1953.

Technical Education News. Various issues.

Thomas, Brinley. Migration and Economic Growth: A Study of Great Britain and the Atlantic Community. National Institute of Economic and Social Research. Economic Studies XII. Cambridge, England, 1954.

U. S. House of Representatives. 82nd Congress, Second Session. Hearings before the President's Commission on Immigration and Naturalization, September 30–October 29, 1952. Washington, 1952.

—— 82nd Congress, First Session. Inquiry into the Operations of the Office of Education . . . with Particular Reference to the Division of Vocational Education. House Report No. 1225, Committee on Expenditures in the Executive Departments. Washington, 1951.

U. S. Senate. 83rd Congress, Second Session. S. 3271, A Bill to Promote and Assist in the Extension and Improvement of Vocational Education . . . Washington, 1954.

—— 82nd Congress, Second Session. Staff Report to the Subcommittee on Labor and Management Relations on State and Municipal Fair Employment Legislation. Document No. 15. Committee on Labor and Public Welfare. Washington, 1953.

Veterans Administration. Education and Training under the Servicemen's Readjustment Act of 1944. Information Bulletin IB 7-58. Washington, 1953.

—— Employment Objectives of Disabled Veterans of World War II. Information Bulletin IB 7-41. Washington, 1953.

War Manpower Commission. Training within Industry Materials. Washington, 1945.

—— The Training within Industry Report, 1940–1945. A Record of the Development of Management Techniques for Improvement of Supervision — Their Use and the Results. Washington, 1945.

Warner, W. Lloyd. Structure of American Life. Edinburgh, 1952.

Weaver, Robert C. Negro Labor: A National Problem. New York, 1946.

Williamson, Harold F., and John A. Buttrick. Economic Development: Principles and Patterns. New York, 1954.

Woodring, Paul. Let's Talk Sense about Our Schools. New York, 1953.

Wool, Harold, "Long Term Projections of the Labor Force," in Studies in Income and Wealth, Vol. 16, Long Range Economic Projection. Princeton, N. J., 1954.

Woytinsky, W. S., and Associates. Employment and Wages in the United States. New York, 1953.

DATE DUE

OCT 6 '72			
JAN 2 6 1975			
DEC. -3.1981			

GAYLORD   PRINTED IN U.S.A.